THE CPA PROFESSION

Opportunities, Responsibilities, and Services

Stephen R. Moehrle, CPA
Associate Professor of Accounting
University of Missouri-St. Louis

Gary John Previts, Ph.D., CPA
Professor of Accountancy
Weatherhead School of Management
Case Western Reserve University, Cleveland, Ohio

Jennifer A. Reynolds-Moehrle, CPA
Associate Professor of Accounting
University of Missouri-St. Louis

WITH A FOREWORD BY
Barry C. Melancon, CPA
President and Chief Executive Officer
American Institute of Certified Public Accountants (AICPA)

AMERICAN INSTITUTE OF CERTIFIED PUBLIC ACCOUNTANTS

Notice to Readers

This publication does not represent an official position of the American Institute of Certified Public Accountants and is distributed with the understanding that the authors, editors, and publisher are not rendering legal, accounting, or other professional services in this publication. The views expressed are those of the authors and not the publisher. If legal advice or other expert assistance is required, the services of a competent professional should be sought.

Internal Revenue Service Circular 230 Notice

To ensure compliance with U.S. Treasury rules, unless expressly stated otherwise, any U.S. tax advice contained in this publication (including examples, exhibits, and illustrations) is not intended or written to be used as, and shall not be considered, a "covered opinion" or other written tax advice, and should not be relied upon for the purpose of avoiding tax-related penalties under the Internal Revenue Code; promoting, marketing, or recommending to another party any transaction or tax-related matter(s), IRS audit, tax dispute or other purposes.

Copyright © 2006 by
American Institute of Certified Public Accountants, Inc.
New York, NY 10036-8775

All rights reserved. For information about the procedure for requesting permission to make copies of any part of this work, please visit www.copyright.com or call (978) 750-8400.

1 2 3 4 5 6 7 8 9 PP 0 9 8 7 6

ISBN 0-87051-624-8

About the Authors

Stephen R. Moehrle, CPA, is an Associate Professor of Accounting at the University of Missouri-St. Louis. He previously held appointments at the University of Southern California and the University of California-Irvine. He received his Ph.D. from Indiana University, master's degrees from Indiana University and St. Louis University, and a baccalaureate degree from the University of Missouri-St. Louis.

Professor Moehrle teaches courses in financial accounting, financial reporting, and financial analysis at both the undergraduate and graduate levels. He was named the Outstanding Educator by the Missouri Society of Certified Public Accountants in 2004 and has won several teaching awards including the prestigious Indiana University Sauvain and Panschar Teaching Awards.

Professor Moehrle is an active researcher in financial accounting and analysis, has won research excellence and best paper awards, and has published articles in scholarly journals such as *The Accounting Review, Accounting Horizons, Research in Accounting Regulation, The CPA Journal, The Journal of Accountancy,* and *The Financial Analysts Journal.* He is married to Jennifer Reynolds-Moehrle and is the father of Elizabeth, Allison, and Jack.

Gary John Previts, CPA, is Professor of Accountancy and Associate Dean at the Weatherhead School of Management, Case Western Reserve University.

He is editor of *Research in Accounting Regulation* and, with Barbara Merino, coauthor of *A History of Accountancy in the United States (1998)*. He also is involved in research related to disclosure and regulation policy, corporate communication and the development of accountancy. Previts has worked on a variety of research projects with doctoral students and with visiting scholars from Holland, Turkey, Italy and Japan. In 2000 he concluded research with Weatherhead colleagues on financial and business reporting, sponsored by the Financial Executives Research Foundation. Previts chaired Working Groups for the Financial Accounting Standards Board's *Business Reporting Research Project*, which published its final report in 2001.

Previts has served as president of the Ohio Society of CPAs, and as a member of the Board of Directors of the AICPA. He has served on the Board of the AICPA Foundation and is an elected member of the AICPA's Governing Council. In March 2001 Comptroller General, David Walker, appointed him to the United States General Accounting Office's Accountability Council, an advisory policy panel.

He has served as an advisor to corporations and major accounting firms, the SEC, and agencies of the Indonesian government on matters relating to accounting, standards, and conduct. He chaired task force initiatives of the AICPA relating to the award of Rule 203 (GAAP) authoritative status to the Federal Accounting Standards Advisory Board and was a member of the Accounting Accreditation Committee of the AACSB.

He is the recipient of the President's Hourglass Literature Award, the Academy of Accounting Historians (1980); Outstanding Ohio Accounting Educator (1986); Distinguished Ph.D. alumnus, University of Florida (1990); Faculty Award of Merit, Federation of Schools of Accountancy (1991); Theodore M. Alfred Distinguished Service Medal, Weatherhead School of Management (1995); Lifetime Achievement Award for Educators, American Institute of Certified Public Accountants, (1996); Faculty Research Award, Weatherhead School of Management (2000); Gold Medal for Service, Ohio Society of CPAs (2002); *Accounting Today*, List of 100 Most Influential Persons in Accounting, 2002 through 2005.

Jennifer A. Reynolds-Moehrle, CPA, is an Associate Professor of Accounting at the University of Missouri-St. Louis. She previously held an appointment at the University of Southern California. She received a master's degree and Ph.D. from Indiana University and earned a baccalaureate degree from the University of Kentucky.

Professor Reynolds-Moehrle teaches courses in financial accounting at the undergraduate level and an innovative accounting research course at the Masters level and earned the prestigious Anheuser-Busch Award for her Teaching Excellence. Professor Reynolds-Moehrle is an active researcher in financial accounting and analysis and has published articles in scholarly journals such as *Accounting Horizons, Research in Accounting Regulation, The CPA Journal, The Journal of Accountancy, The International Journal of Managerial Finance,* and *The Financial Analysts Journal.* She is married to Steve Moehrle and is the mother of Elizabeth, Allison, and Jack.

Acknowledgments

The CPA Profession is the product of the hard work, insight, and dedication of many people, without whom this book would not have been possible. We would like to thank the following professionals for their assistance in reviewing this book, and lending their technical expertise: the AICPA staff and members of the various AICPA Technical Teams, who devoted their personal time and effort to review the manuscript, and my colleague Jeff Tucker, CPA, Immediate Past Chair, the Ohio Society of CPAs Executive Board, and partner, Rea & Associates, Columbus, Ohio. All being accomplished experts in their fields, their depth of knowledge of the subject matter is always impressive and their thoroughness greatly appreciated.

We also wish to acknowledge and thank Marie Bareille, Martin Censor, and the entire AICPA Publications Team, for coordinating and managing the publication of this edition; as well as Karen Coutinho for editing; and Robert DiCorcia and his team, for overseeing production and design.

Last but certainly not least, we would like to thank our families, for their patience and encouragement.

Finally, although many fine people helped to bring this publication to fruition, as is customary in such an eclectic endeavor as painting the portrait of a dynamic profession, errors and inconsistencies may be found by our readers. We invite you to bring them to our attention by your correspondence in letter or e-mail.

Stephen R. Moehrle
Gary John Previts
Jennifer A. Reynolds-Moehrle

Contents

Foreword, xv
Preface, xvii
Introduction, xxi

1 Introduction to the CPA Profession, 1
Introduction, 1
What Is a Profession?, 2
What Is a Professional?, 2
   What Is a Certified Public Accountant?, 3
Defender of the "Information Right", 6
   CPA's Qualities, 7
   CPA's Practice, 8
   CPA's Regulation, 8
Summary, 12

2 Qualities of a CPA: Commitment to Serve, Competence, Integrity, and Objectivity, 15
Commitment to Serve, 15
Qualities of a CPA: Competence, 17
   Education, 17
   Examination, 19
   Experience, 21

Continuing Professional Education, 21
Other Requirements, 21
Qualities of a CPA: Integrity and Objectivity, 22
   Rigorous Examiner/Engaging Diplomat: A Delicate Balance, 32
   The Process of Developing CPA Qualities in Aspirants, 33
Summary, 34

3 CPA Careers, 35
Introduction, 35
CPAs in Public Practice, 37
CPAs in Corporate Practice, 43
   How Does the Corporate CPA Career Evolve?, 46
   What Resources Are Available to CPAs in Corporate Practice?, 47
CPAs in Government Practice and Not-for-Profit Organizations, 48
CPAs in Education, 50
CPA Training Is Great for Virtually All Endeavors, 51
Diversity in the CPA Profession, 52
Summary, 55

4 The Scope of CPA Services, 57
Introduction, 57
Practice Environment, 60
Public Practice Scope of Services: Watchdog and Business Adviser, 61
   Accounting and Auditing Services, 62
   Taxation: Compliance and Planning, 64
   Management Advisory Services (Consulting), 67
   Accredited CPA Consulting Services, 72
   Other CPA Consulting Services, 75
   When Are Nonattest Services Inappropriate?, 77
CPAs in Corporate Practice: Cultural and Career Dimensions, 79
   Financial Measurement and Financial Management, 81
   CPAs in the Communication Function, 82
   CPAs as Financial and Operating Analysts, 83
   Corporate CPAs in Assurance Roles, 83
   Corporate CPAs in Consulting Roles, 84
Summary, 84

5 Accountability: Personal Oversight, 87
Introduction, 87
The Highest Standard: Highly Competent and Highly Ethical, 88

Contents   **xi**

    Learning to Practice Competently and Ethically: The Process, 89
        The Role of the Firm in Shaping the Professional, 90
        The Individual's Role in Developing the Qualities of a CPA, 90
    Ramifications for Failure to Practice up to the Professional Standard, 93
    The AICPA Code of Professional Conduct: A Major Source of Guidance on Ethical CPA Behavior, 95
    The AICPA's Core Concepts Addressing CPA's Ethical Dilemmas, 98
        Confidentiality, 99
    Ethical Decisions—Where Can I Get Help?, 103
        The Bottom Line: It Is up to You, 106
    Summary, 106

6 Accountability: Professional (Peer) Oversight, 107
    Introduction, 107
    Peer Oversight and Quality Control, 108
        Self-Regulation of the Accounting Profession by the AICPA, 109
        AICPA Regulation Activities on Behalf of the Accounting Profession, 110
        The Peer Review Process: A Closer Look, 112
        State CPA Societies, 114
    Setting Accounting Standards: The Role of Public and Private Organizations, 115
        The Financial Accounting Standards Board, 117
        The Auditing Standards Board, 118
    Public or Private Standard Setting?, 120
    Summary, 121

7 Accountability: Public Oversight, 123
    Introduction, 123
    Public Sector Regulation of the CPA Profession, 124
        Regulation by the Securities and Exchange Commission, 125
        Regulation by the Public Company Accounting Oversight Board, 128
        Regulation by State Boards of Accountancy, 129
    Legal Responsibility of CPAs, 131
        What Is the CPA's Legal Responsibility?, 131
        A CPA's Contract Responsibilities and Potential Liability, 132
        A CPA's Common Law Responsibilities and Potential Liability, 133
        A CPA's Statutory Responsibilities and Potential Liability, 134

Legal Liability—A Billion Dollar Problem, 141
   The Causes of the Legal Liability Problem, 142
   The Litigation Storm, 144
   Some Recent Relief, 145
   Insuring a Firm in the Eye of the Litigation Storm, 146
   Competing Incentives: The Commitment to Serve, the Profit
      Motive, Professional Integrity, and Litigation Risk, 146
Other Legal Matters Facing CPAs, 147
   Criminal Guilt, 147
   CPAs' Responsibility to the Public, 148
   Limited Liability Partnerships, 149
   Legislative Intervention and CPA Regulation, 150
Summary, 151

8 Developments in the Profession: Enron, WorldCom, Arthur Andersen, and Sarbanes-Oxley, 153

The CPA Profession—Post 2000, 154
What Led to the String of Corporate Scandals?, 155
What Happened at Enron and WorldCom?, 158
   What Was Going On at CPA Firms?, 160
What Is Sarbanes-Oxley?, 160
   Sarbanes-Oxley Title I: The PCAOB, 161
   Sarbanes-Oxley Title II: Auditor Independence, 167
   Sarbanes-Oxley Title III: Corporate Responsibility, 168
   Sarbanes-Oxley Title IV: Enhanced Financial Disclosure, 170
   Sarbanes-Oxley Title V: Analyst Conflicts of Interest, 173
   Sarbanes-Oxley Title VI: Commission Resources and Authority, 173
   Sarbanes-Oxley Title VII: Studies and Reports, 174
   Sarbanes-Oxley Title VIII: Corporate and Criminal Fraud
      Accountability, 174
   Sarbanes-Oxley Title IX: White-Collar Crime Penalty
      Enhancements, 175
   Sarbanes-Oxley Title X: Corporate Tax Returns, 176
   Sarbanes-Oxley Title XI: Corporate Fraud and Accountability, 176
Impact of Compliance, 176
Summary, 179

9 A View of the Horizon for the CPA Profession, 181

Hiring and Employment Trends, 182
Significant Advances in Technology, 183
Principles Versus Rules-Based Guidance, 184

Private Company Financial Reporting, 186
A Global Accounting Community, 187
   International Financial Reporting Standards, 187
   International Auditing Standards, 188
   Convergence, 190
Summary, 190

Appendix A: AICPA Code of Professional Conduct, 193

Appendix B: CPA Certificate and Permit to Practice Requirements, 195

Appendix C: State Boards of Accountancy, 205

Appendix D: State/Jurisdiction CPA Societies, 213

Appendix E: A Historical Perspective, 221

Appendix F: World Wide Web Sites, 239

Appendix G: Chapter Discussion Questions, 243

Foreword

The CPA profession has quickly rebounded from the concerns of recent years. Once again, our profession sits atop the list of most trusted professions. We are very happy about this, but we cannot rest. Professors Previts, Moehrle, and Reynolds-Moehrle have produced this work to continue our efforts to improve our professional communities' awareness and commitment to this new CPA profession.

In this work you will learn what differentiates a profession from an occupation and what are the distinguishing characteristics of CPAs. The authors' work will help to acquaint this new generation of CPAs about their role in society, a high calling. In my view, I cannot think of a more important effort, as our leaders and members establish the new CPA profession in the new millenium.

There has never been a more exciting time. There are now increasing opportunities for young professionals and professionals seeking a more fulfilling career. Consider the opportunities and challenges addressed in this work. I hope as a result you will be better informed about our profession and inclined to become more involved with it.

Barry C. Melancon, CPA
President and CEO
American Institute of Certified Public Accountants

Preface

This book provides an introduction to the CPA profession. First, it explores factors that distinguish a profession from other forms of employment. You will learn the difference between an occupation and a profession and the difference between an employee and a professional. You will also be introduced to the special role that CPAs fulfill in society and the qualities that a person must develop in order to effectively fulfill this special role. Principal among these are the dedication of the professional to the well-being of clients and a concern for the public well-being. Professionals must place their concern for the well-being of clients and society above their own self-interest. Professionalism is rooted in education in a specialized field of knowledge, guided by a code of ethical behavior and overseen by governmental licensure.

The CPA profession provides countless opportunities to those entering the profession. CPAs are essential to the proper functioning of capital markets and decision making. As a result, CPAs are found in public and in private practice and in organizations of all types and sizes.

Key qualities of CPAs include a commitment to serve, competence, integrity, and objectivity. New college graduates do not spring into the profession fully formed with respect to these qualities. The development of competence and commitment occurs over many years from education, examination, experience, and continuing education. The primary responsibility for the CPA is that commitment, competence, integrity, and objectivity rests with the individual and their understanding of the fiduciary responsibility to the client or employer.

The book explores career opportunities available to CPAs and describes the structure of those careers. We should begin by pointing out that a CPA possesses a "monolithic identity." That is, a CPA is a CPA, whether in public or corporate practice.

The CPA profession is a dynamic one, offering entrants a wide variety of opportunities. CPAs work in public accounting, corporate practice, governmental and not-for-profit accounting, and education. Opportunities are many for CPAs in all of these areas. CPAs enjoy upwardly mobile careers with varied and interesting responsibilities. In addition, many CPA careers are lucrative.

The needs of society and the needs of users of business information constantly change. As a result, the nature, scope, and domain of CPA services are constantly subject to change, and the CPA profession has to be able to continue to "reposition" itself to those places where the highest and best use of its social and professional product are to be employed. The work associated with the requirements of the Sarbanes-Oxley Act of 2002 is the latest example.

Practitioner competence to perform a given service is the initial factor to be considered when evaluating the scope and domain of CPA services. A CPA must possess expertise to agree to perform a service. Attention to competence focuses on making public practice responsive to user needs.

The professional CPA has both a commitment as well as an obligation to protect the public interest. While professional oversight processes (Chapter 6) and public oversight processes (Chapter 7) exist to monitor the quality of CPA activities, the primary self-regulation mechanism is the self! The CPA should aspire to the highest standard of professionalism.

The public depends upon CPAs to ensure the reliability of financial information provided by companies. With so much at stake, how can society be confident that CPAs are fulfilling their responsibility? In most instances, competent CPAs acting ethically provide outstanding service to their clients and to society. However, perfection by all individual practitioners is not possible. Thus, controls are in place to protect society's interests against inferior CPA services.

This book provides a discussion of the regulation of the profession of public accountancy by bodies within the profession (for example, the AICPA, the FASB, and the state societies). Self-regulation of the CPA profession by CPAs is optimal because of the vast and specialized technical skills and knowledge necessary to set and enforce accounting and auditing standards. The profession must be regulated and its activities directed to optimally serve the public interest.

The final level of oversight and regulation of CPA activity is society. Society granted the CPA profession the monopoly attest franchise. In return, the CPA must have a commitment and obligation to serve society and the public interest. Society and the public interest are protected via oversight of the profession by public sector regulatory bodies as well as by laws. Public sector regulators of CPAs and laws governing and controlling CPA practice are examined.

Most states have accountancy statutes, administered by the respective states' boards of accountancy. These boards set rules for entry into the profession, establish appropriate (ethical) behavior during practice, and discipline inappropriate activities by accountants (for example, taking away the right to practice). Collective action and coordination of the policies of the various state boards is facilitated by the National Association of State Boards of Accountancy (NASBA), a private nonprofit organization to which all state boards belong.

The Sarbanes-Oxley Act of 2002 was signed into law on July 30, 2002. The Act, named after its co-sponsors Senator Paul Sarbanes from Maryland and Representative Michael Oxley from the 4th District in Ohio, revised existing securities laws and established new securities laws related to corporate governance, corporate reporting, and regulatory oversight and enforcement. The act is designed to restore investor trust in the capital markets following the string of high profile corporate scandals. The book describes key provisions of Sarbanes-Oxley. Particular attention is given to provisions of the law that affect the CPA profession directly.

An important component of Sarbanes-Oxley is the establishment of the Public Company Accounting Oversight Board (PCAOB). The PCAOB is a private-sector, non-profit corporation created to oversee the auditors of public companies in order to protect the interests of investors and further the public interest in the preparation of informative, fair, and independent audit reports. Section three of Sarbanes-

Oxley empowers the PCAOB by providing that violation of the rules of the PCAOB will be treated as a violation of the SEC Act of 1934 and give rise to the same penalties that arise for violations of that act.

Professions must evolve, adapt, and innovate to continue to provide the expert service that is the hallmark of a profession. The accounting profession is no exception. The first years of the 21st century have already produced profound changes for the profession, and the rate of change is not slowing. Some of the larger efforts currently affecting the profession are examined in this book, including (1) hiring and employment trends, (2) technological advancements, (3) debate about the optimal philosophical basis for accounting standards, (4) debate about the optimal accounting standards for smaller closely-held companies, and (5) convergence of accounting and auditing standards across countries.

Any profession must respond to its changing environment to continue to deliver service worth of the term *professional*. The accounting profession operates in an environment of constant change. As a result, the accounting profession offers continually more opportunities for its members. This book summarizes four areas to watch over the next several years. The first is technology. Technological advances continue to make the accounting profession more effective and more efficient. Advances that we cannot fathom right now will be an integral part of a CPA's toolkit within five years. One such technological advance is XBRL. XBRL has profound potential to change the way companies report to stakeholders and the way CPAs audit the information.

A contemporary debate sets the stage for the second initiative on the horizon for the CPA profession. Currently, much authoritative guidance is written from a rules-based perspective. CPAs across the profession and academe are debating whether a shift to more principles-based guidance is appropriate. Another question being examined is whether small, privately-held companies should use the same accounting rules as large publicly traded companies.

Finally, convergence of accounting and auditing standards across countries is a goal and objective of most accounting regulators. Significant steps toward convergence have occurred in recent years. Current evidence such as the recent joint rule proposal by the FASB and the IASB suggests that convergence will continue and even accelerate in future years.

Introduction

Physicians attend to the healthcare needs of their patients. Lawyers protect and defend the rights of their clients. What do certified public accountants (CPAs) do? This book provides an in-depth examination of the CPA profession: yesterday, today, and tomorrow. You will learn that the CPA profession is very rewarding monetarily. More importantly, you will see that, just like the medical and law professions, the CPA profession provides a service of paramount importance for society. Thus, CPAs find their profession to be extremely rewarding from a personal as well as from a financial standpoint. Most will agree that having a personally fulfilling career is more important than having a financially rewarding career. Fortunately, CPAs usually have both!

    The book begins by distinguishing between an occupation and a profession and by demonstrating what it means to be a member of a profession. You will then learn the qualities of a CPA and how an aspirant CPA acquires these qualities. You will see the career opportunities available to CPAs as well as the variety of services offered by CPAs and CPA firms. You will be amazed at the variety of positions held by CPAs in contemporary business. Obviously, many CPAs run CPA firms. However, CPAs also lead Fortune 500 companies, government agencies, educational institutions, and not-for-profit agencies.

You will learn the processes in place in the profession to ensure that all CPAs are providing outstanding service to their clients or to their employers. Finally, you will learn about the dramatic changes in the CPA profession that have occurred in recent years and the incredible opportunities that these changes have presented for CPAs. The CPA profession is the most trusted profession in the world and is thriving. In this book, you will learn why this is true and how you can become a member of this great profession.

Keep in mind as you read this book that the professional activities described in this book reflect current practice, but this is a dynamic profession and requires that practitioners update their understanding frequently.

1

Introduction to the CPA Profession

A great profession takes a long view. Its members inherit a legacy from the past, derive benefit from it, build on it and pass it to the next generation even stronger than they found it. A great profession occupies a position of trust. When we review our assets, none is as important as our position of trust in the economic marketplace.

Robert L. Bunting, AICPA Chair [1]

Introduction

In this chapter, you will learn the difference between an occupation and a profession and the difference between an employee and a professional. You will also be introduced to the special role that CPAs fulfill in society and the qualities that a person must develop to effectively fulfill this special role.

---

[1] R. Bunting, "Renewing a Great Profession," AICPA acceptance speech reprinted in the *Journal of Accountancy* (January 2005): 58-61.

What Is a Profession?

A *profession* is a discipline practiced by an individual. However, it is also a vital, continuing social organization that lives on after any particular individual leaves the profession. Professions are typically marked by at least the following:[2] (1) professional education (usually at the graduate level), (2) a system of self-regulation based in a code of professional ethics (conduct), and (3) governmental review and/or licensure. Each of these processes serves to develop special qualities in members of professions. Each is examined in depth in this book as they relate to the CPA profession.

A profession is judged by the performance of its practitioners. If one member fails to meet the expectations placed upon the profession by society, the entire profession can be diminished. We see this phenomenon in the case of rogue attorneys, physicians, and CPAs. A delicate and tenuous relationship exists between a profession and society. One minute society might revere a profession. However, if rogue members of the profession soil the good name of the profession, the profession might soon find that it is simply tolerated or even condemned by society. Thus, it is important for a profession to ensure that all its members understand the history, structure, and expectations of the profession.

At the time of this writing, the CPA profession has just regained its status as the most trusted profession following the high-profile financial reporting scandals of recent years (for example, Enron, WorldCom, Global Crossing, and Parmalat). This book is designed to help the new generation of CPAs understand the profession and also the mistakes their predecessors have made, so these mistakes will not be repeated.

What Is a Professional?

There are two key characteristics of professionals. First, they are paid for the endeavor (for example, professional baseball players).[3]

---

[2] Harold L. Wilensky, "The Professionalization of Everyone," *The American Journal of Sociology* (September 1964): 137.

[3] Many professionals, however, also provide free (*pro bono*) services to select indigent clients as a service to society. Such societal contributions can even be viewed as another hallmark of professionals.

Amateurs engage in the activity purely for enjoyment. Second, professionals possess highly developed and specialized skill as well as a desire to serve the public.[4] John L. Carey, then executive director of the American Institute of Accountants, said the following in 1954 about professionals. (Note the use of the word *his*. This says a lot about one significant change in the profession over the past 50 years The profession now features women throughout and at the highest levels):[5]

> When people need a doctor, or a lawyer, or a CPA, they seek someone whom they can trust to do the best he can, not for him, but for them. They have to trust him, since there is no practicable way to appraise the quality of his "product." And so they must believe that his primary motive is to help them.

It is expected that responsibility, wisdom, and concern for the public welfare will override the professional's desire for personal gain if there is a conflict. That is, the professional should not take an action that is irresponsible, that is unwise, or that is not in the public's interest even if the professional stands to gain from the action (for example, be paid cash or make a gain on trade).

What Is a Certified Public Accountant?

A certified public accountant (CPA) is an individual who has been licensed by the state to provide public accounting services. The state license is evidence that the CPA has met a series of requirements that demonstrate *competence* to provide public accounting services. These requirements include college education, successful completion of a standardized qualifying examination, experience in the field, continuing education, and demonstration of ethical behavior. According to the AICPA and the National Association of State Boards of Accountancy (NASBA):[6]

---

[4] Robert K. Mautz, "Public Accounting: Which Kind of Professionalism?" *Accounting Horizons* (September 1988).

[5] John L. Carey, "The CPA and His Profession," American Institute of Accountants, New York (1954): 47.

[6] American Institute of Certified Public Accountants and National Association of State Boards of Accountancy, *Digest of State Accountancy Laws and State Board Regulations* (1996): vi.

State legislators and the courts have determined that it is in the public interest to license and regulate those individuals who have met prescribed requirements and who hold themselves out to the public as qualified to practice public accounting. Accountancy laws governing the licensing of professional accountants have been enacted in all fifty (50) states, the District of Columbia, Guam, Puerto Rico, and the U.S. Virgin Islands. These laws set forth education, examination, experience, and other requirements for licensure and establish a state board of accountancy (or an equivalent public authority) to administer and enforce the law.

Certified Public Accountants (CPAs) are licensed in all 54 jurisdictions. The accountancy law in each of these jurisdictions restricts the use of the title "Certified Public Accountant" to individuals who are registered as such with the state regulatory authority.

Regulatory laws in all but three states prohibit nonlicensees (i.e., persons not registered with the state regulatory authority) from expressing opinions or issuing prohibited forms of reports on financial statements. In other words, the laws restrict the performance of specific professional accounting services to licensees.

Each state or jurisdiction has its own definition as to what services constitute "public accounting." In general, public accounting involves the preparation of reports pertaining to the financial statements of client organizations. These reports might constitute a compilation, review, or audit of the underlying financial information and are intended to provide comfort that financial data reflects the underlying financial condition and performance of the organization (compilations, reviews, and audits will be discussed more fully later in this book). As you shall see in Chapter 3, the practice of public accounting includes a wide array of services, not limited to those previously specified. Additionally, many CPAs do not practice as public accountants, but rather work for businesses, not-for-profit entities, or educational institutions. These CPAs are still professional accountants and are bound by the same rules regarding competence and ethical behavior.

Professor Jamie Pratt depicts the relationship between capital providers and companies as follows:[7]

---

[7] J. Pratt, "Financial Accounting in an Economic Context", 6th ed., John Wiley & Sons, Hoboken, N.J. Chart presented here is a simplified version of Prof. Pratt's schema. Used with permission of the author.

Introduction to the CPA Profession 5

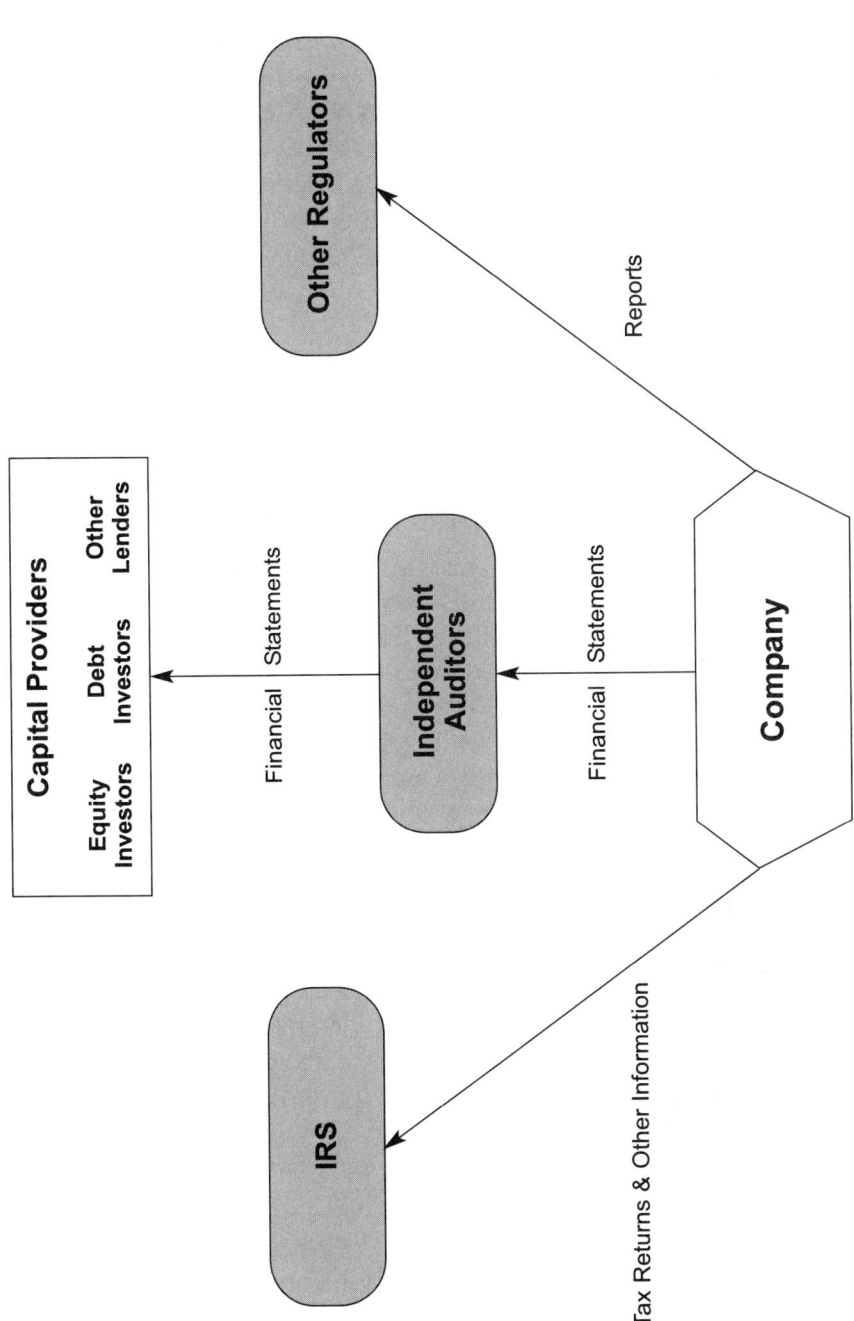

CPAs are active in all of the roles depicted. For example, providers of capital, debt, and equity investor organizations employ many CPAs to read and analyze the financial statements and other financial information provided by companies. Many individual debt and equity investors solicit the advice of CPAs as well. The companies employ CPAs as accountants to produce the financial statements, as tax professionals to prepare required tax reports, as internal auditors, as financial analysts, as business managers, and in a variety of other positions as described in Chapter 3. Companies must periodically issue financial statements to their capital providers. Companies engage auditors to attest to the reliability of the statements, which were prepared by company management. This is the core activity of CPAs.

Defender of the "Information Right"

CPAs are granted by law the responsibility of providing assurance that the information the organization provides by the organization can be relied upon. As you will see later in this book, CPAs are very well compensated for their services and expertise. Should a rational person thus conclude that CPAs do what they do because the law gives them the monopoly right to provide the service and because the compensation is adequate? This may be the case in a limited number of instances. However, in most cases, CPAs are driven by a greater goal: protecting the rights of all individuals to equal access to reliable information (the information right).

Individuals must have equal access to information for capital markets to operate fairly, effectively, and efficiently. An extreme example can be used to demonstrate this concept. Opaque Corporation is a jeweler based in Miami, Florida. Opaque's management reports an inventory of diamonds on the balance sheet totaling $10,000,000. However, in reality, the reported inventory should be $1,000,000. Paul and Sally are a couple living in Wichita, Kansas. Paul and Sally buy shares of Opaque Corporation believing that the shares are slightly undervalued since, among other things, the company has $10,000,000 of diamond inventory and they have always admired the quality of the diamonds offered by Opaque. What Paul and Sally do not know is that the seller of those shares was an individual living in Miami who has heard whispers about the reliability of the information on Opaque's balance sheet. Did Paul and Sally have equal access to information about Opaque? Of course not. Further, if investors believed that such a scenario was commonplace, they would not participate in the capital markets. The few gamblers willing to venture into such a market would not be willing to pay nearly as much for shares of stock because they do not have faith in the credibility of the information being provided about the organization. While this is an extreme example, it demonstrates the information right concept and demonstrates that equal access to information is crucial to functioning capital markets. It is the CPA's role to ensure that the information provided to individuals across the globe can be relied upon for decision-making. The next several chapters describe the role of protector of the individual's information right and demonstrate how the young professional acquires the skills and abilities necessary to competently assume this role. Along the way, you will see other roles that CPAs often fulfill because of their unique skills, abilities, and objectivity.

CPA's Qualities

What qualities must a CPA possess to competently protect the information right of investors? The most important required qualities include commitment to serve the public interest, competence, integrity, and objectivity. These concepts are introduced in this section and explored in depth in the next chapter.

Commitment to serve. Individuals with a specialized technical expertise who place the interest of the client or patient above their own self-interest are acting in accordance with that most important precept of professionalism: a commitment to serve. "The essence of being a professional is a sense of moral authority which places the well being of those we are asked or expected to serve above our own well being."[8]

Competence. Professional competence means having the knowledge, training, and motivation to perform with skill. Competence to practice is developed by the "three Es": education, examination, and experience.

---

[8] Gary John Previts, "A Culture for Accountancy Education: Lessons from Medicine, Law and Management" (Proceedings of the Tenth Annual Meeting, Federation of Schools of Accountancy, 1986): 135.

Integrity. Integrity means that one expresses one's views and recommendations genuinely, truthfully, and free of the artificial influence of another. Without integrity, the other attributes mean little or nothing.

Objectivity. Being objective means being intellectually honest and free from any conflicts of interest.

Chapter 2 describes what it means to be committed to serving the client, to be competent, and to practice with integrity and objectivity. The chapter also explores how CPA aspirants develop these qualities and how CPAs maintain these qualities.

CPA's Practice

Defending the information right of individuals is the core activity of CPAs. This role takes on many forms and is carried out by CPAs in a wide variety of positions in virtually all types of organizations. Chapters 3 and 4 provide an introduction to the practice of CPAs. Chapter 3 examines CPA career alternatives in public as well as private practice. Chapter 4 examines an issue that has taken on additional significance in recent years: what services can CPAs working in public practice provide and under what conditions. This is commonly referred to as the "scope of services" for CPA firms.

CPA's Regulation

To competently protect the information right of investors, the CPA profession must ensure that all its members are competently trained and act in the best interest of investors. The ultimate legal authority for this oversight is granted to the individual states and their respective state boards of accountancy. This regulatory structure is detailed later in this book.

However, the profession strives to a standard greater than the legal minimum. The AICPA's mission statement provides the basis for establishing professional accountancy ideals, and thus the code of conduct for CPAs. It also forms the basis for the AICPA's authority for the regulation of members who voluntarily agree to abide by the precepts and standards of the organization. This mission statement reads as follows:[9]

---

[9] *Mission Statement of the AICPA* (New York: AICPA, November 1995).

The American Institute of Certified Public Accountants is the national, professional organization for all Certified Public Accountants. Its mission is to provide members with the resources, information, and leadership that enable them to provide valuable services in the highest professional manner to benefit the public as well as employers and clients.

In fulfilling its mission, the AICPA works with state CPA organizations and gives priority to those areas where public reliance on CPA skills is most significant.

To achieve its mission, the Institute:

Advocacy

Serves as the national representative of CPAs before governments, regulatory bodies, and other organizations in protecting and promoting members' interests.

Certification and Licensing

Seeks the highest possible level of uniform certification and licensing standards and promotes and protects the CPA designation.

Communications

Promotes public awareness and confidence in the integrity, objectivity, competence, and professionalism of CPAs and monitors the needs and views of CPAs.

Recruiting and Education

Encourages highly qualified individuals to become CPAs and supports the development of outstanding academic programs.

Standards and Performance

Establishes professional standards; assists members in continually improving their professional conduct, performance, and expertise; and monitors such performance to enforce current standards and requirements.

Initially a national code of ethics was officially sanctioned by CPAs in 1917.[10] The Code of Professional Conduct was adopted in 1988 by a vote of the membership of the AICPA. The most recent revision of the code, amended January 14, 1992, is reproduced in Appendix A. The focus of the new code is on professional conduct (hence the name) rather than upon ethics. This code recognizes the unique responsibilities of CPAs in public practice, corporate practice,

---

[10] Joyce Lambert and S.J. Lambert, "The Evolution of Ethical Codes in Accounting" (Working Paper No. 23, The Academy of Accounting Historians Working Paper Series, vol. 2, 1979. School of Accounting, James Madison University).

government, and education, all of whom play a vital role in providing a broad range of information, consulting and "knowledge" services to decision makers. The code sets out principles and rules, which apply to all members of the AICPA. The principles state:[11]

Responsibilities

In carrying out their responsibilities as professionals, members should exercise sensitive professional and moral judgments in all their activities.

The Public Interest

Members should accept the obligation to act in a way that will serve the public interest, honor the public trust, and demonstrate commitment to professionalism.

Integrity

To maintain and broaden public confidence, members should perform all professional responsibilities with the highest sense of integrity.

Objectivity and Independence

A member should maintain objectivity and be free of conflicts of interest in discharging professional responsibilities. A member in public practice should be independent in fact and appearance when providing auditing and other attestation services.

Due Care

A member should observe the profession's technical and ethical standards, strive continually to improve competence and the quality of services, and discharge professional responsibility to the best of the member's ability.

Scope and Nature of Services

A member in public practice should observe the Principles of the Code of Professional Conduct in determining the scope and nature of services to be provided.

Collectively, these rules and ideals constitute the CPAs' code of ethics. The code establishes proper CPA conduct and ethical behavior. It is important that all CPAs conduct themselves in accordance with these standards to uphold the reputation of their fellow professionals. The present code also relates the rules of conduct to technical

---

[11] *Code of Professional Conduct*, as amended January 14, 1992, AICPA, New York, 1992.

standards as a measure of competence. In fact, the AICPA's ethical rules specifically require compliance with relevant technical standards. If a CPA fails to comply with relevant technical standards, the breach is considered to be an ethical violation.

Additionally, the AICPA holds CPAs to the highest level of moral and ethical standards in all aspects of professional life. The AICPA recently issued a statement of their policy on Discrimination and Sexual and Other Forms of Harassment in the Workplace. In this statement, the AICPA condemns discrimination and harassment and encourages all members to adopt policies in their organizations to prevent such behavior.

There is a potential downside to ethical codes. Ethical codes set forth minimum measures of appropriate behaviors. CPAs must recall their professional commitment to serve others. Without this commitment, the professional may view any behaviors not specifically forbidden as acceptable. Ideally, CPAs view the code of conduct as a set of rules to be exceeded in letter and in spirit. Many believe that professionalism suffers in a practice oriented and guided by rules. Professor Zeff observed:

> Also compatible with a possible dilution in professionalism is rule-dominated practice. Professional judgment frequently gives way to an increasing dependence on arbitrary rules.[12]

Nevertheless, a code of ethics is indicative of the self-regulation so necessary to a profession. Society grants professions a monopoly to practice because of their necessary expertise in a field of specialized knowledge—and in return accepts a pledge of ethical behavior. An interesting aspect of self-regulation is that it is far less expensive than oversight by a governing body provided that the self-regulation is successful.

The regulatory and legal framework designed to ensure that CPAs provide quality service is set forth in Chapters 5 and 6 of this book. The respective roles of self-regulatory bodies such as the AICPA and public sector oversight bodies such as the Securities Exchange Commission (SEC), the Private Company Accounting Oversight Board (PCAOB), the Government Accountability Office (GAO), and the State Boards of Accountancy are described.

---

[12] Stephen A. Zeff, "Does the CPA Belong to a Profession?" *Accounting Horizons* (June 1987): 67.

Summary

This chapter provides an introduction to the CPA profession. First, it explores factors that distinguish a profession from other forms of employment. Principal among these are the dedication of the professional to the well-being of clients and a concern for the public well-being. Professionals must place their concern for the well-being of clients and society above their own self-interest. Professionalism is rooted in education in a specialized field of knowledge, guided by a code of ethical behavior and overseen by governmental licensure.

CPAs provide a service critical to society—the competent delivery of objective, unbiased information for the use of decision makers. In short, CPAs protect the right of persons across the globe to equal access to information about an organization (the information right). If individuals do not have equal access to information, capital markets cannot operate effectively and efficiently. Indeed, capital markets cannot operate effectively and efficiently even if individuals simply are not confident that they have equal access to information, regardless of whether they actually do.

Important personal characteristics of an accounting professional include commitment to service, competence in the technical practice of the discipline, integrity, and objectivity. Because moral and ethical considerations in the practice of public accountancy are important, the development of proper habits of conscience and behavior are also crucial. The process of ethical decision making in our complex and ever-changing profession may not be perfect, but we must have high expectations of ourselves and our peers.

The CPA profession provides countless opportunities to those entering the profession. CPAs are essential to the proper functioning of capital markets and decision making. As a result, CPAs are found in public and in private practice and in organizations of all types and sizes.

The CPA has several sources of guidance for determining proper conduct in their practice, for example, the expectations of the public and its elected representatives, coupled with the CPA's mission to serve the public provide guidance about proper conduct. Also, the profession issues technical standards and has developed an ethical code that sets forth minimum standards of ethical behavior. The standards and the Code of Conduct provide guidance to the CPA especially when the CPA appropriately seeks to comply with the spirit as well as the letter of the rules. The CPA gains an understanding of these rules and ideals through formal college education, continuing professional education, and experience in the profession. The experience component provides the developing professional with a recognition of and respect for the culture of the profession in addition to experience applying the skills of the field.

2

Qualities of a CPA: Commitment to Serve, Competence, Integrity, and Objectivity

Integrity has been described as doing the right thing even though no one else is looking.

Niemeier[1] *(quoting countless wise persons throughout history)*

Commitment to Serve

Chapter 1 describes what makes an individual a professional rather than simply an individual working in an occupation. The first distinguishing characteristic is that the individual is paid for the endeavor. Another distinguishing characteristic is that the individual

---

[1] Charles D. Niemeier, Public Company Accounting Oversight Board Member in keynote speech to the AICPA Annual SEC and PCAOB Conference, December 7, 2004.

understands that he or she is serving in an important role for society and, as a result, places the public welfare above his or her desire for personal gain. John L. Carey, then the executive director of the American Institute of Accountants, put the commitment to serve succinctly in an early precursor to this book (keep in mind that Carey was leading a then male-dominated profession. This is certainly not the case any longer):[2]

> Professional men are accepted as men highly skilled in some science or art, who desire to minister to other people—who want to serve the public, and who place service ahead of personal gain. If they were not regarded in this light they would have not patients or clients. Who would engage a doctor, or a lawyer, or a certified public accountant who was known to put personal gain ahead of service to his patient or client? How would anyone know whether to take his advice or not? If the practitioner were mainly interested in selling his services and building up fees, he might be expected to keep his patients sick, or keep his client in litigation, or extend his examination of the clients' accounts beyond the necessary scope. Who would engage such a man?

Society grants CPAs the right to provide audit and attest services. In doing so, society is recognizing the special skills and abilities that CPAs possess and are asking CPAs to apply these skills and abilities to protect the information right of society's members. All CPAs must continuously be grateful for the opportunity to serve, appreciate the confidence placed in them by society, and take the associated responsibility very seriously. This is the essence of the commitment to serve. By the way, outstanding CPAs will do very nicely from a personal financial standpoint despite always putting the welfare of the public first.

Carey went on to point out that a professional attitude must be learned. It is not a natural gift in all that enter a profession. For most, it is natural to place "personal gain ahead of service." Carey expounded on this point:[3]

> That is precisely why people as a whole honor the relatively few like professional men and other true public servants, who have disciplined themselves to follow the nobler way. A professional attitude, like a golf

---
[2] John L. Carey, "The CPA and His Profession," American Institute of Accountants, 1954: 47.
[3] See footnote 2.

swing, must be acquired by self-discipline. The rules of ethics are guides to right action—to action that will develop the professional attitude, and thus win public confidence.

The commitment to serve is arguably the most important quality of a professional CPA. If CPAs are committed to serving the public interest, they will not accept engagements to provide services for which they are not highly competent. For those engagements that they accept, their commitment to serve would motivate them to serve with the highest integrity and objectivity. The process for developing the characteristic of commitment to serve as well as the other characteristics of CPAs is described later in this chapter.

Qualities of a CPA: Competence

Professional competence means having the knowledge, training, and motivation to perform with skill. Competence to practice is developed over several years from the following complementary processes:

1. Education (college education)
2. Examination (the Uniform CPA Examination)
3. Experience (professional experience under the supervision of a licensed CPA)
4. Continuing education

Education

The first step in developing competence to practice is to obtain formal education in the field. The education provides an aspiring professional with the technical knowledge, skills, and abilities needed to competently practice. Since the CPA certificate is awarded by the state, candidates for the certificate must meet the specific educational requirements in the state where they will practice (or states, if they desire to be certified in more than one jurisdiction). Appendix B provides a summary of educational and other requirements for each state. Appendixes C and D provide contact information for state boards of accountancy and state CPA societies. These organizations should be contacted for additional information regarding requirements for your state.

rection of the states in educational requirements has been evolving toward graduate education. All states and jurisdictions require students to earn a baccalaureate degree to obtain a CPA certificate. In addition, 45 of the 54 states and jurisdictions require a total of 150 hours of college credit be completed. The 150-hour rule also has been passed and becomes effective in Minnesota and Virginia on July 1, 2006, and becomes effective in New York on August 1, 2009. Only six states or jurisdiction have not yet passed the 150-hour rule: California, Colorado, Delaware, New Hampshire, Vermont, and the Virgin Islands.

The 150-hour requirement is equivalent to four years of full-time study at the undergraduate level and one year of postgraduate study. A graduate degree is not required. However, many universities structure programs so students can obtain a graduate degree in the 150-hour program if they desire. Many states specify a number of required accounting courses that must be in the 150-hour total.

In addition to providing required knowledge and technical skills, the university education provides an introduction to the "culture" of the profession. The culture of a profession is the qualities or ideals that practitioners possess and habits they follow in fulfilling their distinctive role in society. An appreciation of and respect for the culture of the profession is a requirement for all professionals. For instance, a medical school should assist would-be physicians in developing a sense of obligation and concern for the physical and mental well-being of the patient. The failure to focus on this imperative creates physicians with poor "bedside manner." Similarly, the "culture" imparted by law schools is one of vigorous advocacy on behalf of the rights of the client. Beyond that, of course, is the idea that the purpose of the practice of law is to seek the truth. Thus, an overriding social concern properly may intrude on the lawyer–client relationship.

The "culture" of the public accountancy profession involves an overriding concern for protecting the rights of all capital market participants to reliable information about organizations. To this end, CPAs ensure that organizations competently provide objective (unbiased) information and advice to facilitate decision making in the market-based economy. This information is used by investors, creditors, employees, government agencies, and others in making important decisions. If CPAs ensure that those responsible for key decisions have optimal information for decision making, an efficient allocation of society's limited resources will result. If CPAs fail, dire consequences would result.

Examination

Once an individual has completed the educational requirement and any other general qualifications as required by their state (for example, age or citizenship), he or she generally becomes eligible to take the Uniform CPA Examination. The examination became computer-based on April 5, 2004. The primary reason the exam was computerized was to "achieve a better alignment between the knowledge and skills required of entry-level CPAs and the requirements of current professional practice."[4]

Candidates can take the Uniform CPA Examination during the first two months of each calendar quarter (that is, January, February, April, May, July, August, October, or November). The exam can be taken at any of more than 300 designated testing centers found across the United States and its territories (see www.prometric.com/cpa for a current list of testing center locations). Any or all of the sections of the examination can be taken during any of the testing months, and the sections can be taken in any order. According to a recent survey, 97 percent of candidates who have taken the computer-based test were satisfied with their experience on the new exam.[5]

The exam consists of the four sections described here. The section descriptions are excerpted from the Uniform CPA Examination Candidate Bulletin, which is available at the following Web site: http://www.cpa-exam.org. You will find the Candidate Bulletin as one of the choices on the "Getting Started" button.

Auditing and Attestation. This section covers knowledge of auditing procedures, generally accepted auditing standards, and other standards related to attest engagements, and the skills needed to apply that knowledge in those engagements. Candidates have up to 4.5 hours to complete this section of the examination.

Financial Accounting and Reporting. This section covers knowledge of generally accepted accounting principles for business enterprises,

---

[4] W.W. Holder and P.B. Thomas, "A Vision Fulfilled," *Journal of Accountancy* (July 2005): 35-39.
[5] See footnote 4.

not-for-profit organizations, and governmental entities, and the skills needed to apply that knowledge. Candidates have up to four hours to complete this section of the examination.

Regulation. This section covers knowledge of federal taxation, ethics, professional and legal responsibilities, and business law, and the skills needed to apply that knowledge. Candidates have up to three hours to complete this section of the exam.

Business Environment and Concepts. This section covers knowledge of general business environment and business concepts that candidates need to know in order to understand the underlying business reasons for, and accounting implications of, business transactions, and the skills needed to apply that knowledge. Candidates have up to 2.5 hours to complete this section of the examination.

For additional details, see *The Uniform CPA Examination Candidate Bulletin* and the CPA Exam Web site (www.cpa-exam.org).

A candidate must pass all four parts of the examination with a score of 75 or higher. According to the National Association of State Boards of Accountancy (NASBA), 50,264 candidates sat for the May 2003 exam and 59,608 candidates sat for the November 2003 exam (the last time the exams were offered on only the specified May and November dates).[6] For those candidates sitting for the first time, 21.4 percent passed all of the parts taken on the May exam, and 19.2 percent passed all parts taken on the November exam. Another 29.8 percent and 30.4 percent passed some parts, while the remainder passed no parts. For repeat candidates, 28.1 percent passed all remaining subjects taken on the May exam, and 25.9 percent passed remaining subjects on the November 2003 examinations.

Obviously, completion of the educational requirement is no guarantee of immediate success on the Uniform CPA Examination. The examination is comprehensive and rigorous. Indeed, it must be to provide comfort to the public that successful CPA candidates will possess the technical skills required to fulfill their role for society. The exam requires a great deal of preparation. Many candidates take review courses specifically designed to prepare them for the examination. Candidates should keep in mind that an overwhelming majority of serious candidates successfully complete the exam even if it takes several attempts.

---

[6] "CPA Candidate Performance on the Uniform CPA Examination," National Association of State Boards of Accountancy (2003 Edition): 5.

In 1996, the CPA examination became a "secure" examination. This means that no questions or answers from the exams would be published after the exam. This rule imposes a confidentiality responsibility on those involved with the exam, including the candidates who take the exam. Each candidate now has to sign a declaration that he or she "will not divulge the nature or content of any question to an individual or entity" and that he or she will "report to the board of accountancy any solicitations and disclosures of which I become aware." Failure to report any such incident can result in invalidation of grades, disqualification from future examinations, and possible civil and criminal penalties.[7]

Experience

After completing the educational and examination requirements, a candidate has accomplished the major steps toward earning the CPA certificate. Many states require that the candidate also obtain one or more years of experience prior to receiving the license and permit to practice. The number of years of required experience and the types of qualifying experience vary by state (see Appendix B).

Continuing Professional Education

To practice, a candidate must also have a current license or permit to practice. The license is typically valid for one to three years before it must be renewed. To maintain the license the states usually require that a CPA obtain continuing professional education. In general, approximately 40 hours per year are required. Education never ends for a CPA. To remain professionally qualified, CPAs must keep up-to-date on laws, standards, and regulations in their area of practice.

Other Requirements

Each jurisdiction has its own individual requirements other than education, examination, and experience. Most jurisdictions require that the candidate complete a special examination or course in Professional Ethics. Once these requirements are met, the candidate receives a CPA certificate. The AICPA has developed an excellent

---

[7] American Institute of Certified Public Accountants, *Information for Boards of Accountancy, Implementing the Nondisclosed Uniform CPA Examination* (January 1996): B-7.

Web site that contains information related to each state and jurisdiction including CPA requirements as well as tax forms and information. The URL for this Web site is http://aicpa.org. At that Web site, navigate to the states news link and then click on the state of your interest on the map.

Qualities of a CPA: Integrity and Objectivity

CPAs cannot function in their role as protectors of information rights without integrity and objectivity. Having integrity means expressing one's views and recommendations genuinely, truthfully, and free of the artificial influence of another. Without integrity, the other attributes mean little or nothing. Being objective means being intellectually honest and not compromised by conflicts of interest.

Independence is the quality required of CPAs to create circumstances that are conducive to being objective, acting with integrity, and applying professional skepticism. Thus, independence is the cornerstone ethical concept in the profession. Carey wrote the following about the meaning of independence:

> Independence is an abstract concept, and it is difficult to define either generally or in its peculiar application to the certified public accountant. Essentially it is a state of mind. It is partly synonymous with honesty, integrity, courage, character. It means in simplest terms, that the certified public accountant will tell the truth as he sees it. And will permit no influence, financial or sentimental, to turn him from that course.[8]

Current audit standards require that:

> In all matters relating to the engagement, an independence in mental attitude shall be maintained by the practitioner. The practitioner should maintain the intellectual honesty and impartiality necessary to reach an unbiased conclusion about the subject matter or the assertion. This is the cornerstone of the attest function. In the final analysis, independence in mental attitude means objective consideration of facts, unbiased judgments, and honest neutrality on the part of the practitioner in forming and expressing conclusions. It implies not the attitude of an advocate or an adversary but an impartiality that recognizes an obligation for fairness. Independence in mental attitude presumes

---
[8] John L. Carey, *Professional Ethics of Public Accounting* (New York: American Institute of Accountants, 1946): 7.

an undeviating concern for an unbiased conclusion about the subject matter or an assertion no matter what the subject matter or the assertion may be. The profession has established, through the AICPA's Code of Professional Conduct, precepts to guard against the presumption of loss of independence. Presumption is stressed because the possession of intrinsic independence is a matter of personal quality rather than of rules that formulate certain objective tests. Insofar as these precepts have been incorporated in the profession's code, they have the force of professional law for the independent practitioner.[9]

The AICPA provides a synthesis of the independence rules in its *Plain English Guide*.[10] AICPA professional standards require firms (including the firm's partners and employees) to be independent (in fact and in appearance) from an attest client. Attest services include financial statement audits, financial statement reviews, and other attest services as defined in the Statements on Standards for Attestations Engagements. A CPA firm does not have to be independent to perform services that are not attest services if the firm is only providing nonattest services to that client.

Independence rules are the minimum standards of independence. The independence rules are set forth in AICPA Rule 101, *Independence* (AICPA, *Professional Standards*, vol. 2, ET sec. 101.01).[11] The first section (section A below) sets forth situations in which independence would be considered impaired for CPAs assigned to the audit engagement (covered members). The second and third sections (sections B and C below) are independence rules for all members of the audit firm as well as immediate family of audit firm employees that are not assigned to the audit engagement in question.

Independence would be considered impaired if:[12]
- A. During the period of the professional engagement, a covered member (partner or engagement team member)
  - (1) Had or was committed to acquire any direct or material indirect financial interest in the client.

---
[9] Excerpted from the AICPA Professional Standards Statements on Standards for Attestation Engagements, AT section 101.35-38.
[10] AICPA, *Plain English Guide to Independence*, March 1, 2005 available on the internet at www.aicpa.org.
[11] AICPA, *Professional Standards*, volume 2, ET section 101.01.
[12] AICPA, *Professional Standards*, volume 2, ET Section 101.02.

(2) Was a trustee of any trust or executor or administrator of any estate if such trust or estate had or was committed to acquire any direct or material indirect financial interest in the client.
(3) Had a joint closely held investment that was material to the covered member.
(4) Except as specifically permitted in interpretation 101-5, had any loan to or from the client, any officer or director of the client, or any individual owning ten percent or more of the client's outstanding equity securities or other ownership interests.

B. During the period of the professional engagement, a partner or professional employee of the firm, his or her immediate family, or any group of such persons acting together owned more than five percent of a client's outstanding equity securities or other ownership interests.

C. During the period covered by the financial statements or during the period of the professional engagement, a partner or professional employee of the firm was simultaneously associated with the client as a(n)
(1) Director, officer, or employee, or in any capacity equivalent to that of a member of management;
(2) Promoter, underwriter, or voting trustee; or
(3) Trustee for any pension or profit-sharing trust of the client.

In September 2005, the Professional Ethics Division of the AICPA issued an exposure draft that includes a framework for AICPA independence standards. It identifies and defines seven broad categories of potential threats to auditor independence (self-review, advocacy, adverse interest, familiarity, undue influence, financial self-interest, and management participation) and three broad categories of safeguards against these threats (safeguards created by the profession; legislation, or regulation, safeguards implemented by the attest client; and safeguards within the audit firm's systems and procedures—including policies and procedures to implement professional and regulatory requirements). The draft defines independence in terms of both independence of mind and independence in appearance. Independence of mind, similar to the concept of independence in fact, refers to the state of mind that permits the performance of an attest service without being affected by influences that compromise professional judgment, thereby allowing an individual to act with integrity and exercise objectivity and professional skepticism. Independence in appearance refers to the avoidance of circumstances that would cause a reasonable and informed third party, having knowledge of all relevant information, including safeguards applied, to reasonably conclude that the integrity, objectivity, or professional skepticism of a firm or a member of the attest engagement team had been compromised.

The seven categories of threats to independence are summarized as follows:

1. *Self-review threat*—Members reviewing as part of an attest engagement evidence that results from their own, or their firm's, nonattest work.
2. *Advocacy threat*—Actions that promote an attest client's interests or position (for example, promoting the client's securities as part of an initial public offering or representing the client in U.S. Tax Court).
3. *Adverse interest threat*—Actions or interests that are in opposition to an attest client's interests or position (for example, the auditor suing the client or vice versa).
4. *Familiarity threat*—Members having a close or longstanding relationship with an attest client of their firm or knowing individuals or entities (including by reputation) who performed nonattest work for the client (for example, a member of the audit team whose spouse serves in an officer position with the client or a partner who has provided the client with attest services for a long period of time).
5. *Undue influence threat*—Attempts by an attest client's management or other interested parties to coerce the auditor or exercise excessive influence over the auditor (for example, a threat to replace the auditor over a disagreement with the client, pressure to reduce necessary audit procedures to reduce audit fees, a significant gift from the client to the auditor).
6. *Financial self-interest threat*—Potential benefit to a member from a financial interest in, or from some other financial relationship with, an attest client (for example, having a direct financial interest or a material indirect financial interest in the client, excessive reliance on revenue from a single client, having a loan from a client or a significant investor in a client).
7. *Management participation threat*—Taking on the role of client management or otherwise performing management functions

on behalf of an attest client (for example, serving as an officer or director of a client; establishing and maintaining internal controls for the client; or hiring, supervising, or terminating the client's employees).

The AICPA exposure draft goes on to offer categories of safeguards against these threats to audit independence.

Safeguards created by the profession, legislation, or regulation. These safeguards include education and training requirements on independence and ethics rules for new professionals, continuing education requirements on independence and ethics, professional standards and monitoring and disciplinary processes, external review of a firm's quality control system, legislation governing the independence requirement of audit firms, and competency and experience requirements for professional licensure.

Safeguards implemented by the attest client that would operate in combination with other safeguards. Examples of safeguards in this category include a tone at the top that emphasizes the attest client's commitment to fair financial reporting; policies and procedures that are designed to achieve fair financial reporting; a governance structure, such as an active audit committee, that is designed to ensure appropriate decision making, oversight, and communications regarding a firm's services; and attest client personnel with the skill, knowledge, and experience to make managerial decisions with respect to the delivery of nonattest services.

Safeguards within the firm's own systems and procedures. The list of examples in this category is quite long, but instructive. Thus, all of the examples from the AICPA exposure draft are provided here:

- Firm leadership that stresses the importance of independence and acting in the public interest, policies and procedures designed to implement and monitor audit quality control, documented policies and procedures for identifying and eliminating threats to independence, policies to ensure compliance with the firm's policies, and policies and procedures that are designed to identify interests or relationships between the firm or its partners and professional staff and attest clients.
- The use of different partners and engagement teams that have separate reporting lines in the delivery of permitted nonattest

services to an attest client, particularly when the separation between reporting lines is significant.
- Training on and timely communication of a firm's policies and procedures, and any changes to them, for all partners and professional staff.
- Policies and procedures that are designed to monitor the firm's reliance on revenue from a single client and, if necessary, cause action to be taken to address excessive reliance.
- Designating someone from senior management as the person who is responsible for overseeing the adequate functioning of the firm's quality control system.
- A means of informing partners and professional staff of attest clients and related entities from which they must be independent.
- A disciplinary mechanism that is designed to promote compliance with policies and procedures.
- Policies and procedures that are designed to empower staff to communicate to senior members of the firm any engagement issues that concern them without fear of retribution.
- Policies and procedures relating to independence communications with audit committees or others charged with client governance.
- Discussing independence issues with the audit committee or others responsible for the client's governance.
- Disclosures to the audit committee (or others responsible for the client's governance) regarding the nature of the services that are or will be provided and the extent of the fees charged or to be charged.
- The involvement of another professional accountant who reviews the work that is done for an attest client or otherwise advises the attest engagement team (this individual could be someone from outside the firm or someone from within the firm who is not otherwise associated with the attest engagement).
- Consultation on engagement issues with an interested third party, such as a committee of independent directors, a professional regulatory body, or another professional accountant.

- Rotation of senior personnel who are part of the attest engagement team.
- Policies and procedures that are designed to ensure that members of the attest engagement team do not make or assume responsibility for management decisions for the attest client.
- The involvement of another firm to perform part of the attest engagement.
- The involvement of another firm to reperform a nonattest service to the extent necessary to enable it to take responsibility for that service.
- The removal of an individual from an attest engagement team when that individual's financial interests or relationships pose a threat to independence.
- A consultation function that is staffed with experts in accounting, auditing, independence, and reporting matters who can help attest engagement teams assess issues when guidance is unclear, or when the issues are highly technical or require a great deal of judgment and resist undue pressure from a client when the engagement team disagrees with the client about such issues.
- Client acceptance and continuation policies that are designed to prevent association with clients that pose an unacceptable threat to the member's independence.
- Policies that preclude audit partners from being directly compensated for selling nonattest services to the audit client.

The AICPA exposure draft incorporates these concepts into a risk-based approach to analyzing independence. The approach entails evaluating the risk that the member would not be independent or would be perceived by a reasonable and informed third party having knowledge of all relevant information as not being independent. That risk must be reduced to an acceptable level to conclude that a member is independent under the concepts in this framework. Risk is at an acceptable level when threats are at an acceptable level, either because of the types of threats and their potential effect, or because safeguards have sufficiently mitigated or eliminated the threats. Threats are at an acceptable level when it is not reasonable to expect that the threat would compromise professional judgment.

The risk-based approach involves the following steps:

1. *Identifying and evaluating threats to independence.* Identify and evaluate threats, both individually and in the aggregate, because threats can have a cumulative effect on a member's independence. Where threats are identified but, due to the types of threats and their potential effects, such threats are considered to be at an acceptable level (that is, it is not reasonable to expect that the threats would compromise professional judgment), the consideration of safeguards is not required. If identified threats are not considered to be at an acceptable level, safeguards should be considered as described in the next section.

2. *Determining whether safeguards already eliminate or sufficiently mitigate identified threats and whether threats that have not yet been mitigated can be eliminated or sufficiently mitigated by safeguards.* Different safeguards can mitigate or eliminate different types of threats, and one safeguard can mitigate or eliminate several types of threats simultaneously. When threats are sufficiently mitigated by safeguards, the threats' potential to compromise professional judgment is reduced to an acceptable level. A threat has been sufficiently mitigated by safeguards if, after application of the safeguards, it is not reasonable to expect that the threat would compromise professional judgment.

The AICPA is not the only entity that has issued rules for CPAs related to independence. The Securities and Exchange Commission (SEC) issues independence-related guidance primarily through staff reports, federal rules or regulations, and even some informal policies and positions of SEC staff members. In February 2003, the SEC adopted rules regarding auditor independence for issuers of public securities. The foundation of the SEC independence rules is based on three principles. First, auditors cannot audit their own work. Second, an auditor cannot function in the role of management. Third, an auditor cannot serve in an advocacy role for a client. The details of the rules are consistent with many of the provisions of the Sarbanes-Oxley Act as well as the AICPA exposure draft discussed in this chapter. The rules prohibit auditors from providing the following nonaudit services:

1. Bookkeeping or other services related to the accounting records or financial statements of the audit client.
2. Financial information systems design and implementation.
3. Appraisal or valuation services, fairness opinions, or contribution-in-kind reports.
4. Actuarial services.
5. Internal audit outsourcing services.
6. Management functions or human resources.
7. Broker or dealer, investment adviser, or investment banking services.
8. Legal services.
9. Expert services unrelated to the audit.

The SEC rules also call for management of the audit engagement by the client's audit committee. To this end, the auditor is not considered independent unless (1) the audit engagement is preapproved by designated outside members of the client's audit committee or (2) the audit engagement is entered into pursuant to preapproved policies and procedures established by the audit committee, the audit committee is informed on a timely basis of each engagement, and the policies and procedures followed by the client company do not include delegation of the audit committee's responsibilities to management. The audit committee must also preapprove all other significant services provided to the company by the independent auditor.

The rules require audit firm lead and concurring partner rotation every five years. Partners rotated off a client engagement must remain off that engagement for at least five years. An audit partner can serve on an engagement for seven consecutive years provided he or she is not a lead or concurring partner on that client for more than five years.

Audit independence is also impaired if the client hires a former member of the audit engagement team into a financial reporting oversight role less than one-year after the auditor worked for the audit firm. A financial reporting oversight role is defined as "a role in which a person is in a position to or does exercise influence over the contents of the financial statements or anyone who prepares them." Regarding communication with audit committees, the SEC rules require that the independent auditors report to the audit committee, prior to issuance of financial statements, (1) all significant accounting policies and practices to be used to prepare the statements; (2) all alternative treatments allowed under GAAP for significant transactions that have been discussed with management as well as the ramifications of the alternative treatments and the treatment preferred by the independent auditors; and (3) all other written communications between the auditors and management (for example, engagement letters, management letters, schedules of unadjusted audit differences, internal control recommendations, and letters confirming the accountant's independence).

The SEC rules also call for vastly expanded disclosure by the issuer about the independent auditor. Required disclosures include (1) the aggregate amount of audit fees billed for each of the last two fiscal years for the annual audit and the quarterly reviews; (2) the aggregate amount of audit-related fees billed in each of the last two years as well as a description of the nature of these services;[13] (3) the aggregate amount of tax fees billed in each of the last two years; (4) the aggregate amount of all other fees billed in each of the last two years as well as a description of these services; (5) the audit committee's preapproval policies and procedures; and (6) the percentage of audit-related fees, tax fees, and other fees that were approved by the audit committee using a *de minimis* exception.

The rules provide that an audit partner will not be considered independent if he or she earns any compensation for procuring agreements with the audit client to provide any services other than audit, review, or attest services. This restriction does not apply to specialty partners such as tax or valuation specialists.

The Government Accountability Office (GAO) provides governmental auditing standards for audits of government agencies. These rules are known as Generally Accepted Government Auditing Standards. Less formally, they are often called the "yellow book" requirements because of the color of the book that contains the

---

[13] Audit-related services include assurance and related services such as due diligence services that are traditionally provided by the primary independent accountant.

guidance. Their guidance synthesizes independence to overarching principles that underlie many of the rules presented above. The GAO principles are that *auditors should not* do any of the following:

1. Perform management functions.
2. Make management decisions.
3. Audit their own work.
4. Provide nonaudit services in situations where the amounts or services involved are significant and material to the subject matter of their audit.

The Sarbanes-Oxley Act of 2002 is the most recent law affecting business and CPA practice. Among its many provisions is rule-based guidance related to independence for audits of publicly traded companies. These rules are similar to the AICPA guidance above. These rules are presented in Chapter 8, along with the other provisions of Sarbanes-Oxley. Finally, Sarbanes-Oxley gives the Public Companies Accounting Oversight Board (PCAOB) power to issue additional independence-related rules as deemed necessary. To date, the PCAOB has adopted as interim PCAOB standards on independence, the standards set forth by the AICPA and the SEC.

Rigorous Examiner/Engaging Diplomat: A Delicate Balance

The independent auditor is hired and paid by the client company. Once hired, the CPA serves on behalf of the current and potential capital providers to the company. This can create a dilemma. On the one hand, the primary goal of the CPA is to provide an unbiased informed opinion about the financial statements for the benefit of global capital market participants. To this end, the auditor must rigorously examine the company and challenge its officers and directors to defend their practices, records, and disclosures. On the other hand, in most instances the CPA would like to be retained and provide the audit services in future years. To accomplish this, the CPA must remain respected and hopefully even admired by the client. Thus, the auditor must be a tough advocate for the shareholders, but also an engaging diplomat for client officers and directors.

The Process of Developing CPA Qualities in Aspirants

Individuals do not spring full-blown into professional life, ready at once to take on all challenges in a discipline such as public accounting. Competence and self-confidence take time to acquire. Individuals entering the profession first acquire basic technical knowledge through formal training both in universities and at firms. Professional ethics come from many sources, not the least of which may be family values and/or religious grounding. These carry over into professional life and enhance an individual's ability to function with integrity and self-confidence. Experience and the guidance of mature professionals are the next essentials.

A professional firm furnishes the initial exposure to the working environment. The scope and range of services to clients may differ between larger and smaller firms, but the ethical principles ideally are the same. The ethical foundation consists of written and unwritten (1) rules of conduct, (2) attitudes toward clients, (3) dedication to the profession itself, and (4) encouragement in the development of a sense of individual responsibility. Firms have the duty to provide this support, and aspiring CPAs should demand it. The extent to which these conditions are present in employment outside of public accounting firms varies tremendously, but the necessary environment of dedication to responsible and ethical behavior is the same.[14] A pattern of "professional" behavior should be the norm wherever the CPA is practicing.

This early phase of a CPA's development is "on-the-job-training." But the process is more than just instructions from superiors regarding how to perform some accounting or auditing task. It is during this period that careers are shaped, technically and ethically. Supervisors charged with guiding the development of subordinates have an important task.[15] First, supervisors evaluate subordinates on technical knowledge, and help the subordinates to further their

---

[14] Laws dealing with the qualifications necessary for the granting of a CPA certificate vary widely from state to state in the amount and nature of required experience in public accounting or under the direction of an individual already holding a certificate. Some states have dropped the experience requirement entirely, and grant the certificate based only upon educational attainments and the passing of the uniform CPA examination.

[15] The authors are indebted for some of these notions to a study of social interactions in a medical training environment. Charles L. Bosk, *Forgive and Remember, Managing Medical Failure*, University of Chicago Press, 1979.

knowledge. Second, supervisors evaluate subordinates with respect to the ethical rules of the profession and the personal standards of the superior. Again, supervisors impart their view of ethical standards and norms. Third, since failure of subordinates to measure up to either technical or ethical norms on occasions is to be expected, supervisors evaluate the seriousness of deviations, correct errors, protect the client from adverse effects, and support the development of the subordinates' self-confidence in the face of momentary failure.

Summary

Key qualities of CPAs include a commitment to serve, competence, integrity, and objectivity. New college graduates do not spring into the profession fully formed with respect to these qualities. The development of competence and commitment occurs over many years from education, examination, experience, and continuing education. Education refers to the university education required to enter the profession (150 hours of college). The examination refers to the Uniform CPA Examination that is required to demonstrate technical competence to serve the public interest. Experience refers to professional "on the job training" gained by young CPAs under the supervision of more experienced CPAs. Finally, continuing education refers to the required lifelong learning required of CPAs to ensure that professionals remain competent in the dynamic profession. This chapter examines the process by which young CPAs acquire and polish their professional CPA qualities. The profession requires that practitioners remain independent in appearance and in fact from attest clients to establish an environment conducive to integrity and objectivity. Accounting professors, colleagues, and supervisors all play a role in the development of professional CPAs. However, the primary responsibility for commitment, competence, integrity, and objectivity rests with the individual and their understanding of the fiduciary responsibility to the client or employer.

3

CPA Careers

> CPAs are professionals, distinguished from other accountants by stringent licensing requirements . . . CPAs provide audit, review and compilation services for businesses. They also provide tax assistance, management advisory services and estate and personal financial planning. CPAs act as advisors to individuals, businesses, financial institutions, nonprofit organizations and government agencies on a wide range of finance-related matters. CPAs also work as financial managers in industry, education, and various levels of government.
>
> American Institute of Certified Public Accountants[1]

Introduction

This chapter explores career opportunities available to CPAs and describes the structure of those careers. We should begin by pointing out that a CPA possesses a "monolithic identity." That is, a CPA is a CPA whether in public or corporate practice. This is true for physicians and attorneys as well. They retain their identity as doctors or lawyers whether they work in public practice or in corporate practice (that is, whether they work directly for a patient or client or

---

[1] *A Guide to Understanding and Using CPA Services* (New York: AICPA, 1984).

whether they are a part of corporate management). The AICPA membership and ethical requirements place the corporate practicing CPA under the same expectations as the public practice CPA.[2] Indeed, CPAs in any line of service should adhere to the requirements (for example, a CPA proprietor of an independent business).

Some have stereotyped accountants as "number crunchers, tax geeks, or bean counters." However, these stereotypes do not apply to most positions held by CPAs. The education, examination, and experience required of CPAs distinguish them from non-CPA accountants. These requirements are not simply hurdles that must be cleared. They are activities that provide skills, abilities, and experiences that are valued highly by the job market.

Obtaining a CPA certificate entitles an individual to practice "public accounting." However, the CPA's opportunities are not limited to public accounting by any means. There are a wide variety of opportunities for CPAs in public accounting, private or corporate practice, government and not-for-profit entities, and education. The AICPA has more than 334,000 members (as of 2004).[3] The actual number of CPAs is higher since not all CPAs are members of the AICPA. Of this total, about 42 percent are in corporate practice, 39 percent in public practice, 4 percent in government, 2 percent in education and the remainder (13 percent) is in a variety of other practices or retired. Less than half of the AICPA members actually practice public accounting. Many CPAs start their career with public accounting firms and later move to corporate practice, government/not-for-profit, or education.

There are many opportunities for promotion within public, private, government, and education practices. This chapter explores the typical opportunities, career paths, structure, and lifestyle for CPAs in public practice, corporate practice, government/not-for-profit practice, and in education. Chapter 4 sets forth the scope of services offered by CPAs in public practice.

---

[2] P.B. Chenok, "The New Ethics Code," *Journal of Accountancy* (June 1989): 4.
[3] AICPA Annual Report 2003-2004, Total AICPA Membership (excluding student and other affiliates).

CPAs in Public Practice

CPAs in public practice provide services to corporations, not-for profit organizations, individuals, and governmental units, to name just a few. They fulfill a need for independent, objective review or advice and provide a source of specialized knowledge and experience. CPA firms are typically organized as partnerships, sole proprietorships, professional corporations, or limited liability companies, depending upon the state of organization. Limited liability partnerships provide partnership treatment for tax purposes. Limited liability partnerships and corporations shield partners from most liability other than for professional malpractice.

The firms can range in size from a sole practitioner in a single office to thousands of partners in hundreds of offices worldwide. Table 3.1 presents a summary of the 20 largest firms providing public accounting and tax services as determined by *Accounting Today*.[4] The "Big Four" firms continue to dwarf even their largest rivals. This has created concerns about the potential lack of competition for audit and tax services. William McDonough, the former chairman of the Public Company Accounting Oversight Board (PCAOB), acknowledges the problem but asks, "What can be done about it?"[5] Indeed, there are no easy solutions to the problem.

Table 3.1 also provides a breakdown of firm revenues into accounting and auditing (A&A), tax, consulting (management advisory services, or MAS), and other services. These are the broad categories of services generally associated with public accounting firms. Accounting and auditing services primarily involve the *compilation, review*, or *audit* of an organization's financial statements. In a compilation, the CPA *prepares* a set of financial statements. In a *review* or an *audit*, the CPA attests to the fairness of presentation of financial statements prepared by the organization's management. In the tax area, a CPA may assist clients in preparing required tax filings, perform research on tax rules, and advise clients on how best to structure transactions from a tax perspective. In consulting, the CPA provides services based upon specialized knowledge and experience. Some

---

[4] "The 2005 Accounting Today Top 100 Firms," *Accounting Today*.
[5] J. Goff, "They Might Be Giants," *CFO* (January 2004): 47.

Table 3.1
Top 20 Tax and Accounting Firms

Firm	Revenue (millions)	Offices	Partners	Professionals	Total Employees	Fee Split % (A&A/Tax/ MAS, Other)
Deloitte & Touche	$6,876.0	107	2,568	20,276	29,378	40/26/30/4
Ernst & Young	$5,514.0	95	2,000	16,489	25,089	67/30/3/0
Pricewaterhouse-Coopers	$5,189.5	125	2,200	21,210	23,300	65/30/5/0
KPMG	$4,115.0	95	1,585	11,866	18,331	72/28/0/0
H&R Block	$4,108.0	10,300	N/A	N/A	15,300	0/51/12/37
Grant Thornton	$ 634.8	49	368	2,686	3,923	53/29/18/0
RMS McGladrey	$ 585.8	92	467	2,618	4,024	42/35/20/3
Jackson Hewitt Tax Services	$ 460.1	4,935	N/A	280	377	0/100/0/0
American Express Tax & Business Services	$ 385.0	48	N/A	1,900	2,500	32/36/32/0
Cbiz/Mayer Hoffman McCann	$ 373.5	127	231	1,610	3,633	23/27/50/0
BDO Seidman	$ 365.0	36	258	1,241	1,947	50/33/17/0
Crowe Group	$ 286.2	19	170	1,014	1,502	28/20/36/16
BKD	$ 230.6	27	197	976	1,496	44/35/21/0
Moss Adams	$ 199.0	18	183	835	1,319	38/36/26/0

Firm	Revenue (millions)	Offices	Partners	Professionals	Total Employees	Fee Split % (A&A/Tax/ MAS, Other)
Plante & Moran	$ 198.6	17	161	810	1,255	48/33/19/0
UHY Advisors	$ 174.2	19	98	624	1,039	30/36/34/0
Clifton Gunderson	$ 160.0	50	145	1,012	1,380	44/27/29/0
Virchow, Krause & Co.	$ 136.3	12	128	718	974	35/32/20/13
Larson Allen	$ 105.0	841	82	513	766	47/29/22/2
J.H. Cohn	$ 103.1	9	90	420	629	54/18/7/21

Data represents U.S. operations only.
Adapted from "The 2005 Accounting Today Top 100 Firms," *Accounting Today*, a SourceMedia publication. Reprinted with permission.

CPA firms offer a wide array of services, while others specialize in particular areas of practice. *Accounting Today* reports a wide array of "niche" services provided by the top 100 firms. These services include business valuations, computer systems, litigation support, employee benefits, and personal financial planning, among others.[6]

The AICPA now offers specialty designations in two of these areas: personal financial planning and business valuation. These specialty designations indicate that an individual has obtained both knowledge and experience in the specialty area beyond that required for the CPA examination and certification. The *Personal Financial Specialist* program accredits CPAs who specialize in assisting individuals in defining their financial goals and designing a plan to meet those goals. For example, CPAs often assist clients in planning to pay for a child's college education and/or for the client's retirement. This area requires knowledge of income taxes, estate taxes, insurance, retirement plans, and investments. According to CEG Worldwide, approximately 17 percent of CPA firms currently offer investment management services and nearly half will do so within three years.[7] The AICPA reports that 23,000 of its members provide financial planning services including 15,000 that are NASD licensed to sell investment products.[8] The Personal Financial Planning Division of the AICPA provides educational and other resources for CPAs who practice in this area.

The *Accredited in Business Valuation* program accredits CPAs who specialize in determining an estimate of the value of a business enterprise. This service is used in a variety of circumstances, including buying or selling a business, estate tax work, and in connection with employee stock ownership or option plans. Both of these specialties require that the individual pass an exam and demonstrate substantial experience in the area. The AICPA offers courses to assist individuals in acquiring competence in these areas through its Certificate in Educational Achievement Program.

CPAs in public practice usually follow a standard career path at a CPA firm: staff accountant, senior accountant, manager, and

---

[6] "The 2005 Accounting Today Top 100 Firms," *Accounting Today*.

[7] S. Zimmerman, "Build Customized Bond Portfolios," *Journal of Accountancy* (April 2005): 38.

[8] Barry Melancon, "In Support of CPA Financial Planners," *Journal of Accountancy* (February 2005): 30.

partner. An attractive aspect of public accounting is this generally accepted career path, which features relatively frequent promotions in responsibility and position relative to other careers. A *staff accountant* represents the entry-level position. A staff accountant is typically assigned to a team and is under the direct supervision of a senior accountant. The staff accountant is promoted to senior accountant after he or she has obtained sufficient experience. This usually occurs in two to three years, depending upon the education and experience of the staff member. The *senior accountant* assists in planning the work to be performed as well as supervising the work of staff accountants. As the name suggests, the next level, manager, entails more managerial responsibility. The *manager* is responsible for supervising senior and staff accountants, serving existing clients, and developing new clients. The most senior level of responsibility rests with the *partner*. Depending upon the organizational form, this individual may hold an ownership stake in the firm. Some firms also have designations such as *principal*, which represents an equivalent level of responsibility without ownership.

While there are many nonfinancial rewards to being a professional accountant, the salaries and financial benefits are excellent as well. Salaries in public accounting vary among firms, regions, and specialization. Table 3.2 provides aggregate salary information from Robert Half International.[9] For entry-level positions, candidates usually earn from $34,000 to $47,000 depending primarily upon the size and location of the firm. As you can see, the financial rewards increase to the manager/director level, with salaries ranging from $69,000 to $125,000. Partner compensation is not shown in the table and varies based upon profitability of the firm, individual offices, and practice units within an office.[10]

Recently, recruitment of CPAs has intensified in response to demand for accountants to fulfill additional financial reporting and auditing responsibilities resulting from regulatory changes. According to Andrea Hopkins of Reuters News, "No degree is more in demand than accounting, where the starting salary averages $44,564." Ernst & Young alone expected to hire 4,500 accounting

---

[9] 2005 Salary Guide, Robert Half International (2005).

[10] Practice units in a firm broadly include audit, tax, and management consulting. These units are discussed in greater detail elsewhere in this book.

Table 3.2
2005 Accounting Salaries

Public Accounting: Audit, Tax, and Management Services

Large Firms (Over $250 million in sales)

Experience/Title:	2005 Salary Range:
To 1 year	$41,750–47,000
1–3 years	$47,000–55,000
Senior	$55,000–69,000
Manager	$68,000–92,000
Mgr/Director	$81,750–125,000

Medium Firms ($25 to $250 million in sales)

Experience/Title:	2005 Salary Range:
To 1 year	$35,000–42,000
1–3 years	$42,250–48,000
Senior	$48,250–62,000
Manager	$64,500–80,250
Mgr/Director	$74,000–107,500

Small Firms (up to $25 million in sales)

Experience/Title:	2005 Salary Range:
To 1 year	$34,000–39,250
1–3 years	$38,000–45,000
Senior	$45,000–57,000
Manager	$57,750–69,000
Mgr/Director	$69,000–87,750

2005 Robert Half and Accountemps Salary Guide. Reprinted with permission.

graduates in 2005.[11] The hiring is certainly not limited to recent graduates. The national director of one large accounting firm said, "We would hire every person we could who is experienced enough to tackle work on Sarbanes-Oxley 404." A survey of public accounting recruiters reported that pay is up 10 percent or more and that the base salary for a junior partner with 10 to 12 years experience is $500,000 at the large international firms.[12]

---

[11] A. Hopkins, "Accountants Are Kings Among U.S. 2005 Graduates," Reuters (June 5, 2005).

[12] S. McGee, "CPA Recruitment Intensifies as Accounting Rules Evolve," *Wall Street Journal* (March 22, 2005): B6.

The workload for CPAs varies based on the individual's area of expertise (that is, audit, tax, or consulting), the time of year, the responsibility level of the individual, and the characteristics of the engagement or engagements to which the individual is currently assigned. CPA firms have to compete with the corporate world for talent. As a result, firms are implementing attractive and sometimes creative packages of perquisites for professional staff, including higher salaries, signing bonuses, more vacation, and innovations such as concierge services to help with errands. Individual firms offer other innovations. For example, Deloitte offers leaves of absence of up to five years. New parents have chosen to take advantage of this perquisite in order to remain home during their child's preschool days. During that time, Deloitte provides continuing education to the professional to ensure that he or she remains abreast of professional developments.[13] Other firms, such as Alpern Rosenthal based in Pittsburgh, Pennsylvania, have several parents working part-time schedules. Alpern Rosenthal even allows one shareholding partner to work a part-time schedule.[14]

CPAs in Corporate Practice

More than half of all CPAs do not work in public accounting. These CPAs are said to be in corporate practice, industry, or private accounting. CPAs find that opportunities are virtually limitless in corporations. The CPA designation connotes ability and integrity. These are two very valuable commodities to a corporate employer. As a result, CPAs are found throughout companies right up to the chairman of the board and chief executive officer. In fact, many CPAs find themselves working in important and rewarding positions that have little or nothing to do with the day-to-day accounting activities at the company.

CPAs continue to become increasingly important to their organizations and to the profession. Companies employing CPAs range from small closely held organizations to large publicly traded

---

[13] See for example, "Green Eyeshades Never Looked So Sexy: Raises, Perks, Long Sabbaticals—Auditors Can Write Their Own Ticket These Days," *Business Week* (January 10, 2005): 44.

[14] J. Gannon, "Accounting Firms Earn Plaudits for More Flexible Hours, Schedules for Employees," *Pittsburgh Post—Gazette*, April 15, 2005.

corporations. Within these organizations CPAs work in a variety of areas such as general accounting, financial reporting, cost accounting, internal auditing, information systems auditing, tax accounting, controllership, and treasury operations. CPAs are also found outside of finance in positions such as chief operating officer. The career path is somewhat similar to that in public accounting, although each firm has it own unique terminology for each position. Positions usually filled by accountants include but are not limited to the following.

Staff accountant. This individual is responsible for maintaining the general journal and general ledger, reconciling ledger accounts, and assisting with the process of closing the accounts at the end of reporting periods. This would be an entry-level position for young CPAs, but is also often held by non-CPAs.

Cost accountant. This is a position found primarily in manufacturing firms. This individual is responsible for measuring and monitoring production costs. Often this individual will have responsibility for measuring the cost of production of a particular product or set of products, a particular process or set of processes, and/or a particular plant location or set of plant locations.

Financial analyst. This individual works to develop and monitor operating budgets at the company. In addition, financial analysts are often called upon for special financial analyses on an *ad hoc* basis.

Senior accountant. This individual heads a team of staff accountants in the day-to-day accounting functions described in this chapter as well as taking charge of some of the more complex accounts at the company. Experienced non-CPA accountants or early career CPAs usually hold this position.

Accounting manager. This individual is responsible for overseeing the day-to-day accounting operations, including maintenance of the general journal and the general ledger. The accounting manager is usually a CPA at mid-sized and large companies.

Assistant controller. This individual assists the controller in carrying out the controllership function. The assistant controller is usually a CPA.

Controller. This is the chief accounting officer of the company. The controller is responsible for the accounting organization and the quality and integrity of accounting information. To this end, the controller supervises the accounting manager and prepares and analyzes financial statements and budgets. The controller is also responsible for ensuring that the company's internal control system is sound and that all financial reporting guidelines are followed. The controller is usually a CPA.

CFO/treasurer. This is the chief financial officer (CFO) of the company. The treasurer has ultimate responsibility for the finance and accounting activities at the company, including preparation and monitoring of the operating budgets, maintenance of the accounting systems, generation of relevant and reliable financial reporting, capital budgeting decisions, and financing decisions. The treasurer is usually a CPA.

Chief executive officer (CEO). Many companies promote CPAs to the top position in the company. CEOs that are CPAs usually have spent several years distinguishing themselves as the CFO or sometimes the chief operating officer (COO).

Several CPAs usually constitute the company's internal audit division as well. This division performs operational and financial audits of the company and will work closely with the independent auditors on the outside audit of the company. Position titles in internal audit are similar to those in CPA firms. The director of internal audit will usually report to the company's board of directors via the board's audit committee. Large companies will usually have a tax department that will also employ several CPAs. The tax department is responsible for complying with all required international, national, state, and local tax filing requirements. In addition, the tax department fulfills an advisory role to ensure that transactions are structured to minimize the tax burden faced by the company.

Table 3.3 provides Robert Half International salary data for the corporate practice environment.

The importance of private practice to the CPA profession is highlighted by the AICPA's formation of the *Center for Excellence in Financial Management* (CEFM). The CEFM is an alliance of activities of the AICPA geared toward members in corporate practice. The CEFM provides resources in the areas of professional education, research, benchmarking, information, and publications. It serves as an area where members in corporate practice can obtain new skills, improve existing skills, and compare their company's performance and operations to the best practices of other companies.

Table 3.3
2005 Accounting Salaries

Corporate Practice

General, Audit and Cost Accountants

Large Companies (Over $250 million in sales):	2005 Salary Range:
To 1 year	$31,750–39,750
1 to 3 years	$37,500–48,750
Senior	$48,000–63,000
Manager	$61,250–83,250

Corporate Controller

Company volume in millions:

$500 +	$105,750–147,250
$250–500	$95,000–129,000
$100–200	$81,000–106,750
$50–100	$68,500–87,750
To $50	$44,500–65,750

Tax Director

Company volume in millions:

$250+	$117,000–209,750
$50–250	$86,750–129,250

CFO, Treasurers

Company volume in millions:

$500+	$244,500–347,000
$250–500	$170,250–231,250
$100–250	$111,750–153,250
$50–100	$92,750–122,500
To $50	$84,500–111,000

2005 Robert Half and Accountemps Salary Guide. Reprinted with permission.

How Does the Corporate CPA Career Evolve?

"Cheshire Puss . . . would you please tell me which way I ought to go from here?" asked Alice. "That depends a good deal on where you want to get to," said the Cat."[15]

---

[15] Lewis Carroll *Alice's Adventures in Wonderland.*

Over 80 percent of CPAs working in companies began their career in public accounting. Obviously, since less than 50 percent of CPAs are in public accounting, a CPA's career path often leads to the corporation setting. The CFO position is often the long-term goal. Some CFOs are promoted from within the organization while others are recruited into the company, often from a CPA firm. The following financial press item (detail removed) describes one such career change.

> The "BB Co." a retailer [listed on the New York Stock Exchange] yesterday named "AA" age 36, chief financial officer effective July 1. "AA" has been in training at "BB Co" since last January and . . . is a good selection for . . . [the] post. "bb is not only a CPA but . . . has spent the last 13 years with the public accounting firm of "CC" managing engagements for " DD Co." and "EE Co." [other retailers.][16]

What Resources Are Available to CPAs in Corporate Practice?

As described earlier, the AICPA has vast resources available to support the corporate CPA. In addition to the AICPA, there are several professional associations that seek to serve and support the career needs of CPAs in corporate practice. Although these organizations are not the size of the AICPA, they offer specialty attention to individuals who are identified with their corporate roles. Three examples of such organizations include:

1. The Institute of Management Accountants (IMA), with over 50,000 members, was founded shortly after World War I, and then named the National Association of Cost Accountants. Its headquarters is in Montvale, New Jersey. This organization sponsors programs awarding the Certified Management Accountant (CMA) and Certified Financial Manager (CFM) credentials.
2. The Financial Executives Institute (FEI), currently numbers 15,000 members in the United States and Canada. It was founded in 1931 as the Controllers Institute of America. Its offices are in Morristown, New Jersey.

---

[16] Donald Sabath, "OfficeMax Hires Ex-Revco Execs," *The Plain* Dealer [Cleveland] (June 18, 1997): C1.

3. The Institute of Internal Auditors (IIA), with about 13,000 members, was formed during the time of World War II (December 9, 1941). Its headquarters location is Altamonte Springs, Florida. This organization sponsors programs leading to the Certified Internal Auditor (CIA) designation.

The first two of these national organizations are broader in scope of membership interest than the last. However, it is quite common for an individual to belong to several if not all of these organizations as well as the AICPA. The value each organization, and its particular chapter or national entity, provides in terms of meeting location, program content, and peer contact often are important factors in deciding to select such organizations.

Collectively, these professional organizations have the potential to collaborate and form multidisciplinary groups when matters of public policy cut across the interests of their members. Recent examples of issues engendering collaboration include professional education and accreditation, the cost of compliance with Sarbanes-Oxley, measurement and disclosure of stock options, and taxation of dividends. The "politics" of the CPA profession therefore extend to the need for diplomacy among peer organizations to determine what constitutes the public interest in complex accounting, and reporting matters affecting the capital markets.

CPAs in Government Practice and Not-for-Profit Organizations

The U.S. government and the various state and local governments constitute the largest economic entity in the world. The number of AICPA members working in government or not-for-profit practice is about 15,000. When one considers that many CPAs in public practice, however, are also involved in serving government and philanthropic clients, that number might easily be doubled. The types of entities usually included in this category of practice include the IRS, the Federal Bureau of Investigation (FBI), the Government Contract Audit Agency, several other governmental units, colleges and universities, health care providers, and voluntary welfare organizations.

Since these agencies rely upon the generous donated funds of individuals, it is especially important for the agencies to be responsible stewards of the funds. As a result, CPAs' fiduciary skills are valued greatly. Government accountability legislation suggests that CPAs will become increasingly involved in government practice. Examples of important legislation include the Inspector General Act of 1978, which created the Office of Inspector General in each major cabinet level agency; the Federal Manager's Financial Integrity Act of 1982, which requires involvement of the highest department official in the review of financial accountability and performance of an agency; and the Single Audit Act of 1984, which mandates an annual audit for state and local government programs receiving directly or indirectly $100,000 or more a year in federal financial assistance. Accounting standards promulgated by the Financial Accounting Standards Board (FASB) require not-for-profit organizations to follow many of the same standards as publicly held corporations.

Government practice also includes the important function of policy setting and oversight. CPAs often hold important positions such as comptroller general of the United States, chairman of the Federal Deposit Insurance Corporation (FDIC), chief accountant of the Securities and Exchange Commission, and the inspectors general of cabinet level agencies. CPAs serve in a variety of state and local positions such as the chief fiscal officer for municipal, county, and state governments. CPAs also serve as government auditors in the IRS, the Defense Contract Audit Agency, the Government Accountability Office (GAO), and Defense Department agencies. The FBI recruits CPAs to assist in investigations related to criminal enforcement (especially white-collar crime). With the Government Accounting Standards Board (GASB) as a private sector agency to set governmental accounting standards, and the Cost Accounting Standards Board (CASB), there is great demand by public sector agencies for qualified CPAs to meet the expectation among taxpayers and holders of government financial instruments for more accountability.

Given the significant portion of our nation's assets and activities dedicated to the government and nonprofit sectors, the accounting function and the role of the CPA in these entities and operations may often be underestimated. Much has changed, however, with regard to practice in this sector due to the activities of the Governmental Accounting Standards Board (GASB) and due to the active leadership by recent U.S. Comptroller Generals (for example, Charles Bowsher and David Walker).[17]

The vulnerability of nonprofit entities to fraud and misdeed has also been the subject of attention due to episodes of what is alleged to have been management excesses at the national United Way organization,[18] and fraud in the dealings of the Foundation for New Era Philanthropy (New Era).[19] Professor Albert Meyer, who is credited with leading officials to investigate and ultimately reveal New Era's pyramid, commented as follows: "There is simply no substitute for certified, audited financial statements" as part of the due diligence which should be performed by voluntary agencies undertaking investments of any substantial amount.[20]

CPAs in Education

CPA educators constituted a relatively small percentage, 2 percent in 2004, of the AICPA community. One of the major transformations in the profession has been the development of full-time, fully qualified accounting academics. These CPA educators earn a Ph.D. and become skilled in research, critical thinking, and communication and teaching. As educators first, the full-time demands of academic life often preclude a substantial CPA practice.[21]

However, the use of fully qualified accounting academics is a relatively recent development. During the early part of the 20th century, it was common for practitioners to teach and to staff the accountancy faculty of universities. Most major universities relied on practitioner-teachers through the World War II era. Eventually, collegiate accounting education became, as with other CPA activities, a specialized vocation. In 1967, the Association to Advance

---

[17] Gary John Previts, and Richard Brown, "The Development of Government Accounting: A Content Analysis of *The Journal of Accountancy* 1905 to 1989," *The Accounting Historians Journal* (December 1993): 119-138.

[18] T. McLaughlin, (1995). "Lessons from United Way," *Association Management*, 47(8): 24.

[19] Thomas S. Giles, "'Double-Your-Money' Scam Burns Christian Groups," *Christianity Today* (June 19, 1995): 40-41.

[20] Randy Frame, "The 'Post-New Era' Era," *Christianity Today* (July 17, 1995): 61.

[21] R. J. Bricker, and Gary John Previts, "The Sociology of Accountancy: A Study of Academic and Practice Community Schisms," *Accounting Horizons* (March 1990): 1-14.

Collegiate Schools of Business (then known as the American Assembly of Collegiate Schools of Business), the principal accreditation agency for business programs, established that the doctorate was to be the terminal degree requirement for accountancy faculty.

The role of education in preparing the future CPA professional is a specialized and demanding task. First, CPA educators must acquire a mastery of areas related to practice to provide outstanding instruction to students. Second, CPA educators are relied upon to conduct research into matters relevant to the discipline. Third, CPA educators hold key leadership positions in the profession, such as membership on the FASB and GASB.

Most accounting professors today have earned a doctorate. CPAs interested in exploring an education career should consult the Web sites of university accounting doctoral programs for additional information. Some teaching opportunities do exist for CPAs that don't have a doctorate. For example, community colleges and some universities employ lecturers that have master's-level degrees. Also, many large universities now employ a limited number of "clinical" professors who have vast practice experience. These "clinical" professors are usually retired CPA firm partners or corporate CFOs.

CPA Training Is Great for Virtually All Endeavors

CPAs can employ their skills and abilities in virtually limitless ways. A recent issue of the *Journal of Accountancy* depicted several such examples. Brian Cardozo, one of several entrepreneurs chronicled, was a partner at the CPA firm BDO Seidman. Cardozo used all that he had learned from his days as a practicing CPA to buy and operate a wildly successful Harley Davidson franchise in San Jose, California. Cardozo points out that "my ability to analyze the company's financial data has been enormously helpful." Greg DeVito took his skills and perspective to the high school classroom in Storrs, Connecticut. Students now flock to his high school classes. Heather Johnson-Moreno left KPMG to start a fitness services business. Terry Nolan of Canton, Ohio, has bought 10 companies over the past 20 years. Nolan offers that a CPA "learns to manage money, which helps in becoming an entrepreneur." Joanie Sompayrac, Thomas Kozloski, Greg Geisler, and countless other CPAs left public practice to become university professors. Frank Page, a Florida CPA, has taken his career in arguably the most unique direction. He works as a comedian billing himself as "Florida's Funniest CPA!"[22]

Diversity in the CPA Profession

Because qualified CPAs are continually in demand, the opportunity for individuals of both genders and all backgrounds to succeed are plentiful. This statement is truer now than ever. Entry level positions in accounting, as in medicine and law, require increasing periods of education. The AICPA and state societies have established many educational development programs. The AICPA alone devotes millions of dollars annually for scholarships and assistance programs to support minority education at the collegiate level. Many of the national and international CPA firms also fund millions of dollars of scholarships each year as well. Minorities and women members serve in the highest offices of the profession: as presidents of state societies, on the board of directors of the AICPA, and as deans and professors of accountancy at business schools. For example, the current chair of the AICPA is Leslie Murphy. She is the third woman in the past 10 years to chair the AICPA. Murphy said this about opportunities for women in the profession: "Much has changed in our profession over the past several decades. Most significant is the abandonment of the assumption that women are not willing to make the commitment necessary to be successful."

Women now represent more than half of the graduates in accounting and increasingly are moving into the partner position and assuming leadership roles within firms. The professional service environment provides significant opportunity for flexibility, which is fundamental for striking an appropriate balance between personal and work commitments."[23]

Much remains to be accomplished, however, if the profession is to continue to warrant its reputation as the "opportunity" profession. The profession earned this reputation by providing the structure for thousands of its members to effectively use their skills and education to fulfill societal needs, while simultaneously improving

---

[22] Elizabeth Danziger, "Off the Beaten Path," *Journal of Accountancy* (July 2004): 49-56.

[23] N. R. Baldiga, "Looking Forward: A Talk With Leslie Murphy," *Journal of Accountancy* (September 2005): 34-36.

their own standards of living and position. The future of women in the profession, for instance, is dictated by their relatively recent and increasing presence.

Clearly, with a large number of women entering the profession, the number of women reaching managerial and partnership levels will continue to increase dramatically. Of course, the demands placed on CPAs by the needs of their clients can, at times, place burdens upon the family life of CPAs. CPA firms recognize this problem and are continually innovating to minimize the problem. Examples of recent innovations were previously described (that is, concierge services and sabbaticals).

The AICPA reports that 7 percent of CPAs employed by accounting firms are minorities.[24] One minority population, African Americans, are entering the CPA profession at an increasing rate. Dr. Quinton Booker reported that 4,838, 5,020, and 5,731 African American candidates took the CPA exam between 2000 and 2002. While more recent empirical data is not available, anecdotal evidence suggests that this trend persists.

A majority of these candidates are female (between 62 percent and 65 percent) and just over half of the candidates are less than 30 years of age. Between 5 percent and 9 percent of African American candidates taking the exam during the three years studied passed all subjects attempted the first time. Repeat candidates fared much better with annual passing rates between 15 percent and 17 percent. Thus, as is true for the population of exam candidates as a whole, persistence is crucial.

The good news is that these numbers reflect a nicely increasing trend. The bad news is that these numbers are only about 5 percent of the CPA exam candidates in the respective years. Further, only 40 percent of African American candidates had earned 150 hours of college credit. Candidates must now obtain the 150 hours in most states to qualify to take the CPA exam.[25]

While a study similar to Dr. Booker's has not been published to date related to Latinos in the accounting profession, the number of

---

[24] D. Hobson, "AICPA Diversity Initiatives," *Journal of Accountancy* (May 2005): 63.
[25] Q. Booker, "African American Students and the CPA Exam," *Journal of Accountancy* (May 2005): 60-64.

Latino practicing CPAs seems to be significantly greater than the number.[26]

Clearly, the profession has more work to do recruiting minorities into the profession. The AICPA reports the following initiatives to this end:[27]

- *Advertising.* The AICPA has advertising campaigns designed to attract young people of color to the Accounting profession (for example, "Be a Star in Business" and "Start Here, Go Places"). The Web site for this program is www.aicpa.org/members/div/career/mini/be_star_business.htm.
- *College Residency Programs.* The AICPA conducts week long programs for high school students in which young students and their parents are exposed to opportunities in accounting and other business careers. The Web site for this program is www.aicpa.org/members/div/career/mini/college_residency_program.htm.
- *Minority Scholarship Programs.* In the past 10 years, the AICPA has awarded scholarships totaling over $6 million. In 2004, $488,000 was awarded to 157 students attending 107 different universities. The Web site for this program is www.aicpa.org/members/div/career/mini/smas.htm.
- *Accounting Scholars Leadership Workshop.* These two-day workshops train minority accounting majors leadership, team-building, and communication and presentation skills. The program is designed to develop the next generation of minority leaders in the profession. Over the past 10 years, 800 college students have participated in this program. The Web site for this program is www.aicpa.org/members/div/career/mini/aslw.htm.
- *The PhD Project.* This program is a joint partnership between the AICPA and KPMG to provide financial support to minority candidates for a doctoral degree in accounting. This program is designed to attract minority candidates to university

---

[26] This statement is based on consultation with several human resource professionals at CPA firms and companies located in cities across North America.

[27] D. Hobson, "AICPA Diversity Initiatives," *Journal of Accountancy* (May 2005): 63.

professorships. The Web site for the PhD Project is http://www.phdproject.com/.
- *Minority Doctoral Fellowships.* This program also provides financial support to minority accounting doctoral students. The Web site for this program is www.aicpa.org/members/div/career/mini/fmds.htm.
- *Strategic Partnerships.* The AICPA has partnerships with the following organizations to attract and support minority students interested in pursuing a career in accounting: The Association of Latino Professionals in Finance and Accounting; The National Association of Black Accountants, the Diversity Pipeline Alliance, INROADS and the National Academy Foundation.

For general information about these and other programs, see the AICPA's Academic and Career Development Web site at http://www.aicpa.org/temp/jobres.htm.

Summary

The CPA profession is a dynamic one, offering entrants a wide variety of opportunities. CPAs work in public accounting, corporate practice, governmental and not-for-profit accounting, and education. Opportunities are many for CPAs in all of these areas. CPAs enjoy upwardly mobile careers with varied and interesting responsibilities. In addition, many CPA careers are lucrative. AICPA membership numbers over 300,000 with over half of these members not practicing in public accounting firms. The numbers of women and minorities entering the profession continue to rise dramatically. This has led to a more prominent profile for these groups in all types of CPA practice.

4

The Scope of CPA Services

> Great professions play a vital role in the health of our economy and our society. Each of you—whether you work in academia or government, for a corporation or in a public accounting firm—is involved in the process of providing understandable, reliable and transparent information for decision-makers. This role is vital to our society and its economy.
>
> Robert L. Bunting, AICPA Chair[1]

Introduction

The needs of society and the needs of users of business information constantly change. As a result, the nature, scope, and domain of CPA services are constantly subject to change and the CPA profession has to be able to continue to "reposition" itself to those places where the highest and best use of its social and professional product are to be employed. The work associated with the requirements of the Sarbanes-Oxley Act of 2002 is the latest example. This also has been demonstrated by the increasingly global need for disclosure about

---

[1] R. Bunting, "Renewing a Great Profession," AICPA President acceptance speech reprinted in the *Journal of Accountancy* (January 2005) 58-61.

corporate control[2] and performance measurement information that will affect the price and availability of an important factor of production, *investment capital*.

Practitioner competence to perform a given service is the initial factor to be considered when evaluating the scope and domain of CPA services. A CPA must possess expertise to agree to perform a service. Attention to competence focuses on making public practice responsive to user needs.[3]

CPAs in public, corporate, and government practice are professionals differentiated by specialized functions including (1) traditional attest functions; (2) report preparation; (3) performance and investment analysis (4) tax; and (5) consulting, which is a general category comprising countless types of consulting services. Most generally, the CPA in public practice consults in the role of external adviser and the CPA in private practice serves as a trusted internal expert. These are the general "product lines" which constitute the CPA profession's scope of services. Many firms further specialize within product lines by the specific business or industry to which they are applied. For example, a firm might specialize in audits of banks or hospitals or tax compliance services for farmers.

Research and commentary on the evolution of and debate about the scope of services can be found in several major studies, including Briloff (1965), the Public Oversight Board of the AICPA (1979), Previts (1985), and R.H. Parker (1986), as well as summaries including a report to the Treadway Commission by James B. Edwards (1986), a century-long perspective by Mednick and Previts (1987), and forward-looking views by Mednick (1988) (1991), Wallace (1990), and *The Public Accounting Profession: Meeting the Needs of a*

---

[2] Lori Calabro, "All Eyes on Internal Controls," *CFO* (*August 1993*).
[3] William D. Hall, "An Acceptable Scope of Practice," *CPA Journal* (February 1988): 24, 26-28, 32-33.

Changing World (1991).[4] Professional research periodicals and journals, including *Research in Accounting Regulation* and the *Journal of Accounting and Public Policy*, feature studies and policy discussions about aspects of the subject.

Scope of services is the general term for the activities of the CPA profession. However, scope of services has become a euphemism for the debate over the extent to which CPAs, who serve as principal external auditors for publicly held companies, could undertake nonattest services (NAS), including tax and other forms of advisory and consulting work, without affecting the independence of thought and action expected by the public and required under federal securities laws. In this chapter, the term is discussed in the general as well as the euphemistic context.

Scope of professional services has traditionally dealt with the scope of services for CPAs in public practice. However, in recent years, there has been an increased awareness that the CPA's scope of professional services must consider issues related to CPAs in areas such as corporate and government practice.

The term *scope of services* acquired greater significance after the Securities and Exchange Commission (SEC) issued two Accounting

---

[4] Abraham J. Briloff, "The Effectiveness of Accounting Communication," (Ph.D. diss., New York University, 1965), 227: "Scope of Service by CPA Firms" (Public Oversight Board Report, SEC Practice Section, Division for CPA Firms, AICPA, New York, 1979): "Perceptions of Management Advisory Services Performed by CPA Firms for Audit Clients" (Public Oversight Board Report, SEC Practice Section, Division for CPA Firms, AICPA, New York, 1986): Gary John Previts, *The Scope of CPA Services: A Study of the Development of the Concept of Independence and the Profession's Role in Society* (New York: John Wiley & Sons, 1985): R.H. Parker, "The Development of the Accountancy Profession in Britain to the Early Twentieth Century," Monograph Five (The Academy of Accounting Historians, 1986, School of Accountancy, James Madison University): 46: James B. Edwards, "A Final Report to the National Commission on Fraudulent Financial Reporting; Subject: Expansion of Non-Audit Services and Audit Independence" (A special study sponsored by the National Association of Accountants, University of South Carolina, Sept. 1986): R. Mednick and Gary John Previts, "The Scope of CPA Services: A View of the Future, *Journal of Accountancy* (May, 1987): 220-238: R. Mednick, "Our Profession in the Year 2000: A Blueprint of the Future," *Journal of Accountancy* (August 1988): 54-58: R. Mednick, "Reinventing the Audit," *Journal of Accountancy* (August 1991): 71-78: Wanda Wallace, "The Scope of Services Issue: Food for Thought," *Kent Accounting News*, Boston: Kent-Wadsworth, vol. VIII, (February 1990): 4-5: Chapter II of the monograph is titled, "The Benefits of a Broad Scope of Services," published jointly by Arthur Andersen & Co.; Coopers & Lybrand; Deloitte & Touche; Ernst & Young; KPMG Peat Marwick and Price Waterhouse, January 1991, 30 pp.

Series Releases (ASRs) that required the proxy statements of publicly held companies to disclose the percent of total fees paid to the independent audit firm for nonattest-related services.[5] This requirement had a "chilling" effect on the CPAs' ability to present their case for providing nonattest services to attest clients, since only the fees paid to auditor-CPAs for such services were subject to this disclosure. If the services were provided by competitors, including CPA firms that were not the auditors of record or non-CPAs, no disclosure of the related fees was required. Many publicly traded clients see this disclosure as an additional cost that could easily be avoided by not engaging the auditor to provide desired nonattest services.

Studies to evaluate the issue have not established that nonattest services cause audit quality to drop from compromised independence. Persuasive arguments, including those by a former chief accountant of the SEC, assert that such expanded services in fact are in the best interest of the client, given the need for efficiency and for "one stop shopping for information related professional services."[6] Furthermore, the public is best served, given proper safeguards to independence, by permitting the full skills of CPAs to be employed in concert with market forces. Yet, criticism in the media—some warranted, and some from potential competitors—and in Congress and government agencies will continue. The issue came to the forefront in the Enron case, where some evidence suggests that Arthur Andersen was conflicted in the Enron audit because of the magnitude of fees received from Enron for nonattest services.[7]

Practice Environment

CPAs have been traditionally identified with auditing practice, tax practice, and other accounting services, such as compilation or review of private company reports. Indeed, the attest function remains the unique cornerstone CPA public practice franchise.

---

[5] Securities and Exchange Commission, "Disclosure of Relationships with Independent Public Accountants," Accounting Series Release 250, June 29, 1978, and "Scope of Services by Independent Accountants," Accounting Series Release 264, June 14, 1979.

[6] John C. Burton, "A Critical Look at Professionalism and Scope of Services," *The Journal of Accountancy* (April, 1980): 56.

[7] See for example, "Questioning the books: Companies Mull Separation of Auditing, Consulting," *Wall Street Journal* (February 4, 2002): A6.

However, the domain and scope of CPA services certainly encompass private practice as well. The public responsibilities of a CPA who serves as chief financial officer of a major corporation or in the office of the comptroller general of the United States are as significant to the concerns of society as are the responsibilities of CPAs who are external auditors. As Bunting points out in his banner quote opening this chapter, CPAs participate in the lifeblood function of capital markets—producing, auditing, or analyzing decision information. Maintaining this informational infrastructure as the basis of measurement and disclosure in the capital markets is as essential to the public's well being as a fair and effective court system.

CPAs are expected to conduct themselves as CPAs in any of the principal practice occupations, as reflected in the expanded recognition of duties and responsibilities for AICPA members in its code of professional conduct.[8] CPAs in all practice environments are required to follow reporting standards, to maintain their expertise via continuing education activities, and new entrants must meet the postbaccalaureate educational requirements. And all CPAs are expected to reflect the positive values of competence, integrity, and objectivity in their chosen roles.

Public Practice Scope of Services: Watchdog and Business Adviser[9]

The scope of services in public firms includes audit/attest/assurance services, taxation compliance and planning services, and the general category of other consulting services. The trend in the 1980s and 1990s had been for public practice firms to aggressively pursue growth opportunities in consulting service product lines rather than attest and tax services.[10] The availability of relatively inexpensive, user-friendly software to facilitate preparation of reports and returns allowed CPA firms to provide these services efficiently and freed up

---

[8] *Code of Professional Conduct*, American Institute of CPAs, New York, 1988.

[9] CPA Journal Publisher Louis Grumet described CPAs as delicately balancing two duties: Watchdog and Business Advisor in the January 2003 *CPA Journal*, page 9.

[10] While the engagement of CPA tax services is not technically "mandated," tax compliance is required. Most wealthy individuals and corporations routinely engage in complex transactions such that the services of CPAs are required to comply with the mandated tax laws.

professionals to concentrate on building other revenue sources. Also, growth opportunities in audit and tax services seemed limited. This changed dramatically in recent years. Audit-related services have returned to the forefront as a result of regulatory requirements in Sarbanes-Oxley. Conversely, the Act strictly prohibits CPA firms from providing the following services to publicly held attest clients (see Chapter 8 for the specific code sections).

1. "Bookkeeping or other services related to the accounting records or financial statements of the audit client"
2. "Financial information systems design and implementation"
3. "Appraisal or valuation services, fairness reports, or contribution-in-kind reports"
4. "Actuarial services"
5. "Internal audit outsourcing services"
6. "Management functions or human resources"
7. "Broker or dealer, investment adviser, or investment banking services"
8. "Legal services and expert services unrelated to the audit"
9. "Any other services that the PCAOB determines, by regulation, are impermissible"

Accounting and Auditing Services

The core of a traditional CPA firm practice remains accounting and auditing (A&A) services. For CPA firms with smaller privately held clients, A&A is primarily bookkeeping, compilation, and review services. For larger CPA firms with large publicly held clients, A&A will be primarily audit, attestation, and assurances services.

Audit, Attest, and Assurance

Audit, attest, and assurance are similar terms. Assurance is the most general of the three. Assurance services are defined by the AICPA's Special Committee on Assurance Services as "independent professional services that improve the quality of information, or its context, for decision makers."[11] The assurance services improve the quality of

---
[11] AICPA, Special Committee on Assurance Services, http://www.aicpa.org/assurance.

the information by enhancing the credibility via independent third-party inspection.

Attestation service is a particular type of assurance service. Attestation involves conducting auditing procedures to issue a report on the fairness of financial statements for users of the information (that is, attest to their fairness) or as to the functioning of processes such as internal controls (that is, attest to the functioning of internal controls). Auditing procedures are conducted to provide the necessary evidence to attest as to the fairness of the statements.

CPAs have held the public accounting attest franchise since before World War I. CPA laws, beginning in 1896 in the State of New York, were in existence in all states by the mid 1920s.[12] Until recently, revenue from "core" attest services (annual audits, quarterly reviews, compilations, and others) had become a smaller percent of total fee income. Regardless of the relative percentage of total firm revenues, CPAs must continue to view auditing as " `the very soul of the public accounting profession,' and not stray too far from its core job of policing corporate financial statements."[13]

Compilation and Review

Compilations involve developing financial statements from the client's internal accounting records. Compiled financial statements are the representations of the company. Clients request compilation services in instances where the company does not have the internal expertise or when interested parties such as bank officers prefer to receive financial statements that were compiled by CPAs rather than by company officials.

A review involves "performing inquiry and analytical procedures to provide a reasonable based for expressing limited assurance that there are no material modifications that should be made to the financial statements for them to be in conformity with GAAP."[14] A review is essentially a less thorough and less costly inspection of the accounts than an audit.

---

[12] *Accountancy Comes of Age: The Development of an American Profession*, by Paul J. Miranti, Chapel Hill, University of North Carolina Press, 1990.

[13] "Accountants Cautioned Not to Compromise When Adding Services," *Wall Street Journal* (December 11, 1996).

[14] L. Rittenberg and B. Schweiger, *Auditing Concepts for a Changing Environment*, 5th edition, Thomsen Southwestern, 2005: 630.

These valuable accounting and reporting services are subject to professional standards, just as with auditing. Accountants involved in compilation and review services practice under the Statements on Standards for Accounting and Review Services (SSARS). SSARS No. 1, *Compilation and Review of Financial Statements*, was issued by the Accounting and Review Services Committee of the AICPA in 1978. The statement contains standards for performing a compilation or a review of unaudited financial statements of nonpublic companies, and specifies wording for the accountants report to be issued in each case. To date, 14 standards have been released.

Taxation: Compliance and Planning

CPAs today are associated with tax service as much as or more than they are associated with the core franchise of the profession—auditing. Tax service provided by CPA firms includes both compliance work as well as tax planning. Tax compliance work refers to assisting individuals or client organizations with completing the required tax reporting to international, federal (IRS), state, and local taxing authorities. Tax planning involves the consideration of alternative courses of action designed to minimize the tax liability faced by an individual or client organization.

Tax planning began with income tax planning, but has now expanded to encompass estate taxes—integration of tax strategy with the creation of wills and gifts of property, and the like. The whole field now has even unified under the rubric of financial planning, which can include investment strategy as well as the tax implications of investment and other actions. Here the field is shared with attorneys and a new professional group, non-CPA financial planners and various publicly held enterprises. The AICPA has increased its involvement in this area by development of an accredited specialty devoted to the needs of accounting practitioners in this area (the certified financial planner, or CFP).

In tax practice, competition involving non-CPAs comes from two groups. At the less sophisticated end of the spectrum, there are entities that perform compliance work (the preparation of tax return forms). Examples of these companies are H&R Block and Liberty Tax Service. At the more sophisticated end of the spectrum, there are tax attorneys and financial experts that do compliance work as well as tax planning.

The overlap in tax practice between the profession of law and the profession of public accountancy gives rise to some gray areas. The IRS automatically permits either lawyers or CPAs to practice before them. Other enrolled agents can also practice before the IRS but must first qualify by passing an examination. Not all tax advisers are fully equal in the eyes of the law, however. CPAs are not entitled to the "privileged disclosure" protection of attorneys.[15] Recent state-level attempts to obtain privilege for CPAs in testimony would be of value, not only in tax matters, but also in litigation support.[16] Some form of CPA-client privilege exists in 24 states, including 16 relating to testimonial privilege.[17]

Determining the degree of balance in state and local tax practice also seems to be a current issue. In March 1995, for example, the *Ohio CPA Newsletter* reported that the state supreme court had rejected amendments to the legal profession's proposal regarding the unauthorized practice of law. The proposal contained a "definition that would have greatly restricted the current practices of CPAs . . . the proposed rules would have restricted to attorneys the ability to represent clients before any administrative or governmental body; to give advice on wills, estate plans, trusts, marital property rights, mortgages and leases; and to advise clients on the organization or dissolution of a corporation, partnership, or other organization."

CPA firms provide tax planning services, which relate to structuring complex transactions and assessing tax consequences of business plans and contingencies. However, specialized tax services have come under much scrutiny when the attesting firm is also designing sophisticated tax strategies for their public clients. Supporters say the attest firm has unusual insight, which serves to uniquely inform the tax services. Opponents argue that the relationship impairs the auditors' objectivity. After all, opponents argue, the audit firm is being asked to verify that the tax strategies designed by their firm are proper.

Most tax planning strategies are very astute advice that saves clients great amounts of money. However, occasionally these strategies can be deemed inappropriate and disallowed. For example, the

---

[15] "Tax Notes—It's No Secret," *Wall Street Journal* (May 26, 1993): A1.
[16] R. E. Friedman and D. L. Mendelson, "The Need for CPA-Client Privilege in Federal Tax Matters, *The Tax Adviser* (March 1996): 154-156.
[17] *Ohio CPA Newsletter* (July 1997): 1.

international CPA firm KPMG admitted wrongdoing and agreed to pay fines totaling $456 million for selling certain tax products to clients during the 1990s. KPMG also agreed to discontinue areas of its tax practice, discontinue using any prepackaged tax products, and discontinue accepting fees on any basis other than hourly. Several former KPMG partners also face criminal charges in the case.[18] The tax schemes, with names such as "Bond Linked Premium Structure," "Foreign Leveraged Investment Program," "Offshore Portfolio Investment Strategy," and "S-Corp. Charitable Contribution Strategy," generally involved identifying sham losses to offset taxable gains. KPMG was paid as much as 7 percent of the taxes saved. Resulting revenues were estimated to total between $130 million and $177 million, according to a Senate subcommittee investigation.[19]

Two aspects of the arrangement contributed to the problem. First, in cases in which KPMG was providing the innovative and controversial tax services to attest clients, KPMG auditors were placed in the position of reviewing the work of their colleagues in the firm—an independence concern. Second, KPMG accepted a fee based on dollars saved in several of the tax shelters. Thus, potential commission-based dollars could have impaired the objectivity of the CPAs. IRS Commissioner Mark Everson summed it up as follows: "Accountants and attorneys should be pillars of our systems of taxation, not the architects of its circumvention."[20] To this end, the goal of tax planning remains to devise strategies for minimizing the present value of taxes paid that are substantive and legal.

The Public Companies Accounting Oversight Board (PCAOB), on July 26, 2005, adopted new ethics and independence rules related to tax products titled "Ethics and Independence Rules Concerning Independence, Tax Services, and Contingent Fees." Under the new rules, CPA firms will not be deemed independent of any company to which they have sold tax shelters that the IRS might deem

---

[18] For additional details, see "KPMG LLP Admits Wrongdoing, Agrees to Pay $456 Million for Tax Fraud Conspiracy," *Daily Record*, August 31, 2005, Rochester, N.Y.

[19] E. McClam, "Eight Former Execs Are Indicted as KPMG Admits to Tax Shelters," August 30, 2005 *St. Louis Post Dispatch*: C1. Also see J. R. Wilke, "KPMG Faces Indictment Risk on Tax Shelters," *Wall Street Journal*, June 16, 2005: A1.

[20] E. McClam, "Eight Former Execs Are Indicted as KPMG Admits to Tax Shelters," August 30, 2005 *St. Louis Post Dispatch*: C1.

abusive. Firms will be considered independent, and therefore can conduct the audit if they "reasonably" believe that the tax shelter has a greater than 50 percent chance of being upheld if challenged by the IRS. In questionable cases, the auditors must document an "objectively reasonable and defensible decision that the proposed tax treatment of the transaction is likely to be permitted if challenged."[21] This will be difficult to monitor in practice; certainly a firm (1) cannot audit a client to which it has sold a tax strategy that the IRS has already deemed abusive; (2) will not be deemed independent if it sells personal tax strategies to any senior officials of an audit client that have a financial reporting oversight role; (3) cannot accept a contingent fee based on a percentage of its client's tax savings.; (4) must provide information to the company's audit committee and seek its approval to provide any nonprohibited tax services to the company. The new rules also place other ethical obligations on audit firm personnel. For example, the rules require that CPA firm personnel (1) not conduct themselves in a manner so as to cause the firm to violate applicable rules, laws, and standards relating to the preparation and issuance of audit reports and (2) remain independent of the firm's audit clients throughout the audit and professional engagement period.[22] Rules for tax practice by enrolled agents before the IRS are set forth in Treasury Department Circular 230. This guidance is summarized in Appendix.

Management Advisory Services (Consulting)

Many of the services provided to clients by CPA firms relate to nonrecurring projects that usually take a long time to complete. Since these services are not annually required services, growing nonmandated service revenues requires skills in developing valuable knowledge and marketing it. Consultancy and advisory services have flourished in this way, due in part to the outsourcing phenomenon and the need for firms to develop new value added services based upon their professional skills. Available data indicates

---

[21] Excerpted from an update from the law firm Gibson, Dunn & Crutcher LLP, August 2, 2005.

[22] PCAOB Release No. 2005-014, "Ethics and Independence Rules Concerning Independence, Tax Services, and Contingent Fees." While the PCAOB has adopted this rule, as of this writing, the rule has not been exposed or approved by the SEC. Therefore, it is not yet effective.

that the outsourcing "trend began with the outsourcing of such ancillary functions as building equipment maintenance and progressed to support services, including payroll and data processing."[23] Companies now "outsource" internal audits[24] and large companies, including British Petroleum and Mobil, sought to cut as much as $5 billion from a joint venture by "outsourcing many financial task to international accounting companies."[25] Financial service firms such as J. P. Morgan have identified a seven-year, $2 billion transfer of its computer staff to outside suppliers. The rationale for much of this outsourcing is not mere staff cutting but the elimination of functions that the company cannot do better than someone else, that is, non-core competencies.

The field of advisory services (consulting) was the growth area for the CPA profession until recently. A 1980s survey found four of the then Big Eight firms among the top 10 consulting firms in the United States, with one (Arthur Andersen & Co.) being at the top ahead of such well-known consulting firms as Booz, Allen & Hamilton and McKinsey & Co., Inc.[26] Ten of the top 25 consulting firms were large CPA firms. Andersen's consulting fees, worldwide, in 1988 were $1.1 billion, up from $838 million in 1987.[27] By 1996, seven of the eight largest consulting firms were CPA firms. The following information is taken from the World Survey by *Management Consultants International*.[28]

---

[23] "US Spending on Outsourcing." Source: The Outsourcing Industry, *Annual Report 1996*, Snyder Communication, Inc. [supplement to *US News & World Report* (June 23, 1997)].

[24] Stephen Barr, "Farming Out Internal Audits," *CFO* (June 1995): 69, 71, 72.

[25] Robert Corzine, "BP/Mobile to Contract Out Finance Operations," *Financial Times* (October 21, 1996): 19.

[26] The consulting arm of Arthur Andersen was later spun off. The spun-off unit was renamed Accenture and still operates under that name.

[27] *Consultants News* (October 1983): Arthur Andersen & Co., 1988 Annual Report.

[28] Nicholas Timmins, "Outsourcing," *Financial Times* (June 19, 1997): IV.

10 Largest Consulting Firms in 1996

Firm	FY 1996 Worldwide Revenue ($mill)
Andersen Consulting	5,300
Ernst & Young	2,010
McKinsey & Co.	2,000
KPMG	1,836
Deloitte Touche Tomatsu Int.	1,550
Coopers & Lybrand	1,422
Arthur Andersen	1,379
Price Waterhouse	1,200
Mercer Consulting Group	1,159
Towers Perrin	1,001

Since 1996, many of these firms have sold their consulting practice. The decision to sell was due in certain instances to cultural differences between the audit and tax partners and the consulting partners. However, in most cases, the consulting practice was sold primarily because of the perception (and maybe reality) that independence was impaired when auditors performed nonattest services for attest clients. James S. Turley, chairman of Ernst & Young, explained his firm's sale of its information technology consulting practice thus: "We sold our practice because we thought it was the right and strategic thing to do. And Ernst & Young, as the leader in internal audits services, will be the firm most impacted by the restriction on internal audit services. But again, we think it's the right thing to do."[29] Legislators and regulators agree with Turley's sentiments.[30]

Consulting work is significant to more than just the huge firms. Many companies are outsourcing administrative functions such as internal audit to small and medium-sized CPA firms. It is the small business aspect of consulting services that, in part, also serves to persuade regulators and legislators to be cautious about imposing hard

---
[29] James S. Turley, "How Accounting Can Get Back Its Good Name," *Wall Street Journal* (February 4, 2002): A16.
[30] SEC, Accounting Series Release No. 250 (1978) and No. 264 (1979).

and fast scope-of-service limitations on the CPA profession at large. Also, small and mid-sized CPA firms have earned substantial revenues assisting public clients with documentation and analysis of controls as required by Sarbanes-Oxley.

The market for outsourced expertise is a growth opportunity for many firms. However, there are challenges as well. Some of these are explored in the following sections.

Independence

Some express concern that nonattest services provided to attest clients impair the independence of the attesting firm. For primarily this reason, several of the international CPA firms have sold their consulting practice (for example, Ernst & Young sold its consulting practice to Cap Gemini). Independence concerns will continue to represent a significant challenge to growth of the nonattest services practice.

AICPA Interpretation No. 101-3, "Performance of Nonattest Services," provides guidance related to this challenge. Its general requirements for CPAs involved in nonattest services for attest clients are that (1) the CPA not perform management functions or make management decisions for the attest client and (2) the client must agree to make all management decisions and perform all management functions, designate a suitably skilled individual to oversee the services, evaluate the adequacy and results of the services, accept responsibility for the results of the services, and establish and maintain internal controls, including monitoring ongoing activities. If the client cannot or will not comply with any of these requirements, the auditor's independence would be considered impaired. Before performing the nonattest services, CPAs should establish and document in writing their understanding with the client regarding the objectives of the engagement, the services to be performed, the client's acceptance of its responsibilities, the CPA's responsibilities, and any limitations of the engagement.[31]

Professional Culture

Consulting practice is not defined as clearly as audit and tax. Auditors follow generally accepted auditing standards. Tax professionals adhere to the tax code. CPA consultants simply vow to

---
[31] See AICPA Interpretation No. 101-3 for additional details.

uphold the general standard of professionalism. To this end, CPAs must acquire competence in areas of specialization before offering these services to the market. Some consultants view this culture as an unnecessary impediment to competing with nonaccounting consultants not similarly professional. In essence, they believe that even if they have never provided such services, their skills and abilities will allow them to quickly acquire the knowledge and skills and provide superior service. Indeed, this claim is probably true in many instances. This philosophical difference has contributed to the decision of CPA firms to spin off their consulting practice into an autonomous operating company (for example, Arthur Andersen and Andersen Consulting had culture-related conflict before ultimately splitting).[32]

Litigation Risk

The considerable legal risks of providing attest services (and to a much lesser degree, tax services) have been seen as a financial burden not arising from consultancy practice, and therefore not willingly borne by it. This has led to disputes between audit and tax partners and consulting partners. There are signs, however, that litigation is becoming a factor in consultation. In 1994 for example, a $14.2 million dollar verdict was awarded against a major firm related to work in the litigation support area, which is described elsewhere in this chapter.[33] Even when the outcome regarding consultancy litigation is favorable in legal terms, the legal defense costs and potential reputation damage can be great. Of course, the litigation risk is much less for CPA firms that provide consulting services to privately held companies.

Practice Standards

The determination of the proper standard of care to be employed in consultation may be determined by professional regulation standards for CPAs as advisers or by court rulings. In the Diversified

---

[32] E. McDonald, "Andersen Appears to Rule Out Breakup—Accounting Unit to Remain With Consulting Arm Despite Tensions," *Wall Street Journal*, December 23, 1996: A2.

[33] Don J. DeBenedictis, "Experts Held Accountable," *National Law Review* (June 20, 1994).

Graphics engagement involving then Ernst & Whinney's provision of a "turnkey" computer system, the client sued. The CPA firm argued an ordinary standard of care was appropriate, but the court in deciding the firm had breached that standard, argued the firm was subject to a higher standard of professional care. The court referred to specific MAS Practice Standards (at that time, MAS Practice Standards Nos. 1 through 8) adopted by the AICPA as being the key standards for this type of engagement.[34] Activities of the AICPA's Management Consulting Services Section now provide the information and materials that support improvement of consultation services. The cost-beneficial evolution of consulting guidance issued by the AICPA has evolved now to include Statements on Standards for Consulting Services introduced in 1991. These supersede certain earlier MAS standards and define categories of consulting service.

Accredited CPA Consulting Services

As early as the 1960s, interpretations of the AICPA's ethical precepts affirmed the propriety of organizing separate partnerships with non-CPA specialists.[35] This was consistent with the intent of AICPA Council expressed in 1961 to encourage CPAs to perform the entire range of services consistent with their professional competence, ethical standards, and responsibility. These other CPA services fall broadly under the management advisory services umbrella in addition to the services described earlier.

Practice specializations have created interest in distinctive recognition and identification of individuals' competence to practice in specialized activities. In recent years, three accredited specialties have been authorized by the AICPA. The first, in 1988, was a designation for personal financial planners.[36] In 1996, the AICPA Council[37]

---

[34] Wayne Baliga, "MAS and the Standard of Care," *Journal of Accountancy* (August 1989): 96.

[35] Opinion No. 17: Specialization, *Code of Professional Ethics*, New York: AICPA (1967).

[36] "Should the Profession Recognize Specialization," *LIGNIAPPE* (Louisiana Society of CPAs, November 1993): 3.

[37] The AICPA Council is a member group with the authority to establish the policies and procedures of the Institute and to enact resolutions binding upon the Board of Directors, the Officers, Committees, and Staff. For additional details, see http://aicpa.org/members/council.htm.

approved business valuation as an area of accredited practice. Most recently, the AICPA added a designation for information technology professionals. The Council outlined a program of education, testing, and experience to obtain and maintain an individual's accreditation.[38] Under the current policy, individuals may continue to refer to themselves as "specialists" without having achieved an accredited designation. However, use of the phrase "accredited by the AICPA" with regard to these practices requires successful completion of the approved accreditation program.

Certified Financial Planner

By the early 1980s, financial planning for wealthier individuals was proliferating. The Institute of Certified Financial Planners was organizing the profession, including offering a professional designation, the Certified Financial Planner.[39] Financial planning activities fit well into existing CPA services, including tax planning, estate planning, and advisory services.

The value that CPAs bring to the financial planning environment is their reputation. CPAs are known to be competent and objective. Consistent with all other areas of practice, AICPA members have adopted practice standards, outlined methods for monitoring and updating engagements, and produced guidance for working with other advisers.[40] More information about AICPA programs can be obtained at its Web site (www.aicpa.org). Under the National Securities Markets Improvement Act of 1996, investment advisers who manage over $25 million in client assets are subject to SEC supervision. Advisers who manage less than that amount are regulated by the states.[41] Individuals wishing to learn about SEC policy should visit www.sec.gov.

---

[38] "Council Approves Accrediting Member Providing Specific CPA Services. . . ." *The CPA Letter* (June 1994).

[39] M. Tuttle and N. Opiela, "The Financial Planning Profession and the Institute: An Interview with Judith W. Lau," *Journal of Financial Planning* (February 1997): 60-65.

[40] *Statements on Responsibilities in Personal Financial Planning Practice* (Statements No. 1 through 5) New York: AICPA, 1996.

[41] "Senate Bill Extends Effective Date of Investment Adviser Supervision Coordination Act ," *Planner* (April-May 1997): 8.

Accreditation in Business Valuation

Following the savings and loan failures of the 1980s, federal legislation required expert review of property valuations in transactions involving deposit insured financial institutions. Title XI, *The Financial Institutions Reform, Recovery and Enforcement Act of 1989 [FIRREA]*, reads, "to promote the safety and soundness of insured institutions by requiring that real estate appraisals utilized in connection with federally related transactions be performed in writing in accordance with the uniform standards by individuals whose competency has been demonstrated and whose professional conduct is subject to effective supervision."

This mandate created a need for more valuation experts. As profession leaders developed an AICPA response to these new requirements, they encountered many of the same concerns that were expressed about accreditation of financial planning. Ultimately, the AICPA approved the Accredited in Business Valuation (ABV) designation. Requirements for AICPA members to obtain the ABV include that the candidate:

1. Be a member in good standing and hold an unrevoked CPA certificate or license issued by a recognized statutory authority.
2. Provide evidence of 10 business valuation engagements that demonstrate substantial experience and competence.

To maintain the accreditation, each credential holder is expected to:

1. Successfully complete the Accredited in Business Valuation Examination.
2. Submit documentation at three-year intervals demonstrating substantial involvement in five business valuation engagements.
3. Provide evidence of 75 hours of lifelong learning related to the business valuation body of knowledge.

Again, note the education, examination, experience, and continuing professional education requirements to develop, demonstrate, and maintain competency in the specialization.

Certified Information Technology Professional (CITP)

The CITP designation is awarded to AICPA members who have demonstrated competence and experience providing information technology services. CPAs with the CITP designation specialize in information technology strategic planning, implementation, and management and business strategies. The awarding of this designation involves an innovative point system. There are minimum requirements for business experience as well as lifelong learning in the field of information technology. Members who do not earn enough points in the areas of experience and lifelong learning can take an examination to demonstrate their professional competence. Interested candidates should see the AICPA Web site to see the requirements for earning the CITP.

Other CPA Consulting Services

Litigation Support Services (Forensic Accounting)

"Litigation services are `transaction services, in which the practitioner's function is to provide services related to a specific client transaction, generally with a third party.'"[42] It has become commonplace for CPAs to serve as expert witnesses in business, commercial, and personal financial disputes. Services include damage evaluation and computation, financial analysis, and when needed, expert testimony.[43] In working as a member of a team employed by one or both of the parties in dispute, the CPA seeks to assist in achieving an equitable solution under the law. In some instances court testimony or deposition work is a major facet of the service. In some cases Alternative Dispute Resolution (ADR) procedures are employed. ADR techniques generally include three broad categories: negotiation, mediation, or arbitration.[44] The advocacy nature of these proceedings again distinguishes them from the attest service and the expectation for audit-like independence. A recent AICPA Interpretation No. 102-6, "Professional Services Involving Client Advocacy," provides general guidance for service in this

---

[42] Gerald Hepp, "Litigation Services Standards and Ethics," *Journal of Accountancy* (April 1997): 57ff, and see a clarification *Journal of Accountancy* (June 1997): 24.

[43] Martin Cohen, Michael Crain, and Arthur Sanders, "Skills Used in Litigation Services," *Journal of Accountancy* (September 1996): 101ff.

[44] *Alternative Dispute Resolution A Guide for State Societies*, AICPA, December 1993.

area. Expert witness work may be considered a "nonadvocacy" engagement.

CPAs have been called upon to aid in the court proceedings related to fraud, bankruptcy, business valuations and disputes, divorce, and many other litigation circumstances. The CPA supporting litigation must act with integrity and objectively and apply their knowledge and expertise to the issue. Authoritative guidance on the subject of litigation practice by CPAs advises practitioners to study each situation carefully. Usually, litigation service engagements are subject to the MCS Standards (that is, relating to transaction services).[45] However, any standard could come into play in an engagement, some related to authoritative and some to nonauthoritative literature.

A variety of consulting service practice aids have been developed in recent years to assist CPAs practicing in this area. They address construction of reports, engagement letter particulars, the tasks related to the discovery process, and skills employed in giving expert witness testimony. Noted earlier is the fact that CPAs do not, in some states, enjoy the equivalent of "client-attorney privilege." The AICPA Code of Conduct requirement [Rule 301, *Confidential Client Information* (AICPA, *Professional Standards*, vol. 2, ET sec. 301)], does not protect CPAs in those states when CPAs are required to produce information requested with a valid enforceable subpoena. Therefore, litigation support requires expertise as well as an understanding of state law and AICPA guidance as it relates to advocacy, confidentiality, and privilege.[46]

Fraud Examination

Fraud examination involves assisting in the prevention and detection of fraud (for example, corruption, asset misappropriation, and fraudulent statements). To resolve the fraud allegation, the CPA obtains evidence, interviews witnesses and potential suspects, writes reports, testifies to findings, and assists the client and the courts in any other required ways.[47]

---

[45] *Application of AICPA Professional Standards in the Performance of Litigation Services,* MCS Special Report 93-1, AICPA, 1993.

[46] Michael P. Elkin, "Confidentiality and Privilege," *Florida CPA Today* (July 1994): 22-25.

[47] Joseph T. Wells, "Principles of Fraud Examination," John Wiley & Sons (2005): 4.

When Are Nonattest Services Inappropriate?

At what point does a potential service become incompatible with the role of a CPA? As might be expected, this is a difficult question.[48] The answer is different for clients that are currently attest clients and clients that are not currently attest clients. For current attest clients, a service that conflicts with independence requirements (in appearance or in fact) may be inappropriate and warrants careful evaluation. For clients that are not currently attest clients, the considerations are related more to competency than to independence. There are no perfect guidelines for this type of judgment. The following may be of some value, however. Generally, a service may be inappropriate if:[49]

1. The service presumes a competency at the supervisory level of practice (such as a knowledge of specialized industries) that is not available among the equity holders of the practice unit.
2. The assignment requires acting in the capacity equivalent to a member of management or employee of the client.
3. The service requires having the ability to access, control, or assume custody of client assets.
4. The service requires assuming the role of a promoter or underwriter.
5. The services to be provided are not subject to review by competent individuals within the client organization, so as to determine and evaluate results.
6. A multidisciplinary service entity proposes to offer an inappropriate service using the auditor as a conduit.

---

[48] Fred S. Spindel, "Independence and Non-Audit Services," *The CPA Journal* (January, 1989): 48, 50-2, and SEC Financial Reporting Release (FRR) No. 1, Section 600, Matters Relating to Independent Accountants, Washington D.C. (May 21, 1982).

[49] An AICPA Special Committee chaired by Vincent O'Reilly of Coopers & Lybrand operated from 1995 up through the announcement of the formation of the Independence Standards Board. Its search for principles regarding the management of independence issues in an NAS environment are reflected in some these of items. However no official position exists regarding the authoritativeness of these.

7. The service impact on a workload or schedule configuration is such as to reduce or eliminate proper resources to conduct other engagements.
8. The service is voluntarily prohibited by rules of a professional organization.

Some suggested common-sense safeguards for avoiding offering to provide services that a CPA does not have adequate expertise include questioning whether the services:

1. May cause a violation of professional practice standards;
2. May be difficult to provide with consistent quality on a timely basis; or
3. May be perceived as incompatible with a CPA's occupation (recent interpretations suggest that in such cases, full public disclosure would strengthen the case to permit offering the service).

Certain aspects of tax practice and evolving services such as litigation support and financial advice all have a characteristic that is in contrast to a central culture of the attest service in that these are "advocacy" services.[50] Here the professional "advocates" a particular point of view in support of the employing party. In attest-based service, the third-party user of the statements is relying on an independent opinion supplied by the CPA professional. In all cases the fundamental premise that underlies either advocacy or independence roles is that CPAs offer each service with integrity, objectivity, and competence. Further, under the evolving peer standards in the area, practitioners should disclose clearly to each client their professional role in a service (that is, advocacy versus independence).

---

[50] See for example, William L. Raby, "Advocacy vs. Independence in Tax Liability Accrual," *Journal of Accountancy* (March 1972): 40-47; Betty R. Jackson and Valerie C. Milliron, "Tax Preparers: Government Agents or Client Advocates?" *Journal of Accountancy*, (May 1989): 76-82.

CPAs in Corporate Practice: Cultural and Career Dimensions

Writing over 40 years ago, an American Institute of Accountants officer observed: "Accounting is the principal means of measuring economic relationships. Since accounting is the language of business, it is the best means of conveying public understanding of the economic facts of life."[51] Awareness of this essential information preparation and control responsibility of "in-house" CPAs traces to the beginning years of the organized profession. Writing in October 1930, just a few years after the movement to achieve CPA legislation in all states had successfully concluded, Durand Springer a key figure in the early profession wrote the following on the subject.

> The more certified public accountants representing qualified accountants, are engaged by private business enterprises, the better it will be for the profession of accountancy as a whole. . . . The CPA engaged in private work should feel a responsibility for the maintenance of the ideals of the profession of accountancy just as strongly as the CPA who may be actually practicing as a public accountant.

To Springer, a "CPA was a CPA" regardless of the environment of practice.

> In this respect," he noted, "the practical workings of accountancy do not differ much from those of other professions. Many a lawyer forsakes the public practice of law for the purpose of . . . employment with a business organization. . . . Many a doctor finds that the public practice of medicine is not as alluring as a professorship in a medical school. . . . In fact one can not conceive of any profession in which, for the advancement of the profession itself . . . it is not necessary for individual members to withdraw themselves from its public practice in order that the private demands may be properly met.[52]

Sustaining this viewpoint, an influential textbook writer of the midcentury, Professor Bill Vatter included the following in his introductory comments to *Managerial Accounting*, published in 1950.

---

[51] Maurice Stans, "The Profession of Accounting," *The CPA and His Profession*, New York: AICPA (1954): 10.
[52] Durand W. Springer, "The C.P.A. in Private Practice," *The Certified Public Accountant* (October 1930): 218-219.

One of the basic functions of accounting is to report independently on the activities of others, so that information concerning what has happened may be relevant and unbiased. The major function served by both public and managerial accountants is to use their independent judgment with complete freedom; thus they may observe and evaluate objectively, the fortunes and results of enterprise operations.... This is a highly important aspect of accounting, and it is one of the reasons for the separation of the accounting function from the rest of the management process. The detached and independent viewpoint of the accountant must be keep in mind....[53]

In 1977, in the midst of a new wave of public scrutiny, the third generation of CPAs weighed in on the role and responsibility of corporate CPAs and professionals, with the following observations:

Corporate internal professionals have had professional training in school and many of them have had outside professional experience. They consider themselves to be professionals. Do their professional responsibilities suddenly disappear when they become employees of corporations?[54]

The question here relates to goal conflicts between expectations of the CPA profession and expectations of the non-CPA organization employing the individual CPA.[55] In 1987, the AICPA membership overwhelmingly approved six proposals identified as the "Excellence Vote," which, among other items, established continuing professional education (CPE) as a requirement for AICPA membership for members in corporate practice. As the fourth generation of corporate CPAs establishes itself, these issues have become more important since corporate practitioners now constitute the largest single segment. An event that demonstrates this development is the 1999 election of Olivia Kirtley, a financial officer of Vermont-America Corporation, as the first corporate CPA to serve as chair of the

---

[53] William J. Vatter, *Managerial Accounting*, New York: Prentice-Hall (1950): 8.

[54] Harvey Kapnick, "Corporate internal professionals also have public responsibilities," Before the 16th Annual Institute of the Northwestern University School of Law, October 13, 1977. Two Volumes: Selected Addresses and Articles by Harvey Kapnick: *Accounting and Financial Reporting in the Public Interest*, Chicago: Arthur Andersen & Co, . l979 vol. II: 67-71.

[55] William Campfield, "When the CPA Works for a Non-CPA Organization: Reconciling Role Conflicts," Working Paper 88-1, School of Accounting, Florida International University.

AICPA Board of Directors. Until then, all the principal leaders of this organization, since its inception in 1887, had been CPAs in public practice.

The previous chapter described common positions held by CPAs in corporate practice. This chapter sets forth the scope of services for CPAs in accounting and finance-related corporate practice. These services can be categorized as (1) financial measurement and financial management; (2) communication; (3) analysis (financial and operating analysis); (4) assurance and (5) consulting.

Financial Measurement and Financial Management

Accounting for thousands or millions of transactions in financial and detail terms certainly is one view of what accountants do inside corporations. Such detail work of course is required to track the organization's economic activity. This is the "mass production transaction information" function, which has been greatly transformed by the technological evolution of the personal computer. Top management recognized that the PC could do more than just warehouse data. It could be an analysis tool, generating what-if scenarios, data searches, and real-time reporting.[56] The focus now is not just to cut costs of transaction accounting or report preparation, but to add valuable information useful in achieving competitive advantage. Such value-added services include investment analysis, managing financial instruments, and developing sophisticated projection and performance measurement models. Corporate CPAs are leading a movement to make money, not just count it.

It is easy to understand why corporate management would not outsource this important function. While an airline might be persuaded to outsource even aircraft maintenance, would any business be willing to lose control of its vital and highly proprietary internal information processes? If so, to what extent? Payroll, 401(k) administration, internal auditing, tax filing?[57] Perhaps. Inventory, transactional data bases and archives? Probably not. What does seem vital to evaluating such measures is the ability to have readily available

---

[56] Stanley Zarowin, "Finance's Future: Challenge or Threat?" *Journal of Accountancy*, (April 1997): 38.

[57] "Outsourcing Is Now Common," *The Financial Executives Briefing*, (Vanderwicken's *Financial Digest*, vol. VI, Number A 1997: 8.

and fully committed individuals with the knowledge to provide critical strategic and decision-making information. Routine tasks and tasks viewed as compliance driven seem more likely subjects for outsourcing.

The variety of career paths in corporate practice provides multiple opportunities for successful employment of skills and advancement. As discussed earlier, positions usually held by CPAs include at least the chief financial officer (CFO), the controller, the assistant controller, the director of tax, and the director of internal audit. The chief information officer and the director of pension or compensation positions are often CPAs as well. CPAs often become general operations managers too.

Chief financial officers (CFOs), according to a recent study of 300 chief financial officers around the world, spend nearly a quarter of their time on financial operations issues. This is where their technical background and knowledge and experience are directly called upon. This is the largest single category identified in the survey. Cost planning and budgeting (19 percent) and performance management (16 percent) are the next two major areas, followed closely by treasury and tax management and by performance management. The study revealed that "chief financial officers are taking ever more strategic responsibilities in their companies and . . . it is clear that managing and meeting shareholders expectations is becoming the primary role of top financial executives around the world."[58]

CPAs in the Communication Function

Preparing mandated financial statements and reports, especially for publicly held companies under the jurisdiction of the SEC and other regulators, is one of the higher profile roles of CPAs in corporations. Communicating economic relationships in the language of business sounds easier than it is. On the one hand, the business must provide information to analysts, stakeholders, and owners in the spirit of full disclosure. On the other hand, the business must avoid divulging proprietary information to competitors. This is a difficult trade-off that requires knowledge of the required disclosure rules as well as the firm's competitive risks and opportunities.

---

[58] Diane Summers, "Finance Role Change," *Financial Times* (June 23, 1997).

SEC Regulation FD further complicated the communication process. This regulation requires that if an issuer discloses material nonpublic information to certain individuals or entities (generally securities market professionals, such as stock analysts, or holders of the issuer's securities who may well trade on the basis of the information), the issuer must make public disclosure of that information.[59]

CPAs as Financial and Operating Analysts

Analysts, working to review strategic internal investments and operations or externally in the investment community, acquire and evaluate substantial amounts of information. Market analysts, both as buy side (representing institutional investors) and sell side (representing brokers who typically sell shares to the public) are also involved in the interpretation of corporate communication. CPAs, by virtue of their technical training and understanding of the information conveyed in fina\ncial reports, are frequently recruited into positions such as buy side investment research analysts, merger and acquisition analysts, and general business analysts.

Corporate CPAs in Assurance Roles

CPAs providing assurance services in the public accounting profession were described earlier in this chapter. Assurance services are also provided by CPAs working in private practice (the internal audit function) and governmental auditing. The Institute of Internal Auditors defines internal auditing as follows:

> An independent objective assurance and consulting activity designed to add value and improve an organization's operations. It helps an organization accomplish its objectives by bringing a systematic, disciplined approach to evaluate and improve the effectiveness of risk management, control, and governance processes.[60]

CPAs practicing as internal auditors provide assurance to management and the board of directors that the company is in compliance with policies and regulatory requirements and that operating

---

[59] See Regulation FD at http://www.sec.gov/rules/final/33-7881.htm.
[60] Institute of Internal Auditors, *Standards for the Practice of Internal Auditing*.

processes are effective and efficient. Internal auditors also provide consulting-type services to the company. CPAs in government provide assurance to governmental leaders and their constituents that the financial statements of the governmental unit are presented fairly and that the governmental body or a contractor for the governmental body is complying with relevant policies and regulatory requirements. Governmental auditors also serve in a consulting role for the government and its constituents.

Corporate CPAs in Consulting Roles

CPAs in private practice are being hired with increasing frequency to provide a consulting or trusted adviser role to their employer (large publicly held as well as smaller privately held companies). The advantage of hiring the CPA as an internal adviser is that the organization gains the talents, skills, ethics, and judgment of the CPA without the challenges related to using external advisers (for example, independence and litigation concerns). In addition, the CPA has often obtained very valuable training in various industries and at various companies by virtue of previous positions in public practice. For example, the large investment firms (for example, Credit Suisse First Boston, Edward Jones, and Goldman Sachs) hire CPAs to provide accounting and financial reporting consulting to the investment research department. Also, many large and mid-sized companies hire CPAs in a relatively undefined "special projects" capacity to carry out important projects and efforts designed to move the company forward. CPAs in these positions are also viewed as "bench strength." That is, they are obtaining varied training experiences that develop them for future contributions as senior officers.

Summary

The services that CPAs provide to society through their work in public and corporate practice, government and nonprofit positions, and in education, are shaped by the needs of society, practitioner competence and capacity, and the expectations of peers. CPAs are what they do. In public practice, they are auditors and tax professionals, business advisers, financial planning professionals, and business valuation professionals. The span of CPA services continues to expand over time, and now clearly includes the spectrum of information activities needed to construct and maintain the information system for the free enterprise and capital market system. From consultation services, to report preparation, to assurance through analysis, CPAs are involved.

It is also important for service professionals to remember that when a corporation or client engages them as CPAs, there are certain expectations as a matter of business: timely response, a minimum of "surprises" and the expectation that the CPA will be available or "on call" for advice and consultation. While such expectations exist for all service business providers, the expectations for CPAs as professionals are furthered by the explicit social contract regarding attest services, and by an implicit set of societal beliefs that a CPA should maintain a personal commitment to service, and to integrity, objectivity and competence. It is upon these ideals that society overall will assess our profession's fitness. These expectations provide for what R. K. Elliott refers to as "permissions" given by society to a profession. These "permissions" assist in developing a pattern for decisions about the domain of the profession's scope of services.

5

Accountability: Personal Oversight

> *Greatness comes from aspiring to high expectations and from doing what has to be done to meet them. That is the spirit that has driven the CPA profession, and it demands far more from us than merely complying with the rules set down by regulators.*
>
> Robert L. Bunting, AICPA Chair [1]

Introduction

The professional CPA has both a commitment and an obligation to protect the public interest. While professional oversight processes (Chapter 6) and public oversight processes (Chapter 7) exist to monitor the quality of CPA activities, the primary self-regulation mechanism is the self! The CPA should aspire to the highest standard of professionalism. While peer oversight (Chapter 6) and public oversight (Chapter 7) are key components of CPA regulation, the most important component in regulation remains the regulation of the

---

[1] R. Bunting, "Renewing a Great Profession," AICPA acceptance speech reprinted in the *Journal of Accountancy* (January 2005): 58-61.

CPA's activities by himself or herself. This chapter describes the role of ethical behavior by individual practitioners. Obviously, if everyone understood what constitutes ethical behavior and upheld those principles, no other regulatory or oversight processes would be necessary.

Ethical behavior constraints have traditionally been placed on CPAs in public practice. However, many of the constraints are now placed on CPAs in corporate practice, government, academe, and other occupations as well. The AICPA emphasized this in the introduction to its Code of Professional Conduct:

> The Code of Professional Conduct was adopted by the membership to provide guidance and rules to all members—those in public practice, in industry, in government, and in education—in the performance of their professional responsibilities.[2]

Professionals are nothing without personal integrity—an inner commitment to a course of action in which conflicts are resolved in accordance with the best and highest traditions of their calling and their own conscience. Further, action that upholds one's personal integrity in the context of the CPA profession is almost certainly consistent with society's laws and the profession's Code of Conduct. Indeed, these latter two forces primarily set forth minimum acceptable behaviors.

> Integrity requires a member to be, among other things, honest and candid within the constraints of client confidentiality. Service and the public trust should not be subordinated to personal gain and advantage. Integrity can accommodate the inadvertent error and the honest difference of opinion; it cannot accommodate deceit or subordination of principle.[3]

The Highest Standard: Highly Competent and Highly Ethical

Effective CPAs are competent and ethical. Regarding competence, professionals owe it to clients and society to acquire *and maintain* the

---

[2] AICPA Code of Professional Conduct, adopted January 12, 1988, amended January 14, 1992.

[3] Article III, *Integrity*, Section I, *Principles*, AICPA Code of Professional Conduct, adopted January 12, 1988, amended January 14, 1992.

skills necessary to render professional services with "facility and acumen."[4] In other words, the CPA must only offer to provide services that he or she can provide well. Although a CPA license conveys evidence of at least a basic knowledge in the field, and membership in a professional organization conveys some recognition of collective influences on behavior, only professionals themselves can judge their ability to perform a particular task. This means that true professionals not only recognize and have confidence in their skills but, just as important, recognize and will not undertake those tasks for which they do not have the necessary skills.

This personal responsibility has ramifications in several areas, including continuing professional education. Who wants to be treated by a physician who has not yet heard of antibiotics? It also leads to the necessity for participation in professional society activities, which expose individuals to developments in their profession. State licensing boards recognize this responsibility by adopting continuing professional education requirements as a prerequisite to periodic license renewal and reactivation. Even here, however, the trappings (for example, completion of specified training courses) do not alone evidence necessary skills. Judgments about competency still must be made by the professional.

This chapter first discusses the process by which CPAs are trained in the ethical concepts essential to their practice. Professional "failure" is defined and discussed, as well as the methods by which the profession and society deal with it. The final section of this chapter deals extensively with the AICPA's Code of Professional Conduct on individual behavior.

Learning to Practice Competently and Ethically: The Process

Ethics are learned or at least reinforced by observing appropriate behavior from role models (for example, parents, clergy, professors, and supervisors). These carry over into professional life and enhance an individual's ability to function with integrity and self-confidence. Experience and the guidance of mature professionals are the next essentials.

---
[4] Per Article V of the AICPA Code of Ethics.

The Role of the Firm in Shaping the Professional

Chapter 2 discusses how young CPAs learn professional and ethical norms. Sources of wisdom include the individual's family, religion, university peers and professors, and colleagues at their firms. Of course, some aspirants will not develop the level of competency required by the profession. A difficult but essential part of the judgment exercised by superiors is whether a particular subordinate should succeed, or whether a budding career should be terminated. If the screening process is ineffective, this burden falls on the profession's self-regulatory mechanisms, the states' licensing process, or disciplinary activities as professional failures are surfaced and handled.

Technical errors are always going to be made. If they are made by subordinates performing conscientiously, but in areas where their skills fall short of the task, the lapses usually can be overlooked (particularly if they are acknowledged and nonrecurring). Furthermore, technical errors offer an opportunity for more experienced professionals to teach subordinates. However, continuing inability to acquire higher technical skills is and should be a limiting factor in a career.

Violations of rules of behavior (written or implicit) are more serious since they are an indication of inability to establish proper priorities. Such weaknesses call into question the integrity of the individual and, as a result, injure to the fiduciary relationship between the professional and the client or professional and employer. Indeed, the weaknesses are potentially injurious to the profession as a whole. A concealment of a technical error, an inability to work through ambiguities in relationships and duties, or a refusal on the part of an aspirant to adhere to written or unwritten codes of behavior, act as poison to a CPA career and should be treated as such.

The Individual's Role in Developing the Qualities of a CPA

The relationship between a professional and a client or a professional and an employer is one of trust, since the client's or employer's affairs are entrusted to the skill of the professional in a specialized field of knowledge. Therefore, the CPA must develop an inner sense of the meaning and implications of a fiduciary relationship. This development initially is aided and guided by others, but as we have seen, the final responsibility lies with the individual. It can neither be forced into being nor shared in its application. In other words, ultimately it is up to the individual to do the right thing for the client or the employer. In another context, Thomas P. Holland has suggested five essential ingredients of a fiduciary relationship: honesty, competence, diligence, integrity, and discretion.[5] These certainly correspond to ingredients desired by CPAs in their relationships with clients and employers.

Listings of ethical rules, personal attributes, and personal qualities that should be developed by practitioners cannot provide the professional with clear guidelines in the murky and ambiguous situations found in practice. CPAs, as other professionals, usually must make decisions where knowledge of circumstances may be incomplete, and where uncertainties exist regarding outcomes. Yet, decisions **must** be made. The question is how to do so in a responsible manner.

A Paradigm for Fiduciary Decision Making

Many suggestions have been offered for guidance in decision making. Most suggestions involve a structure for isolating problems and weighing alternative solutions. The following is a framework for making difficult fiduciary decisions.

1. Be as sure of the facts as possible. This is important. It was the financier/philosopher, Bernard M. Baruch, who is reputed to have offered the thought that every man has a right to his opinion, but no man has a right to be wrong in his facts. This is particularly relevant to the process of deciding ethical questions.

2. Once the facts have been clearly established, those with an interest in the outcome should be identified. These persons (concerned parties or stakeholders) usually include the individual professional and/or their firm or employer, as well as stockholders, creditors, regulatory agencies, and perhaps the general public.

---

[5] Thomas P. Holland, "The Social Worker," *The Power of the Professional Person*, Lanham, Md.: University Press of America, Inc., 1988.

3. Once the facts are established and the concerned parties identified, alternative courses of action should be identified.
4. For each identified potential course of action, the possible effects of each alternative on each concerned party should be considered. Ethical questions to consider include the following: Is the course of action fair? Does the course of action violate any party's rights? Is the course of action legal? Does the course of action conform to technical requirements? Does the course of action potentially cause one of the party's financial harm? It is likely that tradeoffs will be necessary in balancing the concerns of all stakeholders. This is usually what is referred to as a "zero sum" calculation; benefits to one may well result in damages to others. It is also a process of setting up a value framework—*value* being defined as that which is perceived as good.[6]
5. Whether the views of constituencies should be solicited ("participatory" decision-making) may depend upon the nature of the problem posed. It is likely impracticable in most cases to do so, particularly since ultimate decisions are the purview of professionals, in light of their trusteeship relationship with a client. Further, most decisions in a professional—as opposed to a commercial or social—environment are not properly subject to a vote. They depend on the exercise of the professional's skill and judgment. Solutions preferred by interested parties (for example, a client) enter into the professional's consideration if offered, but cannot be decisive if objectivity is to be maintained.
6. The last and most important step deals with priorities, and here the professional's inner integrity is most critical. What factors are important in a decision, and which of the CPA's constituents should come first in assessing the benefits and/or penalties related to a particular course of action? Theoretically, in a purely commercial setting, cost/benefit calculations could be made on the assumption that the maximization of

---

[6] A philosophical discussion of what constitutes "good," in the realm of public accountancy or elsewhere, certainly is beyond the scope of this work, or indeed the capabilities of its authors. Suffice to say that the highest ideals attributable to the profession by its leading spokesmen and practitioners can serve as a working definition of the term.

gain is of most benefit to the party most at interest: the business entity. More realistically, the collateral effects of any decision on other parties may be just as or more important, and the individual professional must be able to assess and assign priorities to these effects. Benefits to one party usually involve costs to another. The individual's value system—personal and professional—then is critical to this process.

It is impracticable to explore all the ramifications of this thought, but, for example, should a client be permitted to follow a marginal (but currently acceptable) accounting practice that will maximize share prices, thus benefiting current officers and shareholders? More difficult, does the CPA have a professional responsibility to inform the client of the existence of this option even if then arguing against its use? Should the practice be allowed in the face of a perceived trend leading to the possible future withdrawal of professional approval for the practice? Do the interests of the investing public at large, and in particular potential investors who may be affected by such possible changes, weigh heavily or lightly? The answers to these questions cannot be supplied in the abstract, but the dilemmas they pose are illustrative of the focus on the professional public accountant and the value system that the individual necessarily must have or develop.

Ramifications for Failure to Practice up to the Professional Standard

How is a professional "failure" defined, identified, and treated?

Some attention needs to be given to enforcement mechanisms that protect society in the event of failure by a practitioner. First, there is the question of defining a "failure," next of surfacing it, and finally of the appropriate action to be taken in response to the failure and who should take the action. These issues arise only because professionals are human, and fallible as a consequence. A principal criterion of professionalism is expertise in a specialized field of knowledge. However, expertise does not guarantee perfection. A higher standard is imposed upon the CPA then simply complying with legal minimums. Failure to reach the higher standard can create consequences just as breaking the law will.

Describing professional failure is difficult. Professional rules, laws of the state, and institutional standards of behavior all should be viewed as minimums that the practitioner ideally should strive to exceed in every case. Failure to reach the higher standards may not be directly punishable, but may have consequences nevertheless. The potential consequence is a lack of success because others observe a lack of excellence, rather than any reprehensible technical or moral aberration that causes damage.

There is room for honest differences of opinion on technical matters, areas in which there is no clear consensus, and problems arising from interpretation, analysis, and opinion. The fact that experts disagree, therefore, is hardly cause for action. The fact that damage to a client or others does or does not result likewise is not a determinant of a professional failure but may be taken into account with other factors in deciding on disciplinary action. A somewhat vague reference to "standards of the profession" may be the best measure to be applied in defining failure. This is the standard applied in the event of litigation. Experts (other professionals) usually are called upon to establish those standards in particular circumstances.

Although "damage" may not be an indication of failure, it usually is the method by which failures that have occurred are brought to light. A client complains, an investor is injured, or other parties allege improper performance by a CPA, and an inquiry is launched or a lawsuit is filed. Other, less-visible means are employed as some state boards of accountancy launch positive enforcement programs, routinely investigating and monitoring the performance of licensees. The peer review concept applied by the AICPA and other professional societies is additional evidence of this activity.

An interesting and, some say, perverse development has arisen where professional bodies themselves attempt to respond to outside criticism by setting and enforcing standards. In May 1988, the U.S. Supreme Court ruled that hospital peer review committees are not immune from antitrust suits brought by doctors they penalize and reinstated a lower court antitrust award. In this case a physician claimed the other doctors acted against him because he was a competitor.[7] This would certainly exert a chilling effect on self-regulatory efforts in any profession.

---

[7] As reported in *Professional Ethics Report*, American Association for the Advancement of Science (spring 1988).

Once defined, surfaced, and investigated, professional failures call for action if the public interest is to be protected. This can take many forms and result in a range of penalties, from a simple cautionary warning by a professional society or a state agency, to loss of license to practice, damage awards, or both, as a result of legal action by an injured plaintiff. Voluntary actions by professional societies may be followed by more severe penalties in any event, as the knowledge and implications of failures become known.

The AICPA Code of Professional Conduct: A Major Source of Guidance on Ethical CPA Behavior

An entirely rewritten Code of Professional Conduct was adopted by the AICPA on January 12, 1988, and is revised often to address the changing practice environment. See the AICPA Web site (aicpa.org) for the most current updates.

This Code consists of two sections: principles and rules. The principles are behavioral objectives for CPAs. The rules are enforceable behavioral norms. The rules serve to govern the performance of professional services and provide a basis for disciplinary action where necessary. Among other requirements, the rules require compliance with professional technical standards [for example, Rule 202, *Compliance With Standards* (AICPA, *Professional Standards*, vol. 2, ET sec. 202)]. Therefore, a violation of a technical standard is also an ethical violation.

The principles in Section I of the Code are general in nature. They deal with the responsibilities of professionals to:

1. Exercise appropriate judgment in their activities
2. Serve the public interest
3. Maintain a high sense of integrity
4. Preserve objectivity and freedom from conflict of interest
5. Exercise due care in the performance of professional duties
6. Observe the principles of the Code in determining the nature and scope of services provided clients

The rules in Section II of the Code are enforceable rules of conduct. These rules are more specific than the general principles described in Section I. The rules cover matters of:

1. Independence (Rule 101)
2. Integrity and objectivity (Rule 102)
3. General standards of behavior (Rule 201)
4. Compliance with promulgated (technical) standards (Rule 202)
5. Compliance with accounting principles (Rule 203)
6. Confidential client information (Rule 301)
7. Contingent fees (Rule 302)
8. Acts discreditable to the profession (Rule 501)
9. Advertising (Rule 502)
10. Commissions and referral fees (Rule 503)
11. The form and organization (of practice) (Rule 505)

The Code is included as Appendix A. Other guidance is provided to CPAs by ethics Interpretations and Rulings. The ethics Interpretations are issued by the Professional Ethics Division's executive committee to amplify and explain particular rules and their implications. The rulings are formal rulings made by the executive committee to determine the application of particular rules to particular factual circumstances. Members who depart from rulings in similar circumstances are required to justify the departure. Both interpretations and rulings are made only after exposure to state societies, state boards of accountancy, practice units, and other interested parties. The Code emphasizes the essentially personal nature of institutional ethical constraints, stating, "Compliance with the Code of Professional Conduct, as with all standards in an open society, depends primarily on members' understanding and voluntary actions . . . [and only secondarily on peer pressure and disciplinary action]."[8]

From the beginning, the profession's codes of conduct have dealt with "ethical" (that is, moral) matters, as well as with "commercial"

---

[8] AICPA *Code of Professional Conduct*.

(that is, materialistic) matters. The two long were thought to be inseparable, since commercial activities such as advertising and bidding were not viewed as entirely consistent with the professional's commitment to provide quality service regardless of economic gain or loss, and with the client's need to select a CPA on the basis of that quality, not on the basis of price. The basic issue is one of assuring that the client's welfare—both economic and substantive—is best served. Is the selection of a professional adviser on the basis of price, for example, preferable to the selection based on quality of service? If quality service is the criterion, how is the client to measure "quality" and to be protected against price gouging by unscrupulous practitioners?

For many years, the accounting profession, as with other professions, was believed to be exempt from antitrust (anticompetitive) constraints. Sometime in the late 1960s or early 1970s, however, the Federal Trade Commission (FTC) began to consider whether such laws should not also apply to the professions and began to pressure for the relaxation of professional ethical rules against allegedly anticompetitive activities. Then, in 1975, the U.S. Supreme Court determined that the provisions of the federal antitrust laws applied to professions. In the *Goldfarb* case, the Virginia State Bar Association's minimum fee schedule was held to be illegal price fixing, in violation of the Sherman Act.[9] The FTC then proceeded to move against ethical constraints imposed by professional bodies that were perceived to inhibit free and open competition in the marketplace.

After extended negotiations, in 1990 the AICPA entered into a consent agreement with the FTC. Under this agreement the FTC issued an order[10] requiring modification or repeal of a number of ethical rules. In particular, the AICPA agreed not to interfere if its members wished to accept contingent fees from nonattest clients, accept disclosed commissions for products or services provided by third parties to nonattest clients, engage in advertising or solicitation, make or accept disclosed referral fees, or use trade names. Further, the AICPA cannot discourage or prevent such practices as self-laudatory or testimonial advertising. This is advertising that some in the profession consider "undignified." The AICPA also

---
[9] *Goldfarb v. Virginia State Bar*, 421 U.S. 773 (1975).
[10] Federal Trade Commission, Docket No. C3297, Complaint and Order: *In the Matter of American Institute of Certified Public Accountants*, July 26, 1990.

cannot discourage in-person solicitation of prospective clients. However, it may issue ethical guidelines prohibiting solicitation, advertising, or the use of trade names reasonably believed to be false or deceptive.

The AICPA's Core Concepts Addressing CPA's Ethical Dilemmas

Broadly speaking, any situation involving choices among competing interests could be characterized as an "ethical dilemma." The focus here is on the ethical constraints that arise most frequently in the context of the AICPA's Code of Conduct Section II.

Independence (Rule 101) as well as integrity and objectivity (Rule 102) are arguably the most frequently arising ethical dilemmas for CPAs in public practice. These qualities, key for all CPAs, are discussed in Chapter 2.

General standards of behavior (Rule 201) address professional rules of engagement to assure a consistent public expectation of the client/CPA relationship. The rules regarding contingent fees (Rule 302), acts discreditable to the profession (Rule 501), and advertising (Rule 502) all address specific situations and provide guidance intended to eliminate areas of ethical dilemma.

The rules regarding compliance with technical standards (Rule 202) and with accounting principles (Rule 203) appear to be nonissues with respect to ethical dilemmas, since these rules basically say to "follow the rules," leaving little room for dilemma. However, in the case of Enron, one of the most infamous financial reporting scandals in history, the entire complex scheme depended upon "following the technical rules" while abandoning the spirit of financial reporting objectives. In fact, as a result of the Enron scandal, following the rules is still required, but no longer sufficient in the eyes of the Securities and Exchange Commission (SEC). According to the Sarbanes-Oxley Act of 2002, auditors are required to opine on whether audited financial statements present fairly (without reference to any specific set of rules such as generally accepted accounting principles).

Finally, the rules regarding confidential client information (Rule 301) create frequent and difficult ethical questions for practitioners in both public and private practice. While the overriding requirement of confidentiality applies to all CPAs, the form of confidentiality differs for public versus private practice CPAs.

Confidentiality

CPAs in Public Practice

Any professional relationship depends for its success on the willingness of both parties to establish and maintain an open and uncritical dialogue, in which all pertinent facts and circumstances are freely disclosed. A medical doctor cannot be expected to make an accurate diagnosis unless the patient is forthcoming with symptoms. A lawyer cannot mount a client's case without a full airing of all the circumstances—including, if applicable, knowledge of guilt. A CPA cannot judge the propriety of accounting or reporting practices without being fully apprised of a client's or employer's financial circumstances and plans. The candid exchange of information, advice, and views on a particular matter ultimately depends also on the belief by each party that the discussion will be held in confidence. Any suspicions to the contrary inevitably will degrade the quality of the relationship and the effectiveness of the advice. It is a serious question whether a professional should allow a relationship to continue under such circumstances.

Rule 301, *Confidential Client Information* (AICPA, *Professional Standards*, vol. 2, ET sec. 301), states in part:

> A member **in public practice** shall not disclose any confidential client information without the specific consent of the client. (Emphasis added)

This rule has a number of exceptions. For example, a member is not relieved of the obligation to follow applicable standards for carrying out professional engagements, including appropriate reporting regarding a client's conformity with generally accepted accounting principles. Further, since the confidentiality constraint is only a professional ethical rule, it generally has no standing at law, as does a lawyer's "privileged" communication with clients (disclosure cannot be forced by outside agencies, including the courts). Accordingly, an accountant can be required by appropriate court summons or subpoena to disclose otherwise confidential information regarding a client's affairs. This was underlined by the U.S. Supreme Court in a prominent case granting access to the auditor's working papers by the IRS. The Court focused on the fact that the business of accountants, unlike that of attorneys, clergymen, and physicians, is to prepare disclosures of information for the investing public and regulatory agencies. It said:

> To insulate from disclosure a certified public accountant's interpretation of the client's financial statements would be to ignore the significance of the accountant's role as a disinterested analyst charged with public obligations . . .[11]

This ruling caused auditors to worry that they will not be afforded full access to information necessary to form an opinion on a client's financial statements. The clients had to deal with the possibility that what they told auditors might be forced into public view. A pragmatic balance has been reached, as the IRS administratively has been careful not to upset what is recognized by all to involve public policy issues beyond the immediately perceived need to gain access to working papers.

There is now a growing concern about whether it is ever appropriate for one privy to otherwise confidential information unilaterally to disclose it to third parties in the name of a "greater good." Whatever the individual's personal answer to this question, there is a growing pressure to force such disclosures over the objections of some practitioners. For example, in the 1995 amendments to the securities acts,[12] an auditor who becomes aware that a client has or may have committed an illegal act must:

1. Inform an appropriate level of management, and assure that the audit committee of the board of directors (or the board) is adequately informed.
2. If management or the board does not take "appropriate action," and the failure to do so reasonably would lead to a qualification in the auditor's report, the auditor must promptly so inform the board.
3. The board, within one business day of receiving such information, must inform the SEC, with a copy to the auditor of its notice to the SEC.

---

[11] *United States v. Arthur Young & Co.*, 465 U.S. 805 (1984).

[12] Title III—Auditor Disclosure of Corporate Fraud, *Private Securities Litigation Reform Act of 1995*.

4. If the auditor fails to receive a copy of such notice within the one-day period, he or she must either (a) resign the engagement or (b) furnish the SEC directly a copy of the report to the board.
5. In the event of resignation, the auditor still must furnish the SEC directly a copy of such report.

CPAs offering tax and consulting services are covered by the same Rule 301 applied to those offering attest services, although the public policy aspects of such relationships are more compelling in favor of extending protection to confidential information because of the lesser degree of third party interest. A separate argument may be offered for providing "privilege" (protected communications) in the case of tax advice or tax return preparation. The attorney-client privilege has long been a part of federal law. Clients of CPAs performing the same or similar services are afforded no such protection.[13] For privilege to be invoked, an accountant must work through an attorney, an awkward and seemingly unnecessary complication. Whether working directly with an attorney or an accountant, a client should have the confidence that the full and free disclosure so necessary to competent advice will not result in a disadvantage if one or the other professional is chosen.

CPAs in Corporate Practice, Government, Other Employment, or Academe

As previously stated, independence in appearance is impossible to attain in an employer/employee relationship, but the requirements for objectivity and personal integrity still pertain. Here the principal issue, and ethical dilemma, is whether "other" considerations can or should override loyalty to an employer to the point where the employee is justified in breaking a confidentiality barrier. For example, should a CPA in corporate practice report a perceived breach of an accounting principle to the SEC? This general problem comes under the rubric of "whistleblowing." We all perhaps still have a memory of what it means at a grade school level to "snitch" on a member of a group or class. Society has not traditionally respected snitches, and whistleblowers are a modern version. However, there

---

[13] Some states have provided for accountant-client privilege in tax matters, but this protection does not extend to federal cases.

is indeed a public responsibility borne by a CPA, a responsibility not to participate in a deception. Medical personnel have a legal responsibility to breach the confidentiality barrier to report gunshot wounds, and certain other diseases perceived to offer public dangers. Is there not a similar obligation for CPAs in other situations?

Whistleblowing is a direct and blatant violation of confidentiality. Whistleblowers sound an alarm regarding the very organization where they work, aiming to spotlight neglect or abuses that threaten the public interest. Several assumptions in this definition require comment. The "blower" takes the moral high ground in the name of "public interest." Although he or she may have misjudged that interest or the facts being disclosed, there is an underlying conviction that the good done by the exposure outweighs the damage potentially inflicted on the entity or on the individual's personal career. There is a conflict here that only the individual can resolve, in the light of all that individual's life training and convictions. In any event, the matter is brought into better focus for CPAs by an interpretation of AICPA Rule 102 on integrity and objectivity. Interpretation No. 102-4 states, in part, that a member (not in public practice) who concludes that his or her employer's financial statements could be materially misstated, and appropriate corrective action is not taken, should "consider any responsibility that may exist to communicate to third parties, such as regulatory authorities or the employer's (former employer's) external accountant."[14]

This imperative seems at first blush to be at direct odds with the provisions of the Standards of Ethical Conduct for Management Accountants, promulgated by the Institute of Management Accountants (IMA). These standards require management accountants to "refrain from disclosing confidential information acquired in the course of their work except when authorized, unless legally obligated to do so."[15] It is not clear what "legally obligated to do so" means, nor what constitutes "authorization" to disclose confidential information. A further admonition in the standards does nothing to clear the problem. Under the caption "Resolution of Ethical

---

[14] American Institute of Certified Public Accountants, *AICPA Professional Standards*, June 1, 2002, p. 4442.

[15] National Association of Accountants (now the Institute of Management Accountants), *Statements on Management Accounting: Objectives of Management Accounting, Statement No. 1B*, New York, N.Y., June 17, 1982.

Conflict," the instruction is given that: "Except where legally prescribed, communication of such problems to authorities or individuals not employed or engaged by the organization is not considered appropriate."[16] This creates a conflict of loyalties that cries out for resolution. For example, consider the situation faced by accountants at WorldCom. They recognized that certain accounting entries they were being asked to make were inappropriate and creating misleading financial information. Should they have reported the situation to authorities? The answer depends upon whether they considered such communication to be "legally prescribed." Provisions of the Sarbanes-Oxley Act of 2002 have provided support for the employee by emphasizing the illegality of misleading accounting information and providing protection to those from the organization that bring alleged activities to the attention of authorities.

Interpretation 102-3 relates to the obligation that an AICPA member in corporate practice has to his or her employer's external accountant. Here, the member must "be candid and not knowingly misrepresent facts or knowingly fail to disclose material facts."

This important requirement places a responsibility upon the CPA in corporate practice to avoid intentional misrepresentations on behalf of the employer that could, if uncovered, soil the good name of the CPA profession.

Ethical Decisions—Where Can I Get Help?

Society depends upon CPAs' expertise and ethics. Like doctors, lawyers, engineers, and architects, CPAs frequently must make difficult decisions, and often these decisions involve ethics. Such decisions can be very lonely. For example, the audience was mesmerized as WorldCom Internal Audit Director Cynthia Cooper vividly recalled, in a speech delivered at the American Accounting Association Annual Meetings, ethical choices that she faced.[17] However, there are resources available to help practitioners. In this section, the most important of these resources are described.

The first resource is your family (and your faith, if applicable). They don't want to see you harmed. Thus, they will provide you moral support and quite possibly wisdom as well. Remember, they

---
[16] See footnote 15.
[17] San Francisco, California. August 10, 2005.

will be harmed as well if you act unethically. The second resource is your trusted colleagues and friends. This resource can be the most important because your colleagues like, respect, and admire you and they can probably provide some professional wisdom that will help you with your decision. The third resource is professional information and guidance. Certainly, the AICPA Code of Conduct is foremost. However, there is more guidance available. For example, the AICPA offers much ethics-related guidance on its Web site (see the Professional Ethics Division portion of the Web site).[18] General information about ethics, volumes of ethics resources, frequently asked questions about ethics and specific ethical dilemmas, recent developments related to ethics, email addresses to contact AICPA staff, and even an Ethics Hotline [(888) 777-7077] are all available at this site. There is also a separate site for members in business and industry, which contains information designed to help private practice CPAs make ethical decisions. The ethics decision tree that follows was produced to synthesize the decision making process for CPAs in business.[19]

The International Federation of Accountants (IFAC) is the global organization for the accounting profession. IFAC, a private sector organization that currently has 163 member organizations in 120 countries, works to protect the public interest by encouraging high-quality practices by the world's accountants. To this end, IFAC offers a Code of Ethics for Professional Accountants as well as Statements of Policy of Council regarding the implementation and enforcement of ethical requirements. These documents can be found on the IFAC Web site (www.ifac.org).

---

[18] http://www.aicpa.org/members/div/ethics/index.htm

[19] The AICPA Ethics Decision Tree is available for download from the AICPA, at http://www.aicpa.org/download/ethics/bai/decision_tree_bai.pdf. For additional information, see http://www.aicpa.org/pubs/cpaltr/sept2002/business/busind1.htm and http://www.aicpa.us/audcommctr/guidance_resources/srmgmt_bod_audit_cmte/early_warning_signals/45.htm. See also the Ethics Decision Tree for CPAs in Government, at http://www.aicpa.org/pubs/cpaltr/nov2002/supps/gov1.htm.

Accountability: Personal Oversight **105**

Ethics Decision Tree
For CPAs in Business & Industry

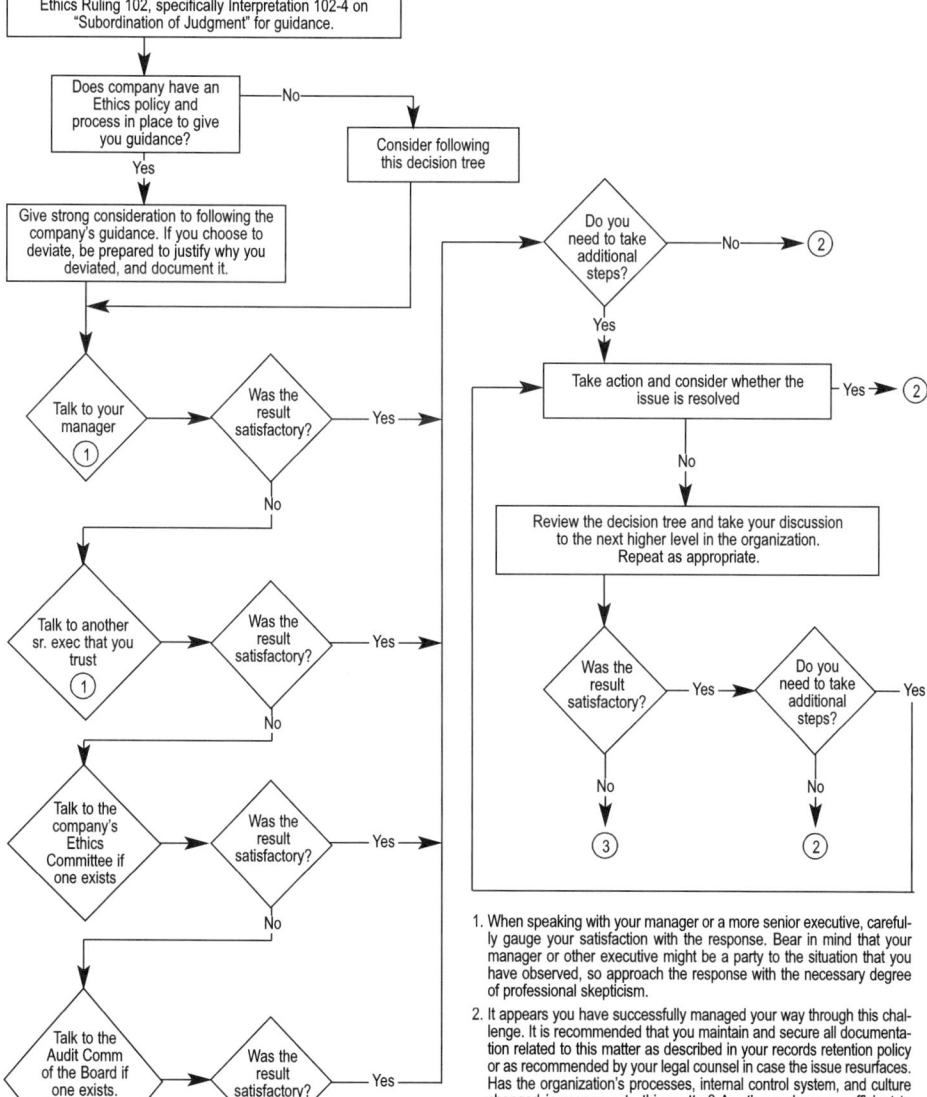

Identify Issue
NOTE: If the issue related to a disagreement or dispute relating to the preparation of financial statements or the recording of transactions, the CPA should refer to AICPA Ethics Ruling 102, specifically Interpretation 102-4 on "Subordination of Judgment" for guidance.

Does company have an Ethics policy and process in place to give you guidance?
- No → Consider following this decision tree
- Yes → Give strong consideration to following the company's guidance. If you choose to deviate, be prepared to justify why you deviated, and document it.

Do you need to take additional steps?
- No → ②
- Yes → Take action and consider whether the issue is resolved
  - Yes → ②
  - No → Review the decision tree and take your discussion to the next higher level in the organization. Repeat as appropriate.
    - Was the result satisfactory?
      - Yes → Do you need to take additional steps? → Yes / No → ②
      - No → ③

Talk to your manager ①
- Was the result satisfactory?
  - Yes →
  - No → Talk to another sr. exec that you trust ①
    - Was the result satisfactory?
      - Yes →
      - No → Talk to the company's Ethics Committee if one exists
        - Was the result satisfactory?
          - Yes →
          - No → Talk to the Audit Comm of the Board if one exists. If not, talk to the BoD
            - Was the result satisfactory?
              - Yes →
              - No → ③

1. When speaking with your manager or a more senior executive, carefully gauge your satisfaction with the response. Bear in mind that your manager or other executive might be a party to the situation that you have observed, so approach the response with the necessary degree of professional skepticism.

2. It appears you have successfully managed your way through this challenge. It is recommended that you maintain and secure all documentation related to this matter as described in your records retention policy or as recommended by your legal counsel in case the issue resurfaces. Has the organization's processes, internal control system, and culture changed in response to this matter? Are these changes sufficient to minimize the recurrence of a challenge like this one? Evaluate your answers and consider consulting with management, an outside mentor or other neutral party whom you respect.

3. Consider whether it is appropriate for you to continue your employment at this company. Consider the severity and implications of the issue you have identified and whether it should be reported to the outside accountants, regulatory agency, bank or other lending institution, owner or investor committee, BoD, or another party.

The Bottom Line: It Is up to You

In the end, it is you who makes the decision. You must ask yourself what your highest aspiration is. Professor Murphy Smith offers this wisdom: "The answer might be wealth, fame, knowledge, popularity, or integrity. Be on guard, if integrity is secondary to any of the alternatives, it will be sacrificed in situations in which a choice must be made. Such situations inevitably occur in every person's life."[20] Lincoln put it this way: "Honor is better than honors."[21] The writer of Proverbs put it best: "A good name is more desirable than great riches; to be esteemed is better than silver or gold."[22]

The bottom line is this:

> Do not make any decisions, take any actions, write anything, or say anything that you would not be perfectly comfortable reading about on the front page of your local newspaper and defending in court. As recent events have demonstrated, each is entirely possible.

Summary

Personal integrity is the key attribute of any professional. This chapter deals with the development of a personal code of behavior for a CPA, and the factors that guide and influence it. Ways are suggested to think about ethical problems and to establish priorities in circumstances where there are competing claims to be resolved. Institutional ethical codes were viewed as minimums, and as not necessarily representing the best measure of proper activity in particular circumstances. Indeed, reliance on codes or laws to establish proper norms tends to reduce all judgments to the lowest common denominator. Reliance on codes or laws is the final refuge of those who have failed to reach for the higher standard that is the hallmark of the true professional. This in the final analysis is a personal problem, and the solutions can only be personal, as each individual weighs the values of competing interests and the effects of choosing one against the others.

---

[20] L. Murphy Smith, "A Fresh Look at Accounting Ethics (or Dr. Smith Goes to Washington)," *Accounting Horizons* (March 2003): 48.

[21] Quoted in Smith (2003). See footnote 20.

[22] Proverbs 22:1.

specialized body of knowledge. It would be difficult and probably impossible for a person who is not an expert in the field to assess whether the services of a CPA were performed in a professionally competent manner. Thus, a CPA's peers, who also possess the professional knowledge, are best qualified to understand the behavioral expectations and to monitor compliance with the expectations.

Peer oversight and quality control begins with standard setting. Select members of the profession are actively involved in the process of developing financial accounting and reporting standards and the auditing standards to which CPAs must conform. Also, many members of the profession provide input used by standard setters to develop relevant standards. The profession also generates resources to help individual practitioners to recognize and comply with all of the standards. In addition, the profession puts quality control mechanisms into place to identify any practitioners that are not complying with the professional standards. The institutions that accomplish these self-regulation and oversight initiatives in the CPA profession are primarily the AICPA and the state CPA societies. These organizations also advocate on behalf of the profession in matters of public policy.

Self-Regulation of the Accounting Profession by the AICPA

The AICPA is the principal professional organization of CPAs in the United States. The AICPA and its predecessor organizations (the first of which was organized in 1887) have served as a mechanism for the development of professional ethics, accounting and auditing practice, a forum for professional concerns, and a focal point for self-regulation. All CPAs are eligible for personal membership in the AICPA. The primary requirement for continued membership is that the CPA is a member in good standing and meets continuing professional education requirements. Members that perform attestation engagements must also undergo periodic peer reviews as well.

AICPA efforts are divided into Audit Quality Centers, Member Interest Centers, technical resources, self-regulation activities, other member interests resources, and external relations activities. The collective efforts of these centers, resources, and activities are designed to provide profession members with the resources necessary to provide consistently outstanding quality, to provide professional oversight of peers to ensure quality, and to advocate on behalf of the profession in matters of public policy and external relations.

Audit Quality Centers. The Audit Quality Centers include the Center for Public Company Audit Firms (CPCAF), the Employee Benefit Plan Audit Quality Center, and the Governmental Audit Quality Center.

Member Interest Centers. Member Interest Centers include Accounting Education, Business Valuation and Forensic and Litigation Services, Financial Management, Information Technology, Personal Financial Planning, and Private Company Practice Section Firm Practice (PCPS).

Technical Resources. The AICPA offers the following technical resources to help practitioners: Accounting and Auditing Hotline Team; Accounting Standards Team; Antifraud Resource Center; Assurance Services technical resources (SysTrust™ and WebTrust™); Audit and Attest Standards Team; Enhanced Business Reporting; and Taxation Topics.

Other Member Interest Resources. The AICPA has resources for other member interests such as the Audit Committee Effectiveness Center, the CPA2Biz Resource Centers, and a vast array of Continuing Professional Education courses.

Self-Regulation Activities. To regulate the activities of member CPAs, the AICPA has Examination Teams, Peer Review, the Professional Ethics Division, and the Center for Public Company Audit Firms Peer Review Program.

External Relations and Advocacy Activities. The AICPA has a Communications/Public Relations Team, a Congressional and Political Activities Team, International Services-related resources, Minority Initiatives-related resources and activities, State Societies and Regulatory Affairs Team, and Work/Life and Women's Initiatives-related resources and activities.

AICPA Regulation Activities on Behalf of the Accounting Profession

Self-regulation in the accounting profession requires an effective mechanism for (1) establishing standards of behavior, (2) exposing substandard performance, and (3) taking appropriate disciplinary action. As the primary self-regulatory body of the CPA profession, the AICPA engages in technical activities (for example, generation of auditing standards) and oversight activities (for example, the peer review process) to regulate the profession.

AICPA technical activities. The following are several of the key technical AICPA activities:

1. Issuing authoritative pronouncements on auditing standards, quality control standards, and accounting and review services (for example, AICPA Code of Professional Conduct).
2. Providing commentary to the Financial Accounting Standards Board (FASB), the Securities and Exchange Commission (SEC), and others organizations on accounting standards.
3. Issuing and enforcing ethical rules and interpretations.
4. Preparing and grading the Uniform CPA Examination for all CPA candidates.
5. Maintaining relations with educators and with federal and state agencies and legislators.
6. Preparing and distributing courses for use in continuing professional education.
7. Dealing with the practice problems of CPAs in areas outside the attest function such as management advisory services, income taxation, and personal financial planning.

AICPA professional oversight activities. Individual members of the AICPA are bound to follow the provisions of the AICPA Code of Professional Conduct (both to remain AICPA members and to comply with state accounting laws that often mandate compliance with the Code of Professional Conduct). The peer review process is the process by which substandard performance under the Code and under all other practice regulations is identified and rectified. To this end, CPAs (and CPA firms) in public practice that fall under the AICPA's practice-monitoring standards and issue reports that purport to be in accordance with AICPA professional standards must be enrolled in an approved quality control (practice monitoring) program. The AICPA approves two practice-monitoring programs: the

Center for Public Company Audit Firms Peer Review Program (CPCAF PRP) and the AICPA Peer Review Program 9PRP).[3]

Firms registered with and inspected by the Public Companies Accounting Oversight Board (PCAOB) must enroll in the CPCAF PRP and undergo a CPCAF PRP peer review. The CPCAF PRP includes a review and evaluation of the portion of firms' practices not inspected by the PCAOB (that is, the portions of the practice not related to publicly traded companies). This oversight enables these firms to meet applicable state licensing requirements, federal regulatory requirements, and AICPA membership requirements. Firms that are members of the CPCAF, but not required to register with and be reviewed by the Public Companies Accounting Oversight Board (PCAOB) can also choose to be reviewed by the CPCAF PRP or, alternatively, by the AICPA PRP.

The AICPA PRP is dedicated to enhancing the quality of accounting, auditing and attestation services performed by AICPA members in public practice, but not evaluated by the PCAOB and the CPCAF PRP. The standards and other guidance for performing and reporting on CPCAF PRP or AICPA PRP peer reviews are available on the AICPA Web site (www.aicpa.org).

The requirements of the two groups are similar. First, members must file an annual report that contains a broad range of information about the firm. Second, members must undergo a peer review of the firm's accounting and auditing practice quality control system. Third, members must adhere to the pronouncements of the AICPA's Quality Control Standards Committee.

The Peer Review Process: A Closer Look

Note: While peer review activities as represented herein reflect current practice, this is a dynamic area and requires that practitioners update their understanding frequently.

Each member firm must undergo a peer review once every three years. The objective is to determine whether the reviewed firm is

---

[3] A firm that is registered with and inspected by the Public Companies Accounting Oversight Board (PCAOB) is required to be enrolled in the Center for Public Company Audit Firms Peer Review Program (CPCAF PRP). Firms that are members of the CPCAF that are not required to be registered with and inspected by the PCAOB may enroll in either the CPCAF PRP or the AICPA Peer Review Program. (Note, discussions are underway that may lead to merger of the CFCAF PRP and the AICPA Peer Review Program).

conforming with substantially all applicable professional standards. To this end, the reviewing firm must determine whether the reviewed firm (1) has a system of quality control that meets the objectives of the AICPA's quality control standards, (2) complied with its stated quality control standards during a specified period (usually a year), and (3) was in conformity with the center's membership requirements. The peer review reports of CPCAF and PCPS member firms are publicly available.

The peer review consists of two elements. First, it includes a consideration of the quality controls in key functional areas such as:

1. Independence, integrity, and objectivity
2. Personnel management
3. Acceptance and continuance of clients and engagements
4. Engagement performance
5. Monitoring

Second, it consists of a review of selected professional engagements. These engagements are reviewed to test the output of the functional controls (that is, to see whether there is reasonable assurance that performance in the field conforms to professional standards). Minor deficiencies are verbally communicated to the peer reviewed firm. More substantive suggestions by reviewers to reviewed firms regarding deficiencies in controls or their application are furnished in a "letter of comments" at the conclusion of each peer review. These letters, together with the reviewed firm's responses, are filed with the Center's Peer Review Committee, and are publicly available.[4]

What Happens If Substandard Performance Is Discovered?

The peer review process is designed to help practitioners and firms to constantly improve. If significant deficiencies are identified by peer reviewers, the Peer Review Committee will develop recommendations to rectify the deficiency. Thus, the peer review process is designed to produce positive outcomes for both the reviewed firm

---

[4] The CPCAF PRP was established on January 1, 2004, as the successor to the SEC Practice Section (SECPS) Peer Review Program. For more information, please visit the CPCAF PRP Web site at http://www.aicpa.org/centerprp/index.htm.

(recommendations for improvement) and for the profession (quality maximization across the profession).

Does the Profession Ever Discipline Practitioners?

In rare cases, CPAs can face disciplinary action from the profession. Although failure to observe the Code of Professional Conduct is the only basis for discipline of AICPA members, the Code requires compliance with professional technical standards. Thus, it addresses technical as well as behavioral violations. If litigation involving a particular issue is pending, and a member's legal rights might be prejudiced by an investigation by the profession, active investigation is deferred until litigation is completed.

Once litigation, if any, is completed, an ethics investigation is begun. Initial determinations are made by staff and in certain cases, a subcommittee representative (technical standards or independence/behavioral standards). Final disposition may be made by the Joint Trial Board unless the member agrees to a proposed disciplinary action at an intermediate point. The penalty for a less serious infraction is usually some sort of private censure requiring certain remedial measures, such as continuing professional education in the area of the deficiency. More serious infractions can result in suspension or expulsion from the AICPA (and the resulting negative publicity).

Since state societies have similar ethical codes and take similar actions for ethical violations, the AICPA has entered into a Joint Ethics Enforcement Program (JEEP) with most of them. Under JEEP, investigations may be carried out either by the AICPA or by state ethics committee representatives. This program not only avoids the problem of dual investigations of the same event, but also greatly expands the ability of the profession to pursue actions. The AICPA usually takes cases of broad or national interest.

State CPA Societies

Although not formally affiliated with the AICPA, the various state CPA societies complement and reinforce the AICPA's activities at the state and local level. Most AICPA members are also members in their respective state societies. With some generally unimportant differences, the AICPA and the state societies have in the past adhered to the same code of conduct. Both the AICPA and the various state societies contribute heavily to the continuing professional education and to other activities of their members.

Setting Accounting Standards:[5] The Role of Public and Private Organizations

Setting accounting and auditing standards is one key aspect of self-regulation of the accounting profession. Before the turn of the 20th century, accounting practices were developed, *ad hoc,* by business enterprises and their accountants to meet business needs. These practices initially were influenced by Scottish or English accountants who came to this country following investments made by entrepreneurs from the United Kingdom. The accounting practices were not organized into any theoretical pattern or paradigm, and it is doubtful whether initiatives at the time went much beyond bookkeeping techniques. Auditing standards were largely nonexistent.

Increased industrial and financial activity in the early 20th century, and the growing need to report to shareholders and other third parties, began to put pressure on accountants to consider the theoretical underpinnings of their craft. Legislation relating to income taxes, banking, and antitrust matters had a profound effect on the accounting profession, which now was required to set methods to be used in handling legal reporting requirements. Early encounters between the accounting profession and emerging regulatory agencies over establishment of accounting principles clearly left the accounting profession in charge. "What the practicing accountants got was . . . disciplinary control over their profession . . . and rejection of a uniform system of accounting that would have reduced their control over accounting practices and thus reduced the value of their services."[6]

An interesting exception to the profession's domination of the standard setting process was the Interstate Commerce Commission (ICC), which promptly exercised its authority by establishing a

---

[5] The terms *principles* and *standards* are used more or less interchangeably today. *Standards* connotes perhaps a somewhat higher level of authority, but the auditor's standard report still refers to conformity with generally accepted accounting *principles*.

[6] Robert Chatov, *Corporate Financial Reporting: Public or Private Control?* (New York: The Free Press, 1975); 50.

uniform accounting system for railroads. The rigidity and theoretical infirmities of this system have been cited as prime examples of the dangers of allowing accounting matters to be handled by a bureaucracy.[7]

The dominance of the private sector in the establishment of accounting standards was legitimized in 1938 with the SEC's issuance of ASR No. 4. In that release, the SEC stated that financial statements would be considered misleading unless prepared in accordance with accounting principles having "substantial authoritative support." It was intended that the authoritative support be developed and expressed by an appropriate professional accounting body. The AICPA undertook that task and formed the Committee on Accounting Procedure (CAP). The CAP began to issue Accounting Research Bulletins (ARBs). These were pronouncements on specific accounting problems drawn to the attention of the Committee, and did not pretend to be issued within any theoretical framework. Before its demise some 20 years later, the Committee issued 51 ARBs. A companion Committee on Terminology issued four bulletins on its topic.

In 1959, the Committee on Accounting Procedure was succeeded by the Accounting Principles Board (APB), which was expected, with the support of a new research capability, to develop a theoretical framework within which particular accounting problems could be addressed. However, the APB was quickly drawn into the same pattern as the old CAP of dealing with emerging problems without being able to integrate its decisions. The APB did not issue a pronouncement until 1962 (on depreciation) and suffered the indignity of having its second opinion (on the investment credit) in effect overturned scarcely a month after issuance by the SEC in ASR No. 96. This defeat was acknowledged a year later by the APB's fourth opinion, negating the position taken earlier in the second opinion.

Several studies were published by the research staff,[8] but were never incorporated into the APB's agenda. The APB issued 31 Opinions and four Statements (on broad accounting topics) before

---

[7] See, for example, Leonard Spacek, *A Search for Fairness in Financial Reporting to the Public* (Chicago: Arthur Andersen & Co., 1969): 22-23.

[8] For example, Maurice Moonitz, *The Basic Postulates of Accounting*, Accounting Research Study No. 1, (New York: AICPA, 1962).

being replaced by the Financial Accounting Standards Board (FASB) in 1972.

The Financial Accounting Standards Board

The apparent inability of the APB to deal with fundamental accounting issues, and growing criticism in the 1960s of accounting practices related to increasingly complex and innovative business practices, led the AICPA to initiate a study of the standard-setting process itself. At a conference to discuss this matter, the then president of the AICPA observed: "If we are not confronted with a crisis of confidence in the profession, we are at least faced with a serious challenge to our ability to perform a mission of grave public responsibility."[9]

Shortly thereafter, at the direction of the AICPA's Board of Directors, a study group was appointed under the chairmanship of Francis M. Wheat, an attorney and former SEC Commissioner, to consider the whole issue of the institutional structure by which accounting principles should be determined. Included in the study group, in addition to the chairperson, were three CPA-practitioners, an investment banker, a corporate financial vice-president, and an accounting academician. The recommendations of this group led to the formation of the Financial Accounting Foundation (FAF), an organization separate from all existing professional bodies, which appointed a full-time Financial Accounting Standards Board (FASB) with seven members to issue pronouncements on accounting standards,[10] and a Financial Accounting Standards Advisory Council (FASAC) to work with the FASB in an advisory capacity. In addition, the AICPA established an Accounting Standard Executive Committee (AcSEC) to present the consensus of AICPA members regarding important matters.

The structure and organization of these entities has been the subject of much attention over the years, and changes have been made from time to time to accommodate developing views on the

---

[9] Report of the Study on Establishment of Accounting Principles, *Establishing Financial Accounting Standards* (New York: AICPA, 1972): 3. (Usually referred to as the "Wheat Report," after the chairman of the group.)

[10] A companion and similar agency, the Governmental Accounting Standards Board (GASB), began operating in 1984, also under the aegis of the Financial Accounting Foundation. The GASB establishes financial accounting and reporting standards only for state and local governmental units.

formulation of accounting standards. Most recently, at the urging of the SEC, the composition of the FAF has been altered to increase the number of "public" members from three to five, thus providing for more input from nonprofessionals.

The FASB was recognized as the appropriate authority for the formation of accounting standards by the AICPA, which designated the FASB's Statements on Financial Accounting Standards as being enforceable under the institute's Code of Ethics. The SEC followed in 1973 with ASR No. 150, reiterating that agency's support for private-sector accounting standard setting and noting that the FASB's standards would be recognized as representing "substantial authoritative support," while contrary principles would have no such support. Notwithstanding this reaffirmation of support for the private sector, the SEC has overruled FASB pronouncements a few times, with at least some diminishing effect on the FASB's prestige.[11] It is clear that the ultimate authority in such matters lies with the SEC, should that agency choose to exercise it.

Although not untouched by controversy, the FASB has in the main been successful in its mission. The process by which the FASB issues accounting guidance (including exposure of proposed Statements for comment and public hearings) is designed to provide for due process and input from reporting entities and financial statement users. The FASB has issued over 150 pronouncements to date on a variety of difficult questions.

The Auditing Standards Board

Sarbanes-Oxley gives the PCAOB ultimate authority to establish the auditing procedures for publicly held enterprises (commonly known as issuers). Such audits number currently around 17,000 per year. However, audits of non-publicly held enterprises number in the hundreds of thousands each year. The Auditing Standards Board (ASB) sets the standards with which these audits must comply.

The ASB is an AICPA committee formed in 1978 and designated by the AICPA Council to promulgate auditing and attestation, and

---

[11] For example, in 1978 the SEC issued ASR No. 253 (financial and reporting requirements for oil and gas producing activities) directly overturning FASB Statement of Financial Accounting Standards No. 19, which had previously been developed by the FASB at the SEC's request to meet a congressional mandate to develop standards in this area.

quality control standards applicable to the performance and issuance of audit and attestation reports for enterprises that are not subject to the Sarbanes-Oxley Act or the rules of the SEC (known as nonissuers). The ASB derives its authority from Rule 202 of the AICPA Code of Professional Conduct, which requires AICPA members who perform professional services to comply with standards promulgated by bodies designated by Council.

The mission of the ASB is "to develop and communicate comprehensive performance, reporting, and quality control standards and practice guidance to enable auditors of nonissuers to provide high quality, objective audit and attestation services at a reasonable cost and in the best interests of the profession and the beneficiaries of those services, with the ultimate purpose of serving the public interest by improving existing and enabling new audit and attestation services."[12]

The ASB accomplishes this mission by "(1) developing auditing, attestation, and quality control standards that inspire public trust, (2) contributing to the development of high quality international auditing standards, and (3) responding timely to the need for guidance and communicating clearly to the profession and to users."[13]

The ASB comprises 19 members including public practitioners, members with state board of accountancy experience, users, and public members. Up to one-quarter of the board members may be non-AICPA members. Typically, five of the members are from local, regional, and other non-big four national firms, five are state board of accountancy representatives, four are from big four firms, and five are users and/or public members. Usually, one seat will be held by a government official or an auditor of government entities and one seat will be held by an academician. The Director of the AICPA Audit and Attest Standards Staff, in consultation with the ASB Chair, nominates the members of the ASB and the AICPA Board of Directors approves the nominations. Elected members normally serve three one-year terms, with reappointment each year dependent upon satisfactory performance.

---

[12] See the AICPA Auditing, Attestation, and Quality Control Standards Setting Activities Operating Policies at www.aicpa.org/members/div/auditstd/index/htm.
[13] See footnote 11.

The ASB issues Statements on Auditing Standards, Statements on Standards for Attestation Engagements, and Statements on Quality Control Standards. Statements proposed by the ASB are subject to an exposure process that includes deliberation in meetings open to the public, public exposure of the proposed statements and a formal vote. Comments are sought from other affected committees and boards and the general AICPA membership before the vote is conducted. All ASB proposals are made available free of charge on the AICPA Web site. Once approved, the standards become authoritative guidance that must be followed by all AICPA members providing these professional services to nonissuers. The final standards can be viewed on the AICPA Web site as well.

Public or Private Standard Setting?

Challenges to private sector standard setting continue to arise. These challenges come from those who are understandably upset with accounting abuses, alleged cases of audit failures (particularly where major corporate bankruptcies are involved), and similar instances that are believed to represent an inability of private institutions to deal with matters of public interest. Criticism coming from federal legislative bodies focuses also on the asserted improper delegation of the SEC's authority in this area to private bodies such as the FASB.

A significant challenge came during congressional hearings in 1976 and 1977 held by subcommittees under the direction of Senator Metcalf and Representative Moss, and have resurfaced again in calls for subcommittee investigation by Representative Dingell. The issue of public versus private determination of accounting principles was addressed directly in the Wheat Report. Reasons cited for public control included the belief that (1) accounting matters are too important to be left to a body not responsible to Congress, (2) that conflicts of interest (between standard setters and reporting entities) can only be avoided through the interposition of governmental agencies, and (3) that accounting principles have the effect of law and should only be established by bodies charged with responsibility in this area and following all procedures prescribed for rule making.

The report, however, came solidly down on the side of continuing standard setting in the private sector. Principal reasons for this decision were the fear that (1) otherwise accounting principles would be set primarily to accomplish political goals (for example, the employee stock option cost debate); (2) rules would be inflexible and unresponsive to emerging problems; (3) such a move would sap the vitality of the profession; and (4) the focus of the rule making body necessarily would be on reporting by public companies and to governmental agencies, whereas the true domain of accounting is significantly broader.

Private control of standard setting is once again being challenged. For example, provisions of the Sarbanes-Oxley Act of 2002 give significant audit and accounting standard setting power to the PCAOB. However, private sector standard setting remains relevant as the PCAOB relies heavily on the existing private sector standards (for example, FASB and ASB pronouncements).

Summary

This chapter provides a discussion of the regulation of the profession of public accountancy by bodies within the profession (for example, the AICPA, the FASB, and the state societies). Self-regulation of the CPA profession by CPAs is optimal because of the vast and specialized technical skills and knowledge necessary to set and enforce accounting and auditing standards. The profession must be regulated and its activities directed to optimally serve the public interest.

The role of professional organizations and their rules of conduct in this process was described. The AICPA is the key element here, as it sets the code of conduct and standards and facilitates peer reviews. The various state societies also provide codes of conduct, which are typically substantively equivalent to that of the AICPA.

The topic of the appropriate mechanism for the development of accounting standards was also considered. This responsibility has historically rested with the private sector (now in the form of the FASB and the ASB). However, recent reforms such as those in Sarbanes-Oxley convey significant standard setting authority to the public sector. The debate of whether standards should be set by the private sector or by governmental (or quasi-governmental) agencies is likely to continue.

7

Accountability: Public Oversight

> *Today effective practitioners of public accounting not only must be aware of the possibility of legal involvement, but also must be able to deal effectively with the litigious environment in which they operate. Practitioners who ignore the possibility of legal involvement, or who fail to understand the legal duties that they owe to the users of their work product, will soon find themselves unable to conduct their professional practices in a profitable manner.*
>
> Jonathan J. Davies[1]

Introduction

The final level of oversight and regulation of CPA activity is society. Society granted the CPA profession the monopoly attest franchise. In return, the CPA must have a commitment and obligation to serve society and the public interest. Society and the public interest are protected via oversight of the profession by public sector regulatory

---
[1] Jonathan J. Davies, *CPA Liability: A Manual for Practitioners* (New York: John Wiley & Sons, 1983), v.

bodies as well as by laws. Public sector regulators of CPAs are examined in the first part of this chapter. Laws governing and controlling CPA practice are examined in the second part of the chapter.

A regulator is a governing or superior body charged with the responsibility to oversee or control a specified activity. In the context of a profession, this usually means the development and enforcement of various rules to direct behavior and to assure clients and employers of an individual's qualifications. For example, the Federal Transportation Administration regulates airlines on society's behalf so travelers have some assurance that the airplane will function properly and the pilot will be qualified to fly the plane. Regulators of any crucial profession must hold members of that profession to a high standard of performance. In the case of the accounting profession, this model is complicated by the nature of the activity itself. CPAs deliver services in a field where they have particular expertise and knowledge and it is difficult for regulators to acquire the knowledge necessary to assess the quality of the CPAs work. As a result, private sector organizations help the public sector regulators. Oversight and regulation by private sector organizations was examined in Chapter 6. In this chapter, oversight by public organizations is examined. Public sector regulation includes licensing by state boards of accountancy and oversight by administrative agencies. Like peer review activities, public oversight activities are dynamic. The activities described in this chapter reflect current practice. Practitioners should update their understanding of these activities frequently.

Public Sector Regulation of the CPA Profession

Because states sanction the activities of CPAs, they require evidence that CPAs are qualified and are protecting the public interest. This is why state governments grant (and revoke) licenses to practice, establish regulatory boards, and monitor the profession. Some express frustration that society relies too much on the knowledge and good faith of the accounting profession since members of the profession largely set the rules and conduct the oversight. This frustration results in attempts at control through restrictive legislation, and by the mandatory inclusion of non-CPAs on professional regulatory boards.

CPAs, like many professions, actively seek governmental participation and assistance in their affairs for justification and image enhancement. State licensing, for example, is sought because it carries at least the implication of official quality control and sanction for an activity. It is this phenomenon that provides value to the title "certified" public accountant. Indeed, one of the earliest initiatives of the first professional accounting organization in the United States (the American Association of Public Accountants, AAPA) was to seek legislative recognition from the state of New York. In 1896, the New York legislature passed a bill "to Regulate the Profession of Public Accountants," the first such statute in this country.[2]

Regulation by the Securities and Exchange Commission

The SEC was created by Congress in 1934 as an independent regulatory agency to administer the federal securities laws. The most important of these laws for the accounting profession are the Securities Act of 1933 and the Securities Exchange Act of 1934. In these acts, the term *independent public accountant* is used to describe the individual or firm given the responsibility to perform the audit function in connection with the issuance and trading of securities in interstate commerce. Either certified public accountants or public accountants[3] may perform this function. The critical qualifications are (1) the possession of a current and valid state CPA license and (2) independence from the client or registrant.

The SEC is headed by a five-member commission. The members of the commission are appointed for five-year staggered terms by the President of the United States with the consent of the U.S. Senate. One member is designated by the President to be the Chairman. The SEC's staff includes accountants, lawyers, securities analysts,

---

[2] James G. Cannon, Presentation at Annual Banquet, *Twenty-First Anniversary Year Book*, the American Association of Public Accountants, New York, 1908, 120.

[3] In most states, public accountants (PAs) are accounting practitioners who are licensed as such, but who have not otherwise complied with the full educational and examination requirements established for CPAs. This class of individuals usually consists of those who were in practice at the time accountancy acts were adopted and who were "grandfathered" in with the expectation that no further PA licenses would thereafter be issued. In a few states, however, a two-tier system prevails in which the PA license is a license to practice granted to CPAs after they have completed specified experience or other requirements not initially necessary for the issuance of the CPA certificate.

engineers, and other experts who review filings by companies that have issued, are currently issuing, or intend in the near future to issue securities to the public. The Office of the Chief Accountant is a staff group within the SEC. The chief accountant is the principal expert adviser to the Commission on accounting and auditing matters. The Enforcement Division of the SEC also is important to the accounting profession, since the outcome of enforcement actions provide guidance about appropriate auditing procedures and independence questions. The Office of the Chief Accountant and the Enforcement Division collaborate to develop professional, ethical, and technical guidelines that CPAs can follow in their practice.

The SEC and Accounting Regulation

The SEC has statutory authority to establish accounting principles and to prescribe the form of reports to be filed under the Securities Acts. The SEC largely delegates the standard setting responsibility to the CPA profession.[4] The SEC has concentrated mostly on disclosure requirements (rather than on matters of accounting measurement) and frequently has moved into new ground (for example, segment reporting) ahead of the profession. The principal SEC publication affecting accountants is Regulation S-X. This regulation sets forth (1) the general form and content of financial statements to be filed with the Commission, (2) the necessary qualifications of accountants, and (3) the technical requirements for the auditor's report.

Although, technically, the SEC has jurisdiction over the financial and reporting practices of only SEC registrants (publicly traded companies), in practice the SEC influences smaller, nonpublic entities as well because the accounting practices of public companies become the *de facto* standards applied by all companies.[5] Also, these standards provide a benchmark for judicial and professional judgments made by auditors and CPA employees.

---

[4] ASR No. 4 (April 25, 1938) expressed the SEC's view that financial statements will be considered misleading unless they are prepared using accounting principles having "substantial authoritative support." A reference to ASR No. 4 in ASR No. 96 (January 10, 1963) stated that "this policy [was] . . . intended to support the development of accounting principles and methods of presentation by the profession. . . ."

[5] A professional task force is currently examining whether an alternative set of reporting rules should be developed for nonpublic companies.

In the very early years, the SEC's role was relatively passive but became more active beginning in 1972, when John Burton took over as chief accountant. Burton's view of the Commission vis-à-vis the accounting profession was as a "creative irritant," prodding, pushing, and punishing where necessary. He did not believe that movement from the *status quo* otherwise would result. He stated that "the accounting world has tended to exhibit comfortable conservative commitment to the *status quo* in the absence of external stimulus for change," and "if there is to be innovation, the Securities and Exchange Commission must be the principal source...."[6] Burton's philosophy still prevails today.

The SEC and Auditing Regulation

The statutory basis for action by the SEC in the development of auditing standards and procedures is less clear than for accounting standards. As a result, SEC oversight of auditing has been less definitive, limited largely to influencing the general content of the auditor's report on financial statements and to matters of auditor independence. While the SEC's input is less direct regarding auditing matters, its influence often is strong, particularly as exerted in connection with disciplinary proceedings under its Rule 2(e), which allows the SEC to suspend or disbar certain persons practicing before it. Strictly speaking, few if any of the major findings in such situations are the result of a Rule 2(e) *proceeding* (investigation followed by formal hearing before the full Commission leading to a judgment in a matter). Instead, the auditor-respondent usually consents to the issuance of a document detailing the facts and the SEC's conclusions without admitting or denying any culpability in the case. This information at one time was issued in the form of Accounting Series Releases (ASRs). Today, disciplinary reports are called Accounting and Auditing Enforcement Releases (AAERs).

Observations made by the SEC as a result of investigations and reports thereon generally are critical of audit performance in areas of concern, and thus caution auditors against potential deficiencies in similar circumstances in the future. CPAs (not just the "guilty" firm) use these reports for guidance. For example, one early such instance led directly to the profession's subsequent adoption of the so-called

---

[6] John C. Burton, "The SEC and Financial Reporting: The Sand in the Oyster," *University of Florida Accounting Series, Number 11*, University Press of Florida, 1980.

"extended" auditing procedures related to direct confirmation of customer accounts receivable and observation of inventories.[7]

Regulation by the Public Company Accounting Oversight Board

Chapter 8 of this publication provides a description of the watershed events in accounting and financial reporting over the past several years (for example, the Enron and WorldCom fiascos and the Sarbanes-Oxley Act of 2002). Arguably, the most significant provision of Sarbanes-Oxley was to establish and empower the Public Company Accounting Oversight Board (PCAOB). The PCAOB is a private nonprofit organization established to register and inspect auditors of public companies. The organization also has some standard setting and investigatory powers. In Chapter 8, the laws prescribing the various activities of the PCAOB are detailed. The regulatory oversight role of the PCAOB is summarized here.

All public accounting firms that audit public companies are required to register with the PCAOB. Even non-U.S. public accounting firms must register with the PCAOB if the firm audits U.S. public companies or foreign subsidiaries of U.S. public companies. The PCAOB is responsible for establishing auditing, quality control, ethics, independence, and other standards relating to the preparation of audit reports for publicly traded companies. The PCAOB will also conduct periodic inspections of registrant public accounting firms. If substandard practices are discovered during the inspection, the PCAOB is empowered to conduct disciplinary proceedings and impose sanctions on the substandard firm. The PCAOB is also responsible for enforcing the provisions of Sarbanes-Oxley, rules established by the PCAOB, professional standards, and securities laws relating to the preparation and issuance of audit reports. Sarbanes-Oxley gives the PCAOB the option to adopt standards proposed by other private sector rule making bodies (for example, the AICPA and the FASB) or to promulgate their own standards.

Firms that conduct more than 100 public company audits are to be reviewed annually. Firms that conduct 100 or fewer public company audits are to be reviewed at least once every three years. The

---

[7] ASR No. 19, *In the Matter of McKesson & Robbins, Inc.*, December 5, 1940.

review assesses the firm's compliance with the requirements of Sarbanes-Oxley, with PCAOB rules, with SEC rules, and with relevant professional standards. The PCAOB issues a report to reviewed firms with a section that can be viewed by the public and a section that is confidential. The section available for public viewing contains general information about the inspection and possibly observed departures from GAAP or PCAOB auditing standards. The confidential section contains any criticism or observed weaknesses in the firm's quality control system. The firm is then given a year to cure the deficiency.

Disciplinary actions that can be imposed by the PCAOB for violation of provisions of Sarbanes-Oxley include:

1. Temporary suspension or revocation or registration.
2. Temporary or permanent suspension or bar of a person from further association with any registered public accounting firm.
3. Temporary or permanent limitation on the activities, functions, or operations of such firm or person.
4. A civil monetary penalty for each violation.
5. Censure.
6. Required additional professional education or training.
7. Any other appropriate sanction provided for in the rules of the PCAOB.

Regulation by State Boards of Accountancy

All 50 states (plus Puerto Rico, Guam, the Virgin Islands, the District of Columbia, and the Commonwealth of the Northern Mariana Islands) have accountancy statutes, administered by the respective states' boards of accountancy. These boards set rules for entry into the profession, establish appropriate (ethical) behavior during practice, and discipline inappropriate activities by accountants (for example, taking away the right to practice). Collective action and coordination of the policies of the various state boards is facilitated by the National Association of State Boards of Accountancy (NASBA), a private nonprofit organization to which all state boards belong.

Boards of accountancy are agencies of state governments. Members of state boards are generally appointed by the governor. The boards usually contain primarily licensed CPAs, plus a representative of licensed public accountants, if any, and often public members, or nonlicensees to look after the public interest.[8] Arguably, the most important duty of the state boards is to establish the requirements for obtaining a CPA license. The vigilance with which discipline is exercised is increasing. Boards are increasingly adopting aggressive enforcement strategies, actively seeking out evidence of substandard performance rather than passively waiting for complaints to be filed.

The National Association of State Boards of Accountancy and CPA Regulation

NASBA has in recent years been a strong force in the regulation of the profession. NASBA and the AICPA have cooperated in developing the Uniform Accountancy Act, and all state boards are urged to adopt its provisions as statutes are amended over time. NASBA also evaluates the CPA exam preparation, administration, and grading, to provide assurances to state boards that the exam can be relied upon as part of the licensing process.

Internationally, the joint NASBA/AICPA International Qualifications Appraisal Board (IQAB) has been actively reviewing the qualifications of other countries' public accounting practitioners, and, in turn, the other countries have been doing the same with ours. This has resulted so far in signing reciprocal agreements with Australian and Canadian Chartered Accountants. Under the General Agreement on Trade in Services (GATS), participating countries are encouraged to break down barriers to reciprocity and the free flow of professional services across international borders. One of the principal impediments to CPA reciprocity is the longer experience requirement to gain a CPA license in most non-U.S. jurisdictions. U.S. CPAs must obtain the additional experience before being granted reciprocal practice rights abroad.[9]

---

[8] Interestingly, the California State Board of Accountancy recently became the first to have a majority of its members not be CPAs.

[9] See footnote 8, December, 1996.

Legal Responsibility of CPAs

Laws are the social contract by which professionals are entrusted with the public welfare in a particular area of expertise. Laws provide professionals with the exclusive right to practice that expertise and regulate their activities. Laws prescribe acceptable behavior and punish transgressions. This section discusses legal responsibilities and potential liabilities that are of particular concern to CPAs. Most regulation and laws affecting accountants in public practice deal with their reporting responsibilities as auditors (for example, the various federal securities acts). Further, most cases alleging violations of those statutes or relevant common law duties relate to auditing. However, recent actions related to controversial tax products reinforce that legal liability is present in all aspects of CPA practice.

CPAs in corporate practice, government agencies or academe also have legal responsibilities and potential liabilities, but these usually do not arise because of public practice or professional designation. For corporate CPAs, legal liability most often arises from financial reporting responsibilities imposed by the federal securities acts.

As a survey of important legislative factors affecting CPAs, this section does not purport to be exhaustive or to cover all aspects of the topic. Most important, the authors are not engaged in offering legal services, and readers should not attempt themselves to apply the principles outlined herein to particular factual circumstances, but should seek legal counsel.

What Is the CPA's Legal Responsibility?

The legal responsibilities and potential liabilities arising from the practice of public accountancy may be imposed by contract, by common law (accumulated judicial precedent), by statutory law, or by a combination. They may involve a breach of contract, a tort (a private wrong against a person, resulting from breach of a legal duty), or a crime (any act contrary to the public good; a wrong that the government has determined is injurious to the public). They are different with respect to clients and nonclients. Where contractual relationships are involved the question of privity arises, since persons who are not parties to a contract (nonclients) may be precluded from asserting rights under that contract.

Legal liability usually involves some failure by the CPA to exercise due care in carrying out professional activities, and this failure causes damage to others. *Due care* is the exercise of at least that degree of skill and competence possessed by members of the profession and required by professional standards. Failure to exercise that due care constitutes negligence. The nature of liability, and the parties to whom it extends, depends upon the degree of that negligence, which exists along a continuum from ordinary negligence through gross negligence and recklessness to fraud. *Ordinary negligence* connotes an intention to exercise due care, but a shortcoming in fulfilling that intention. *Fraud* connotes a conscious knowledge of a falsity and action with intent to deceive.

A CPA's Contract Responsibilities and Potential Liability

The principles of law relating to contracts in general also apply to contracts between a CPA and a client, and to contracts negotiated by and between CPAs in industry or academe on their own or on an employer's behalf. Examples of these principles are the necessity for offer and acceptance, and for consideration, in order for an enforceable agreement to be in place. Failure to perform under or to complete a contract, say for an annual audit, without good cause may give rise to damage claims. CPAs, therefore, should be cautious in withdrawing from a contracted engagement. Consulting with counsel before making such a decision is wise. There are also several contract-related factors that are particularly relevant to CPAs. Traditional common law principles do not permit third parties to sue for breach of contract. However, as discussed later in this chapter, some states allow third parties to sue for negligence.

A contract may be either written or oral. This is not unique in its application to CPAs. However, the difference is of critical importance if it becomes necessary to establish the parameters of any arrangement, which is bound to be required in any dispute.[10] Therefore, it behooves the CPA to establish the agreement with a client in writing (an engagement letter), regardless of whether the

---

[10] See, for example, *1136 Tenants' Corp. v. Max Rothenberg & Co.*, 36 AD 2nd 804, 319 NYS 2nd 1007 (1971). Here the accountants suffered the consequences of (among other things) the failure to document their understanding of the nature and scope of an engagement as being limited to "write-up" work (rather than auditing) and were held responsible for failure to detect irregularities (defalcations).

services to be furnished relate to auditing, accounting, tax, or other services.

A CPA's Common Law Responsibilities and Potential Liability

Legal actions alleging common law violations are based in tort, and the plaintiffs must allege some misrepresentation (or withholding) of a material fact relied upon to their detriment. Regarding auditing or accounting services, this misrepresentation generally arises in connection with financial statements and notes, and reports thereon. Whether the accountant's actions constitute negligence, gross negligence, or fraud depends upon the circumstances of the case. Even where the accountant is an innocent participant in a misrepresentation, liability may exist because of a duty to know the truth, which was breached.

The auditor's common law liability to clients can be differentiated from liability to third parties that are not party to the contract for professional services. A CPA may be liable to clients for ordinary negligence as well as for breach of contract. A CPA is potentially liable to both clients as well as to third parties for gross negligence or fraud.

The CPA's liability to third parties for ordinary negligence has expanded over time. Until well into the 20th century, CPAs were only liable to their contractual clients at common law for ordinary negligence in the performance of their professional engagements. The rule in this country regarding CPAs was based on the *Ultramares* case. Here the court limited an auditor's responsibility to the client because of the hazards of a business conducted under the burden of possible liability to third parties for negligence.

The court in *Ultramares* also stated that liability to third parties for negligence should not be imposed if the audit report was "primarily for the benefit of the [client]." This "primary benefit" rule recognized that financial statements are prepared for many purposes, not all of which should justify breaking the barrier of privity. In so doing, however, the court opened up the notion of some liability to third parties if the financial statements were prepared and audited for the primary benefit of third parties. This rule was applied strictly to insulate accountants from third-party liability for ordinary negligence even where the auditor knew the audit report was to be furnished to a third party who might be expected to rely upon it in making an investment or lending decision.[11] After *Ultramares*, third parties had difficulty suing CPAs. This barrier to lawsuit by third parties has eroded over the years as auditor liability has expanded to ever-widening classes of financial statement users.

Despite the subsequent actions expanding auditors' liability to nonclient users of financial statements, a 1985 case in the same court as *Ultramares* seems to reaffirm, in modified form, the privity barrier.[12] In this case, three prerequisites were established that must be satisfied before liability for negligence to noncontracting third parties will be imposed:

1. The accountants must have been aware that the financial reports were to be used for a particular purpose or purposes.
2. The CPA knew of a third party or parties that intended to rely on the reports, for such purpose.
3. Some conduct on the part of the auditors links them to the parties and demonstrates an understanding of the proposed reliance.

A CPA's Statutory Responsibilities and Potential Liability

Although the common law affects many areas of a CPA's practice, statutes (legislative enactments) are equally or more important. Among the statutes affecting CPAs are federal mail fraud laws and state blue sky laws. However, in this section, we focus on the most important federal statutes affecting CPAs: The Securities Act of 1933, the Securities Exchange Act of 1934, the Private Securities Reform Act of 1995, the Racketeer Influenced and Corrupt Organizations Act (RICO), and the Sarbanes-Oxley Act of 2002.

Both of the securities acts deal with transactions in interstate commerce involving securities. The interpretation of the meaning of each of the key phrases here (interstate commerce and securities) is beyond the scope of this chapter. Generally, the term *security* may include any investment in which a person turns his money or

---

[11] *C.I.T. Financial Corp. v. Glover*, 224 F. 2d 44 (2d Cir. 1955).
[12] *Credit Alliance Corp. v. Arthur Andersen & Co.*, 65 N.Y., 2d 536 (1985).

property over to another to manage for profit,[13] not just stocks or bonds. Also, interstate has been interpreted quite broadly. Thus, a CPA must realize the diversity of circumstances in which potential liability under the securities acts may arise.

The Securities Act of 1933

The 1933 Act sometimes is characterized as a disclosure law. That is, its provisions basically are intended to supply information to potential purchasers of new issues of securities so they can make an informed decision. With certain exceptions (such as for intrastate transactions) the sale of securities requires the prior existence of an effective registration statement filed with the SEC. Section 11 of the Act gives purchasers of registered securities a right of recovery for resulting losses against various persons—including the attesting CPA firm—if the registration statement contains any misstatement of a material fact or omits a material fact necessary to keep the statements from being misleading (the registration must tell the whole truth and nothing but the truth).

A purchaser of registered securities who sustains a loss need only prove a material misstatement or omission in the audited financial statements in order to proceed against the auditor.[14] The purchaser does not have to prove auditor negligence, reliance on the audit report,[15] or a causal relationship between the omission or misstatement and the loss sustained. At this point the burden of proof shifts to the auditor. The auditor must prove that due care was exercised (that is, no negligence) in the work, there was no causal relationship between any misstatement or omission and the plaintiff's loss, or that the plaintiff knew of the misstatement or omission when acquiring the security.

---

[13] Floyd W. Windal and Robert N. Corley, *The Accounting Professional* (New Jersey: Prentice-Hall, Inc., 1980), 259.

[14] This seems to be the common understanding of the basis for the auditor's potential liability. However, Gormley correctly asserts that the proper basis should be misstatements or omissions in the auditor's opinion, not the financial statements. (R. James Gormley, op. cit., 7-12.) In most cases, the result likely would be the same.

[15] Proof of purchaser reliance on the audit report is required if the securities were acquired after the registrant had issued an earnings statement for a year beginning after the effective date of the registration statement.

Some view the burdens of proof placed upon the auditor by the 1933 Act to be overly burdensome. George O. May, a leader of the CPA profession at the time, expressed it this way:

> I cannot believe that a law is just or can long be maintained in effect which deliberately contemplated the possibility that a purchaser may recover from a person from whom he has not bought, in respect of a statement which at the time of his purchase he had not read, contained in a document which he did not then know to exist, a sum which is not to be measured by injury resulting from falsity in such statement.[16]

In the usual audit engagement, the date of the auditor's report signals the end of all significant audit field work, including inquiry into events after the balance sheet date (subsequent events), which may affect or should be disclosed in the financial statements under examination.[17] Section 11(b) of the 1933 Act extends the time of responsibility for knowledge regarding subsequent events. As a result, the auditor must make a specific review for this purpose up to the effective date[18] of the registration statement. This is often called an S-1 review, after the name of the SEC form used for the filing. See the professional literature for details about the content and extent of the S-1 review.[19]

The Securities Exchange Act of 1934

The 1934 Act can be synthesized by pointing out how it differs from the 1933 Act. First, the 1934 Act applies both to purchasers and sellers of securities already issued (transactions in the secondary market). The 1933 Act applies only to purchasers of new issues. Second, Section 18(a) of the 1934 Act requires more in the way of proof by plaintiffs than Section 11 of the 1933 Act. For example, a defendant's liability is limited to errors or omissions in reports filed with the SEC. Also, plaintiffs have a larger burden of proof. The plaintiff must

---

[16] George O. May, *Twenty-Five Years of Accounting Responsibility*, vol. 2 (New York: American Institute Publishing Co., 1936), 69.

[17] AU section 530, *Dating of the Auditor's Report*, and AU section 560, *Subsequent Events*, AICPA, *Professional Standards*, vol. 1.

[18] The date following review of the filing by the SEC and any changes by the registrant, when offers to sell securities legally may be made and purchase orders accepted.

[19] Section AU section 711, *Filings Under Federal Securities Statutes*, AICPA, *Professional Standards*, vol. 1.

prove that they relied on the false information (or improper omissions) in the SEC filing, and the plaintiff must prove that damages were caused by that reliance.

The auditor's defense against a complaint under Section 18(a) is to prove that the auditor acted in good faith and had no knowledge that the statements were false or misleading. The auditor doesn't have to prove that he or she wasn't negligent, only that he or she had no knowledge of the misstatement or omission and its use with intent to deceive. This is a lighter burden than the proof of due care necessary under Section 11 of the 1933 Act.

A more active cause of action under the 1934 Act is Section 10(b), especially SEC Rule 10b-5. This rule provides that in connection with the purchase or sale of any security, it is unlawful to do any of the following:

1. To employ any device, scheme, or artifice to defraud.
2. To make any untrue statement of a material fact or to omit to state a material fact necessary in order to make the statements made, in the light of the circumstances under which they were made, not misleading.
3. To engage in any act, practice, or course of business that operates or would operate as a fraud or deceit upon any person.

Although the words in *connection with* have been broadly construed, and the definition of fraud or deceit is not entirely clear, the application of this Section and Rule to CPAs has been affected by cases such as *Hochfelder*.[20] Here the U.S. Supreme Court held that negligence is not enough to impose liability on the CPA. However, the court did not resolve exactly what does lead to liability for the CPA.[21] Since *Hochfelder*, courts have in some instances substituted recklessness as a standard, thus inferring culpability without a finding of motive.[22] "The amount of litigation based on Section 10(b) does not seem to be decreasing since the *Hochfelder* decision. Courts have been applying varying degrees of recklessness as a substitute for

---

[20] *Ernst & Ernst v. Hochfelder*, 425 U.S. 185 (1976).
[21] R. James Gormley, op. cit., 9-24.
[22] Andrew H. Barnett, and F. Fulton Galer, "Scienter Since Hochfelder," *The CPA Journal*, November, 1982.

scienter with recklessness being defined as everything from 'inaction' to 'knowledge of the falsity.' "[23]

Another decision by the U.S. Supreme Court may serve to limit some actions brought under Section 10(b), although only time will tell whether potential plaintiffs can find alternative theories for asserting claims. In *Central Bank of Denver*, the court held that parties alleged to have aided and abetted a securities fraud cannot be held liable for civil damages in a private action under Section 10(b).[24] This had been the basis for much of what the accounting profession has regarded as "strike suits," seeking damage awards from those perceived to have financial resources, without regard to the degree of culpability, if any.

Private Securities Litigation Reform Act of 1995

The Private Securities Litigation Reform Act of 1995 was passed in December, 1995 over the veto of President Clinton. This represented the culmination of intensive efforts by business and professional groups over a number of years to reign in what had become perceived to be abusive use of the legal system by plaintiffs' attorneys. Some of the more important provisions of this Act are as follows:

1. Joint and several liability (under which any one defendant can be forced to bear the entire brunt of any damages) is replaced with a modified form of proportional liability (under which each defendant is responsible only for that portion of the damages corresponding to its own culpability).
2. Certain provisions impose stricter pleading standards on plaintiff's counsel, eliminate abusive discovery practices, and control the use of "professional plaintiffs," among other things.
3. "Safe harbor" provisions are included that exempt companies from liability under federal securities law when the company makes forward-looking statements and projections in good faith. This provision is intended to encourage companies to offer forward-looking statements that are highly

---

[23] See footnote 22.
[24] *Central Bank of Denver, N.A. v. First Interstate Bank of Denver, N.A.*, 114 S Ct 1439 (1994).

relevant, but inherently not as reliable as backward-looking information.
4. Securities fraud is eliminated as a "predicate act" under the Racketeering and Corrupt Organizations Act (RICO), thus eliminating the ability of plaintiffs to claim treble damages in securities suits.

This legislation has driven more cases to state courts, where the protections of the new federal legislation are not available. A study by two Stanford University law professors found that in the year following the passage of the Reform Act, there was no significant variation in the number of companies sued for securities fraud in class action cases from previous years. A decline in federal court filings was offset by a comparable rise in those filed in state courts.[25]

Securities Litigation Uniform Standards Act of 1997

The 1997 Act was passed to address perceived weaknesses in the 1995 Act. Following passage of the 1995 Act, cases that would have been litigated in Federal Courts were instead taken to various State Courts. This bill establishes uniform national standards for class action lawsuits involving publicly traded securities. It is designed to stop plantiffs' attorneys from shifting securities fraud lawsuits to state courts for the purpose of avoiding the "safe harbor" provisions of the 1995 Act.

However, these efforts have done little to protect the CPA profession. Richard Painter, Megan Farrell, and Scott Adkins of the Federalist Society for Law and Public Policy Studies find a dramatic increase in the percentage of class actions involving allegations of accounting fraud after passage of the Private Securities Litigation Reform bills. Further, class actions were settled for higher amounts that include allegations of accounting fraud (29 percent higher), have an accounting firm codefendant (79 percent higher), or have a finding of accounting irregularities (90 percent higher). In the case of the accounting codefendant, the accounting firm paid, on average, 32 percent of the settlement.[26]

---

[25] As reported in *The Arizona Republic*, April 4, 1997.

[26] R. Painter, M. Farrell, and S. Adkins, "Private Securities Litigation Reform Act: A Post-Enron Analysis," The Federalist Society for Law and Public Policy Studies, working paper.

Sarbanes-Oxley Act of 2002

Chapter 6 discusses the influence of the PCAOB on CPA activities. From a legal perspective, violations of the provisions of Sarbanes-Oxley are treated as violations of the SEC 1934 Act. Section 303 of Sarbanes-Oxley provides leverage for independent auditors by making it illegal for management to attempt to "fraudulently influence, coerce, manipulate, or mislead" any auditor to make financial reports misleading. Title VIII of Sarbanes-Oxley, entitled "Corporate and Criminal Fraud Accountability" creates several new securities-related crimes and increases the punishment for violations of some existing laws. Title IX of the Act, entitled "White-Collar Crime Penalty Enhancements" provides for harsher penalties and more criminal statutes for White-Collar crime. Title XI, "Corporate Fraud and Accountability", makes it easier to prosecute obstruction of justice in corporate fraud cases and stiffens the penalties for securities fraud, accounting fraud, and related offenses. The individual provisions of Sarbanes-Oxley are summarized in Chapter 8 of this book.

Sarbanes-Oxley will likely be revised slightly over the next several years. For example, co-sponsor Representative Michael Oxley commented that some aspects of the law are, in retrospect, excessive. Oxley commented that, "if I had another crack at it, I would have provided more flexibility for small- and medium-sized companies."[27]

Racketeer Influenced and Corrupt Organizations Act

Congress passed the Racketeer Influenced and Corrupt Organizations Act (RICO) in 1970, primarily to provide a weapon against organized crime. RICO specified certain activities considered racketeering, including mail fraud and fraud in the sale of securities, as well as murder, arson, bribery, and the like. RICO made it unlawful for a person to engage in a "pattern of racketeering," which was defined as the commission of two or more of the proscribed activities in a 10-year period. Provisions of the act that are particularly important to accountants and others charged as defendants are the

---

[27] S. Tucker and A. Parker, "Oxley Regrets Tough Law: Sarbanes-Oxley Law's Co-architect Says Some of Governance Are 'Excessive': Would Have Given Small Business More Flexibility," *Financial Post*, July 8, 2005: 4.

following: civil suits by private citizens are permitted and plaintiffs need prove their case only by a preponderance of the evidence (rather than by the standard required in a criminal case of "beyond a reasonable doubt"). RICO also provided for the awarding of treble damages, but the Securities Reform Act of 1995 exempted CPAs from treble damages under RICO in securities suits.

Legal Liability—A Billion Dollar Problem

The legal responsibilities and potential liabilities are of great concern to CPAs. Certainly, no serious student of these matters would suggest that practitioners be insulated from responsibility for their actions. Yet, there remains a difference between what CPAs view as their duty and what others view as the duty of the CPA. This has become known as the "expectation gap." This issue is periodically tested by the courts, and the results so far have expanded the audience for the CPA's work greatly by imposing huge damage awards for failure to meet an unforeseen expectation.

An early and often quoted expression of the feared ultimate consequences of this trend can be found in Judge Cardozo's reasoning in the *Ultramares* case,[28] rejecting the imposition of an auditor's liability to third parties (not in privity) for ordinary negligence:

> If liability for negligence exists, a thoughtless slip or blunder, the failure to detect a theft or forgery beneath the cover of deceptive entries, may expose accountants to a liability in an indeterminate amount for an indeterminate time to an indeterminate class. The hazards of a business conducted on these terms are so extreme as to enkindle doubt whether a flaw may not exist in the implication of a duty that exposes to these consequences.

What is now being explored is a contemporary definition of that duty—and, indeed, the development of tools (procedures) to meet it—which it is hoped will satisfy the reasonable expectations of those who use professional accounting services. This is an ongoing task, since definitions and expectations are ever changing.

---

[28] *Ultramares Corp. v. Touche*, 255 N.Y. 170, 174 N.E. 441 (1931).

The Causes of the Legal Liability Problem

CPAs were not a high-profile part of the business world even as recently as the 1960s.[29] Since that time, economic and societal changes have affected professions such as public accounting and medicine in a way that troubles these professions.

Henry R. Jaenicke attributed these developments to (1) the rise of consumerism, (2) the implementation of new concepts of insurance, and (3) the increasing presence of auditors in all aspects of commercial transactions.[30] The first can be seen as an attempt to redress what may have been viewed as an imbalance between the rights of consumers and commercial interests. The second involves, among other things, the so-called "deep pocket" theory (sue anyone who appears to have economic resources regardless of the degree of culpability), the increasing view of auditors as guarantors rather than as objective observers and reporters, and the "socialization of risk" (the placing of liability on those who are perceived to be in a position either to prevent loss or to shift its costs through higher charges to all users). And finally, the third cause involves the growing importance of accounting information in the investment process and the resulting publicity the accounting information gets in the press when accounting abuses are alleged.

Underlying all these changes seems to be a continuing evolution in the tort concept. A tort is "a private or civil wrong or injury independent of contract, resulting from a breach of duty. . . . The essential elements of a tort are the existence of a legal duty owed by the defendant to the plaintiff, breach of that duty, and a causal relationship between defendant's conduct and the resulting damages to plaintiff."[31] The broadening of the legal duties of CPAs, the broadening of the classes of persons to whom the duties extend, and the erosion of the notion that fault (causal relationship between conduct and damage) on the part of the defendant is a necessary condition to monetary recovery, have contributed to the "litigation explosion." Those concerned with halting or reversing the trend are calling for nothing less than reform of the tort system. Victor M. Earle III asserts that:

---

[29] T.A. Wise, "The Auditors Have Arrived," *Fortune*, November and December, 1960.

[30] Henry R. Jaenicke, "The Effect of Litigation on Independent Auditors," *Research Study No. 1*, Commission on Auditors' Responsibilities, New York, 1977, 3-5.

[31] Steven H. Gifis, *Law Dictionary* (New York: Barron's Educational Series, Inc., 1975).

We must restore fault as the principal basis for tort liability and adopt reforms consistent with that objective. More specifically, both the state and federal courts should return to common law concepts of fault and contributory fault.[32]

Because so many of the suits filed against CPAs arise in cases involving business bankruptcies or other failures where investors have lost money, it is evident that confusion exists regarding the distinction between a *business* failure and an *audit* failure. It is not an entirely unreasonable conclusion that this distinction, intentionally or innocently, is blurred by plaintiffs' attorneys. The fact that an auditor's client encounters business difficulties and is unable to overcome them without loss is entirely unrelated to the question of whether the auditor carried out attest responsibilities in a professional manner and in conformity with professional standards. An auditor examines and reports on a client's financial statements. The auditor is not responsible for the client's decisions or acumen in handling business affairs. Indeed, the auditor has no authority in this area. Nevertheless, as a result of fuzzy concepts of an auditor's duties and responsibilities, the stigma of client failure seems to carry over and become, in the minds of others, audit failure.

The problem is exacerbated where there is undetected management fraud, and where this fraud comes to light because of a business failure or otherwise. Auditors have long contended that they had no responsibility to find fraud, indeed, that the very nature of auditing based upon tests and samples of accounting data made detection of fraud unlikely—although such detection could occur and would be dealt with as necessary.

Because of a continuing belief on the part of the public that the purpose of an audit is to catch criminals, the AICPA's Auditing Standards Board (ASB) in 1988 attempted to clarify this situation by saying that an auditor indeed had the responsibility to "design the audit to provide reasonable assurance of detecting errors [unintentional mistakes] and irregularities [intentional misstatements, including fraud] that are material to the financial statements."[33] This

---

[32] Victor M. Earle, III, "The Fantasy of Life Without Risk," *Fortune* (February 16, 1987): 116.

[33] AU section 316.05, *Consideration of Fraud in a Financial Statement Audit*, AICPA, *Professional Standards*, vol. 1.

is quite a logical step, since the audit opinion deals with the "fair presentation" of financial information. If this fairness is materially distorted by undetected irregularities, the opinion is as much at fault as in the case of undetected errors. The fact that irregularities can be more difficult to detect because of the possibility of collusion and the like is largely beside the point. In 1997, the ASB issued further guidance to the auditors in fulfilling this responsibility.[34]

The Litigation Storm

A major concern of the profession with the legal aspects of its environment is the number of suits (principally by or on behalf of non-client third parties) against CPA firms and individuals, alleging professional malpractice. Another is the amount of damages awarded to plaintiffs in these actions.

T.J. Fiflis asserted that "[i]n 1967, the statement was made correctly that 'suits against accountants by persons other than their clients have been almost uniformly unsuccessful.' "[35] Then, after citing several subsequent seminal cases to the contrary in the late 1960s, he further stated that "[t]his trickle of cases has swollen to hundreds of pending suits against accountants."[36] In its annual report for 1973, Arthur Andersen & Co. estimated then pending suits or claims in process against accountants to number 500. Shortly thereafter, in 1974, Carl D. Liggio estimated 500 to 1,000 cases.[37]

Now, stories about lawsuits against the large CPA firms are virtually a daily occurrence in the *Wall Street Journal*. Large firms have been forced into bankruptcy in recent years (Arthur Andersen and Laventhol & Horwath, among others) in part because of legal troubles. Further, this is not just a problem for the large international CPA firms. Smaller and medium size firms increasingly are considering the risks of providing attest services, especially to public corporations. The consequences to our free private enterprise system of resulting CPA firms' risk aversion may be severe if significant numbers of them withdraw or limit their attest services, and in effect

---

[34] AU section 316.

[35] T.J. Fiflis, "Current Problems of Accountants' Responsibilities to Third Parties," *Vanderbilt Law Review*, January, 1975, 32.

[36] See footnote 35, p. 33.

[37] Carl D. Liggio, "Expanding Concepts of Accountants' Liability," *California CPA Quarterly*, September, 1974, 18-19.

deny corporations the ability to raise capital by denying them audits.[38] Indeed, in 2002 and 2003 PriceWaterhouseCoopers and Deloitte and Touche reported that each had decided not to continue providing attest services to over 500 clients because of liability concerns.[39] Ernst & Young dropped 200 clients during that period as well.

Many believe that the CPAs' predicament reflects fundamental changes in public attitudes that are affecting accountants and other elements of society. One author states that "the liability crisis results from the adolescent desire to blame someone else for everything that goes wrong."[40] This comment must have some meaning to anyone who reads of the countless lawsuits against doctors, accountants, other professionals, businesses—and, in some cases against governmental bodies, universities, law enforcement agencies, and the like.

Some Recent Relief

In April 2005, another important case came before the Supreme Court. In *Broudo v. Dura Pharmaceuticals, Inc.* the Supreme Court raised the bar somewhat for winning class actions suits alleging violations of federal securities laws. The Supreme Court reversed a ruling by the Ninth Circuit Court of Appeals that plaintiffs can satisfy the "loss causation" requirement for suits brought under Section 10(b) merely by showing that the price of the security on the date of purchase was inflated because of the alleged misrepresentations without showing that the later price declines or trading losses were caused by the allegedly false statements, or both. The Supreme Court ruled instead that proof of the inflated stock is a necessary but not sufficient condition to prove "loss causation." The Supreme Court did not indicate how loss causation must be proved. However, it did indicate approval for cases in which losses where shown to result from a stock price decline that occurred upon disclosure of the fraud.

---

[38] From 1994 through April 1997, the Big Six accounting firms dropped a total of 275 publicly traded audit clients because of perceived unacceptable legal risks. *The Wall Street Journal*, April 26, 1997.

[39] B. Hindo and I. Sager, "Audit Clients Get the Heave-Ho," *Business Week*, December 1, 2003: 7.

[40] See footnote 32, p. 113.

Insuring a Firm in the Eye of the Litigation Storm

A byproduct of the litigation storm is the radical increase in the cost of professional malpractice insurance—or in some cases, its unavailability at any cost. Changing concepts of tort liability have had their effect. Increased insurance payouts inevitably result in higher insurance premiums. A related factor may be the perceived tendency of jurors in a malpractice trial to assess damages in large amounts on the basis that the costs will be paid by an insurer and not by the defendant. Victor M. Earle III asserts that jurors "typically justify their largess by assuming the defendant was insured. Jurors apparently also assume that the premiums are paid by the tooth fairy."[41]

The more obvious consequences of increased awards in cases involving tort law ultimately may not be as important as the indirect consequences. Ronald C. Horn sees the real crisis as involving serious and unaddressed public policy problems. These include (1) "legal-flation" (staggering increases in the cost of goods and services to cover insurance premiums); (2) "defensive medicine" (the application of procedures and tests merely to protect against possible future malpractice claims); (3) "public health" (withdrawal of doctors from certain areas of practice such as obstetrics; limitation of production of vaccines); (4) "corporate insolvencies" (bankruptcies that have serious consequences for employees and stockholders); and (5) other effects such as the closing down of child care centers, amusement parks and other facilities where insurance costs cannot reasonably be passed on to customers or the risks even with insurance are deemed unacceptable.[42] Although not so dramatic in terms of their effect on human life, similar problems arise for CPA firms.

Competing Incentives: The Commitment to Serve, the Profit Motive, Professional Integrity, and Litigation Risk

Just as clients have the right to seek a new independent CPA firm for their attestation services, CPA firms have the right to turn down potential business. This is not an easy decision for CPAs. First, it goes against the CPA's fundamental commitment to serve. CPAs hold the franchise to provide an audit and every firm has the right to an

---

[41] See footnote 32, p. 113.
[42] Ronald C. Horn, "America's Lawsuits and Liability Insurance Headaches," *Baylor Business Review*, Winter, 1987.

audit. Of course, this does not translate to a right to receive an unqualified opinion from the audit! Some CPA firm has to serve the company. Second, turning down business goes against the profit motive of CPAs.

Nevertheless, CPAs periodically face a decision whether to forego the revenues to avoid the risk associated with a particular client. In some instances, the CPA firm concludes that it is not willing to serve a client. Chapter 8 discusses how Arthur Anderson & Co. debated long before making the fateful decision to continue to serve as the Enron auditors. In that case, Andersen stood to earn tens of millions of dollars in billings from the client. This certainly is a difficult dilemma for the practicing CPA.

Other Legal Matters Facing CPAs

Other developments in connection with a CPA's legal responsibilities and liabilities include a significant case finding criminal, rather than civil, misbehavior by three public accountants, the assertion by the United States Supreme Court that an accountant's duties to the public on occasion may override duties to clients, and an alternative organizational form for the CPA firm (limited liability partnership) that provides protection against unlimited liability for negligence of professional associates in the same firm.

Criminal Guilt

CPAs can face allegations of criminal behavior. Conviction in a civil case may result in monetary fines, but conviction in a criminal case carries with it the additional possibility of imprisonment and loss of certain rights of citizenship such as the right to vote. Also, subsequent actions by professional societies and state boards of accountancy could result in loss of membership for a civil infraction and loss of the right to practice for a criminal conviction. For example, Arthur Andersen lost the right to practice following criminal conviction for obstruction of justice (a finding that has been overturned by the U.S. Supreme Court).

General mail fraud statutes, laws prohibiting false statements to government personnel or departments, and behavior constituting aiding and abetting others who commit crimes, may give rise to criminal liability. Also, the Securities Acts of 1933 and 1934 and

Sarbanes-Oxley include provisions imposing criminal liability in certain circumstances. State statutes vary, but usually contain prohibitions against making false or misleading statements to state authorities. A common element in all the statutes is the concept of *willful* and *knowing* behavior.

A significant, but still perhaps not widely appreciated, result of a leading criminal case against a CPA is the proposition that compliance with generally accepted accounting principles, while important, will not necessarily insulate an accountant against liability (civil or criminal). This issue turns on whether the language in the auditor's report that the financial statements "present fairly [for example, financial position or results of operations] . . . in conformity with generally accepted accounting principles" means that fairness is attained by conformity alone, or whether another, more subjective meaning of fairness is the appropriate standard. The judge and jury in the *Continental Vending* case[43] decided on the subjective fairness criteria, which weakens the defense that GAAP was followed regardless of whether the resulting information was a fair representation. Two partners and an audit manager of the accounting firm were convicted in this case, and the conviction was upheld on appeal. Terminology in Sarbanes-Oxley certifications further reinforces the notion that fair presentation rather than adherence with GAAP is required. Under Sarbanes-Oxley, company officials certify that "financial statements present fairly . . ." without reference to conformity with generally accepted accounting principles.

CPAs' Responsibility to the Public

A Supreme Court decision in 1984 in the case of *United States v. Arthur Young & Co.* continues to influence the development of the law.[44] The key question in this case was whether tax accrual working papers prepared by an accountant for the purpose of issuing an audit report may be subpoenaed by the IRS (yes, they may). However, the case has more significant ramifications. Justice Burger's statement regarding a public accountant's duties was troubling to the accounting profession because of its seemingly open-ended reach:

---

[43] *United States v. Simon*, 425 F2nd 796 (2d Cir. 1969), *cert. denied* 397 U.S. 1006 (1970).
[44] Burton, Palmer, Kay, op. cit., 1985 edition, 44-2.

In certifying the public reports that depict a corporation's financial status, the accountant performs a *public* responsibility transcending any employment relationship with the client, and owes allegiance to the corporation's creditors and stockholders, as well as to the investing public. (Emphasis in original.)[45]

Critics of the opinion believe it to be a simplification of the auditor's role that might indicate that the accountant was "liable to the world."[46] On the other hand, leaders of the profession for years have emphasized the public responsibilities of the CPA.

Limited Liability Partnerships

While seeking legislative solutions to the general question of the liability of CPAs, accountants also have made changes in the forms of organizations under which they may practice their profession. Once, ethical rules allowed CPAs to practice only as sole practitioners or in partnership with other CPAs. Now Rule 505 of the AICPA's Code of Professional Conduct provides, in part, that "[a] member may practice public accounting only in a form permitted by state law or regulation." As of May, 2005, 48 jurisdictions (out of 50 states, the District of Columbia, Guam, Puerto Rico, and the Virgin Islands) had passed legislation allowing professionals (including accountants) to form limited liability partnerships (LLPs).[47]

Although the particulars in each state differ, the most significant feature of LLPs is that their members (partners) have some form of limited liability. ". . . [M]ost LLP statutes provide that LLP partners are not individually liable for the negligence or other misconduct of other partners or employees unless the partner participated in or supervised the wrongdoing. . . . Under most statutes LLP partners *are* liable for several categories of conduct, particularly including conduct that is no more than a breach of contract. Under other

---

[45] As reported in *Taxation and Accounting*, (Washington: The Bureau of National Affairs, March 22, 1984).

[46] Burton, Palmer, Kay, op. cit., 1985 edition, 44-3.

[47] AICPA *Journal of Accountancy*, September, 1996, 58.

statutes LLP partners have limited liability for all categories of claims."[48]

Another form of organization, limited liability company (LLC), is also available to CPAs and other professionals, and many states have enacted statutes regarding them. For some rather technical reasons, however, it is easier for CPAs to form LLPs, and many have done so. In either case, the effect is to move from the partnership form of organization, with its unlimited liability for all partners, to a form providing some shield for personal assets from damage and other claims. In this respect, LLPs and LLCs provide some of the same benefits of the corporate form of organization, while being treated generally for tax and other purposes as a partnership.

Legislative Intervention and CPA Regulation

The federal securities acts and state accountancy laws always carry with them the possibility of further legislative attention to their scope and coverage if they are not perceived as appropriately comprehensive to protect the public's interest. Oversight committees of the U.S. Congress from time to time have inquired into the administration of the securities acts for this purpose.

The first such investigations of particular importance were made in the late 1970s by the so-called Metcalf and Moss Committees.[49] These investigations resulted in some sharp criticisms of the SEC (for "failure to exercise its authority on accounting matters") and of the accounting profession for a number of alleged performance deficiencies. More recently, Congress intervened following the high profile frauds of recent years. This intervention resulted in the wide sweeping Sarbanes-Oxley reforms.

---

[48] Bromberg and Ribstein, *Limited Liability Partnerships and the Revised Uniform Partnership Act*, Little, Brown and Company, 1995 edition, 15.

[49] *Improving the Accountability of Publicly Owned Corporations and Their Auditors*, Report of the Subcommittee on Reports, Accounting and Management of the Committee on Governmental Affairs, United States Senate, Lee Metcalf, Montana, Chairman, (Washington, D.C.: U.S. Government Printing Office, 1977). *Federal Regulation and Regulatory Reform*, Report by the Subcommittee on Oversight and Investigations of the Committee on Interstate and Foreign Commerce, House of Representatives, John E. Moss, California, Chairman, (Washington, D.C.:U.S. Government Printing Office, 1976).

The mere indication of this continuing interest in the profession on the part of Congress is sufficient to cause the profession to examine and reexamine its practices and institutional structure for possible improvements.

Summary

This chapter considers the various ways that CPAs are regulated by society in the public interest. Foremost here is licensure by state boards of accountancy. The SEC also plays an important role in the development and monitoring of auditing and accounting standards. Finally, Congress and the courts regulate CPA activities. Contracts with clients, common law and statutory law together create the legal environment in which the CPA must operate. In addition, this chapter considers particular laws (for example, the Federal Securities Acts and Sarbanes-Oxley) that have specific professional practice implications, particularly for those CPAs who are employed by companies issuing securities to the public or who have them as clients. Efforts of CPAs and other professionals to effect changes in their statutory responsibilities and potential liabilities have been discussed, along with changes made in forms of practice for CPAs in public practice. Some continuing proposals for further changes in this area were outlined, but movement in this area is likely to be slow and of uncertain direction.

8

Developments in the Profession: Enron, WorldCom, Arthur Andersen, and Sarbanes-Oxley

The profession's response in the face of some very difficult times has been exceptional. We have improved the independence rules, finalized certain auditing and accounting changes and initiated others in ethics, enforcement and peer review standards affecting private companies.

Leslie Murphy, AICPA Chair, 2005–6[1]

Appendix E provides a historical perspective on the CPA profession in America through 1999. It is crucial that current professionals understand the history of the profession so the profession continues

---
[1] N. R. Baldiga, "Looking Forward: A Talk With Leslie Murphy," *Journal of Accountancy*, September 2005: 34-36.

to evolve optimally. The CPA profession has experienced periods of dramatic changes at a couple of times in its history. Recent years constitute one such period. This section summarizes the catalyst for these changes and highlights the key changes as they pertain to the day-to-day operations of CPAs in public or private practice.

Anyone who casually follows the news has heard the names Enron, WorldCom, and Arthur Andersen. While these are not the only organizations embroiled in business scandals over the past several years, they are arguably the most high profile. Billions of dollars were lost by investors in these and other scandal-ridden companies. As a result, the public called for the profession to recommit itself to its core attest function. To revive the full faith of investors, dramatic reforms have been enacted exceeded in magnitude only by those of the early 1930s (that is, the Security and Exchange Commission's (SEC) Securities Act of 1933 and the Securities Exchange Act of 1934). These changes have led to great opportunities for CPAs. Indeed, the profession appears to have rebounded nicely.

The CPA Profession—Post 2000

At December 31, 2000, Enron's 752 million outstanding common shares were valued at just over $83 per share (a market capitalization in excess of $62 billion).[2] Enron was the seventh largest company in America[3] and among the most admired.[4] By December 2001, Enron's market value was approaching zero following the revelation of one of the largest frauds in corporate history. Several other corporate frauds followed (for example, Global Crossing, Adelphia Corporation, Parmalat, Tyco, and Vivendi).

As a result of corporate scandals, Congress was contemplating additional regulatory measures related to the capital markets and publicly traded companies. In June 2002, another financial reporting scandal at WorldCom, another huge company, became the tripwire

---

[2] Per the Enron Annual Report, December 31, 2000.
[3] L. Everest and L. Innes, "The Rise and Fall of Enron," page 1, available at http://www.zmag.org/ZMag/articles/march02everest-innes.htm.
[4] Enron was 22nd on the 2000 *Fortune* 100 "best companies to work for" list and had the highest total return of all the *Fortune* 100 companies, over 300 percent, in the year before its collapse. See http://www.csrwire.com/article.cgi/525.html for details.

for governmental and regulatory action. President George W. Bush called the accounting irregularities "outrageous."[5] Congressman W. J. Tauzin of Louisiana declared that "this latest accounting scandal only highlights the importance of Congress working together to pass tough new laws which will prevent future abuses and restore investor confidence."[6] As a result, soon after the WorldCom fraud was unmasked, Congress passed a sweeping regulatory reform bill named after its principal sponsors: Senator Paul Sarbanes and Congressman Michael Oxley (the Sarbanes-Oxley Act of 2002).

What Led to the String of Corporate Scandals?

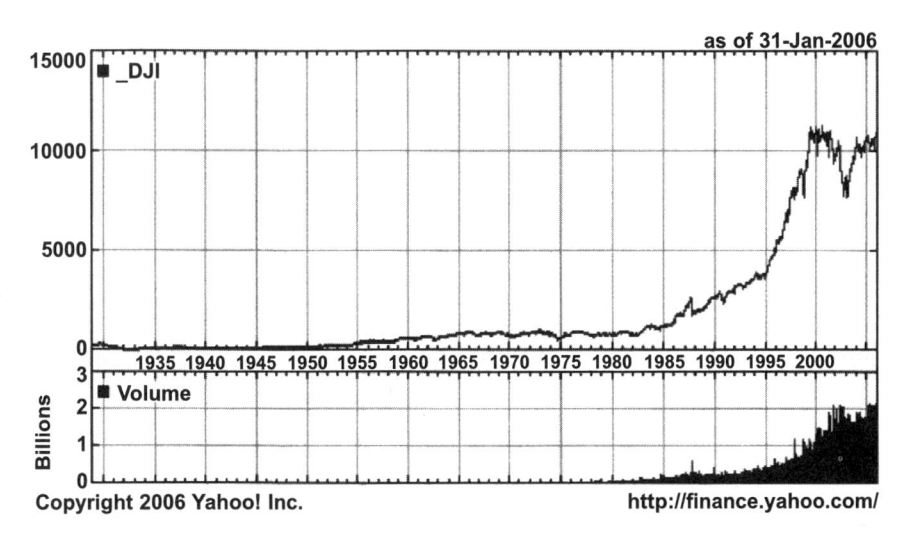

The last half of the 1990s featured a roaring stock market. The Dow Jones Industrial Index increased from 2,753 at the beginning of the decade to nearly 11,500 by the end. More dramatically, the technology and Internet heavy NASDAQ market soared from 453 to over 4,000 in the 1990s. Ultimately, the NASDAQ would reach a high of just over 5,000 in March 2000 before plummeting. This is known

---

[5] J. Sandberg, D. Solomon, and R. Blumenstein, "Inside WorldCom's Unearthing of a Vast Accounting Scandal," *Wall Street Journal* (June 27, 2002): A1.

[6] T. Hamburger, G. Hitt, and M. Schroeder, "WorldCom Case Boosts Congress in Reform Efforts," *Wall Street Journal*, June 27, 2002: A8.

as the "Internet bubble."[7] Internet-related stocks seemed to increase daily for no apparent reason. Federal Reserve Board Chairman Alan Greenspan used the term *irrational exuberance* to describe the pricing of such stocks.[8] While not at the rate of Internet stocks, the stock prices of large companies were increasing dramatically as well. Large company stocks were increasing especially strongly when the companies reported earnings that exceeded key targets (for example, earnings in the same quarter of the prior year and the consensus forecast of analysts).[9] As a result, top company officers were under intense pressure to meet or exceed these targets. In addition, this was a time when companies were awarding tremendous numbers of stock options to their key officers. This presented the officers with even more incentive to keep the stock price up. Reporting solid earnings was necessary to keep the stock price rising and earnings management was the best way to ensure that the company continued to report solid earnings (meet or exceed earnings expectations).[10]

Current FASB board member Katherine Schipper defines earnings management as a "purposeful intervention in the external financial reporting process, with the intent of obtaining some private gain."[11] Healy and Wahlen define earnings management as occurring when "managers use judgment in financial reporting and in structuring transactions to alter financial reports to either mislead some stakeholders about the underlying economic performance of the company or to influence contractual outcomes that depend on reported accounting numbers."[12] Earnings management

---

[7] See for example J. J. Siegel, "After the Bubble," *Financial Planning*, September 1, 2002: 1.

[8] Greenspan termed the run up in stock prices "irrational exuberance and unduly escalating stock prices" in a speech to the American Enterprise Institute in December 1996.

[9] This is demonstrated by research findings. See, for example, Kasznik and McNichols 2002, "Does Meeting Earnings Expectations Matter? Evidence From Analyst Forecast Revisions and Share Prices," *Journal of Accounting Research* (June 2002): 727-759.

[10] See, for example, A. Berenson, "The Number: How the Drive for Quarterly Earnings Corrupted Wall Street and Corporate America," Random House, New York, 2003.

[11] K. Schipper, "Commentary: Earnings Management," *Accounting Horizons* (December 1989): 92.

[12] P. Healy and J. Wahlen, "A Review of the Earnings Management Literature and Its Implications for Standard Setting," *Accounting Horizons* (December 1999): 368.

was pervasive in response to incentives to report ever increasing earnings. SEC Chairman Arthur Levitt called earnings management a "game among market participants" that "if not addressed soon, will have adverse consequences for America's financial reporting system."[13] Complicit in the earnings management craze were CPAs. CPAs inside companies were carrying out the earnings management activities as members of upper management or, in some cases, at the behest of upper management and independent CPAs were approving the earnings reports.

Among the profession's responses to the problem of earnings management was to revise the way auditors were to view materiality. Previously, auditors largely viewed materiality as some percentage of assets, net assets, or net income (for example, 5 percent of net income). However, in SEC Staff Accounting Bulletin No. 99, *Materiality*, the SEC called on auditors to consider qualitative as well as quantitative factors when considering whether a questionable amount represents a material misstatement.[14] For example, if a slightly understated expense amount causes only a two cent or 0.5 percent increase in earnings per share, this amount could still be considered a material misstatement if the two cents is what the company needed to go from missing a relevant earnings target to exceeding it (for example, prior year earnings or analysts expected earnings). This response has been generally effective at curbing earnings management abuses.

Sometimes, companies needed more than a slightly revised accrual amount to meet an earnings target or avoid reporting a net loss. Most of these companies simply reported earnings amounts that missed the target and the stock price dropped as a result. However, a few companies looked for more creative ways to avoid disappointing the markets. Regrettably, some of these companies chose to perpetrate a fraud, and several of these frauds were financial accounting and financial reporting frauds. Eventually these frauds were uncovered and these companies became infamous.

---

[13] A. Levitt, The Numbers Game. Speech delivered at the New York University Center for Law and Business, New York, NY, September 28, 1998.

[14] Available from the Securities and Exchange Commission (SEC) Web site (http://www.sec.gov/interps/account/sab99.htm).

What Happened at Enron and WorldCom?

Enron was an aggressive energy company. During the 1990s, the company made some bad investments and became debt heavy. In an attempt to conceal its financial position, Enron entered into several elaborate transactions using special purpose entities (SPEs), some of which were designed primarily to conceal debt. At that time, an SPE did not have to be consolidated if it met certain conditions (for example, outside investors had at least a 3 percent financial interest in the SPE and the SPE was actively managed by one of the outside investors). In several of these arrangements at Enron, the supposed third-party investor was actually a related party or even the company itself. Enron was also found to be perpetrating other frauds as well to keep the stock price strong.

In October 2001, Enron announced a $1 billion charge for asset impairments, restructuring costs, and investment losses. Enron also announced a $1.2 billion downward restatement of equity due to accounting treatment of a stock transaction that was not allowed for SEC registrant companies. Other restatements followed. These restatements revealed a financially troubled company and also revealed a management integrity problem. As a result of the deteriorated financial position and operating results, debt-rating agencies downgraded Enron's debt. This downgrade placed Enron in technical default of a $690 million note payable at one of the SPEs. Given the deteriorated financial condition and the management integrity questions, the lending bank required immediate repayment upon learning of the technical default. Soon thereafter, Enron's debt rating was reduced to below investment grade, which placed other SPE-related notes in technical default. At the same time, Enron's stock price was plummeting as investors dumped the shares. The falling stock price caused yet another technical default event. Enron's stock quickly fell to worthless. Several Enron executives have been convicted of felony criminal charges for their role in the scandals. The trials on securities law violations by two top officers, Chairman Jeffrey Skilling and Board Chairman Kenneth Lay are still underway. For additional details regarding the facts of the Enron case, see the Powers Report or other Enron-related books and articles.[15]

---

[15] The Powers Report is available at http://energycommerce.house.gov/107/hearings/02052002Hearing481/report.pdf.

Enron's auditor, Arthur Andersen & Company (Andersen), would also be convicted of obstruction of justice. Even before the criminal conviction, clients of Andersen left in droves because of the bad publicity surrounding Andersen. In May 2005, the U.S. Supreme Court overturned the Andersen conviction, but unfortunately the firm had already ceased operations.[16] Also, several banks and brokerage firms have been sued by Enron shareholders in a class action for allegedly aiding Enron in the fraud. The lead plaintiff in the class action is the University of California. To date, J.P. Morgan Chase & Co., Citigroup, and Canadian Imperial Bank of Commerce have paid a total of over $7 billion to settle the suit. Several others have not yet settled.[17]

While the scandal at Enron involved a complex nexus of elaborate financial contracts involving many counterparties, the scandal at WorldCom was quite simple. WorldCom was a large telecommunications company. The telecommunications industry had gone through a period of tremendous growth, led by WorldCom. However, the industry overestimated the ultimate demand for its services. WorldCom was no exception, as the company had spent billions of dollars to lease capacity that would prove worthless.[18]

Analysts that followed the fast evolving telecommunications industry relied heavily on the performance measurement known as EBITDA (earnings before interest, taxes, depreciation, and amortization) to assess telecom companies. EBITDA is an unaudited or *pro forma* measure of firm performance. At that time, analysts believed that it was virtually impossible for companies to manipulate the reported EBITDA. WorldCom proved this belief wrong. WorldCom reported consistently strong EBITDA results by recording ordinary operating expenditures with no future benefit (the line lease costs) as capital assets and depreciating them over time. EBITDA was high because depreciation of the inappropriately capitalized assets (billions of dollars) was not included. In addition, the cash outlays were reported as investing rather than operating activities. Thus,

---

[16] See for example, Bravin, J. "Justices Overturn Criminal Verdict in Andersen Case," *Wall Street Journal* (June 1, 2005): A1.

[17] Sinclair Stewart, "CIBC to Pay $2.4 Billion (U.S.) in Enron Settlement," *The Globe and Mail* (August 2, 2005), Bell Globe Media and Publishing.

[18] Cynthia Cooper, in a speech to the American Accounting Association, August 10, 2005, San Francisco.

WorldCom reported strong cash flow from its core operations. Unfortunately, the strong cash flows were a financial reporting myth. As a result of this fraud, investors lost billions of dollars and several WorldCom officers have been convicted of criminal wrongdoing.

What Was Going On at CPA Firms?

Professor Paul Williams presented the view of many when he reflected on the CPA profession in the 1980s and 1990s. He lamented that accounting was not revered by its practitioners as a profession, a calling that is "inherently worth doing because it is an essential social function."[19] Instead, he viewed the profession as dominated by firms that were first concerned with growing revenues rather than protecting the public interest and serving clients. As a result, tax and consulting revenues skyrocketed, but commitment to serve, competence, integrity, and objectivity were, in some instances, compromised.

What Is Sarbanes-Oxley?

The Sarbanes-Oxley Act of 2002 was signed into law on July 30, 2002.[20] The Act, named after its co-sponsors Senator Paul Sarbanes from Maryland and Congressman Michael Oxley from the 4th District in Ohio, revised existing securities laws and established new securities laws related to corporate governance, corporate reporting, and regulatory oversight and enforcement. The act is designed to restore investor trust in the capital markets following the string of high-profile corporate scandals. The following paragraphs describe key provisions of Sarbanes-Oxley. Particular attention is given to provisions of the law that affect the CPA profession directly.

An important component of Sarbanes-Oxley is the establishment of the Public Company Accounting Oversight Board (PCAOB). The PCAOB is a private-sector, nonprofit corporation created to oversee the auditors of public companies to protect the interests of investors

---

[19] P. Williams, "Association for Integrity in Accounting Enters the Discussion of Accounting Reforms," *CPA Journal*, New York, (April 2003): 14-15.

[20] The Act is available online at various Web sites, including http://pcaob.org/About_ Us/Sarbanes_Oxley_Act_of_2002.pdf.

and further the public interest in the preparation of informative, fair, and independent audit reports. Section three of Sarbanes-Oxley empowers the PCAOB by providing that violation of the rules of the PCAOB will be treated as a violation of the SEC Act of 1934 and give rise to the same penalties that arise for violations of that act.

Sarbanes-Oxley Title I: The PCAOB

Sections 101 through 109 direct the activities and establish the authority of the PCAOB. Creation of the PCAOB is a response of Congress to the perceived failure of the accounting profession's self-regulation mechanisms. Section 101 of Sarbanes-Oxley sets forth the PCAOB membership. The PCAOB has five financially literate members that are appointed by the SEC after consultation with the Chairman of the Federal Reserve Board and the Secretary of the Treasury. Two of the members of the PCAOB must be CPAs. Three of the PCAOB members must not be CPAs.

Section 102 of Sarbanes-Oxley requires public accounting firms to register with the PCAOB. The names of firms registered with the PCAOB and applicant firms are available on the PCAOB Web site. According to PCAOB member Kayla Gillan, as of June 2005, the PCAOB has registered 1,520 firms. Of these, 935 are U.S.-based. The rest are international firms representing more than 75 different countries. Nine of the PCAOB registrant firms have more than 100 U.S. traded clients. Over 70 percent of the PCAOB registrant auditing firms have less than five publicly traded clients and 46 percent of them have none but participate in such audits or intend to do so in the future.[21] Information provided as part of the registration requirements includes:

1. The names of attest clients from the preceding year and the names of expected attest clients for the upcoming year
2. The annual fees received from the previous year attest clients for audit services, other accounting services, and nonaudit services
3. Other information as requested by the PCAOB

---

[21] K. J. Gillan, "Auditing Oversight: Where We've Been and Where We're Going," delivered at the SEC Institute Mid-Year Reporting Forum, San Francisco, June 20, 2005.

4. A statement of the quality control policies of the firm for its accounting and auditing practices
5. The state license number of the firm and the names and license or certification numbers of all accountants at the firm that participate in or contribute to the preparation of audit reports
6. Information relating to criminal, civil, or administrative actions or disciplinary proceedings pending against the firm or members of the firm in connection with any audit report
7. Copies of any periodic or annual disclosure filed by an SEC registrant with the SEC during the preceding year, which discloses accounting disagreements between the audit firm and the client
8. Other information as deemed important by the PCAOB for the public interest and/or protection of investors.
9. A registration fee and an annual fee for firms registering with the PCAOB

Section 103 of Sarbanes-Oxley sets forth the activities of the PCAOB. The PCAOB will:

1. Register public accounting firms
2. Establish auditing, quality control, ethics, independence, and other standards relating to the preparation of audit reports for issuers of publicly traded securities
3. Conduct inspections of accounting firms
4. Conduct investigations and disciplinary proceedings and impose appropriate sanctions for substandard work
5. Enforce compliance with the provisions of Sarbanes-Oxley, rules of the PCAOB, professional standards, securities laws relating to the preparation and issuance of audit reports and the related obligations and liabilities of accountants
6. Set the budget of the oversight board
7. Manage the operations of the oversight board
8. Staff the oversight board

Section 103 also prescribes the relationship of the PCAOB with other professional groups. Under Sarbanes-Oxley, the PCAOB can adopt standards proposed by other private sector rule making bodies (for example, AICPA, Financial Accounting Standards Board (FASB), and the Accounting Standards Executive Committee) if the PCAOB deems them appropriate. The PCAOB can amend, modify, repeal, and reject any standards suggested by other rulemaking bodies if it does not fully support the existing guidance. The PCAOB must report to the SEC on standard-setting activity on an annual basis.

On April 16, 2003, the PCAOB adopted several preexisting standards as its interim standards:

- *Interim PCAOB Auditing Standards:* Under PCAOB Rule 3200T, the PCAOB adopted as interim auditing standards, the generally accepted auditing standards as described in the AICPA's Auditing Standards Board's Statement of Auditing Standards (SAS) No. 95;
- *Interim PCAOB Attestation Standards:* Under Rule 3300T the PCAOB adopted the AICPA's Auditing Standards Board's Statements on Standards for Attestation Engagements, and related interpretations and Statements of Position;
- *Interim PCAOB Quality Control Standards:* Under Rule 3400T the PCAOB adopted the AICPA's Auditing Standards Board's Statements on Quality Control Standards and certain of the SEC's Practice Section's Requirements of Membership;[22]
- *Interim PCAOB Ethics Standards:* Under PCAOB Rule 3500T, the PCAOB adopted the AICPA's Code of Professional Conduct Rule 102 and interpretations thereunder; and
- *Interim PCAOB Independence Standards:* Under PCAOB Rule 3600T the PCAOB adopted the AICPA's Code of Professional Conduct Rule 101, and interpretations and rulings thereunder, and Standards Nos. 1, 2, and 3, and Interpretations 99-1, 00-1, and 00-2 of the Independence Standards Board.

---

[22] Specifically, the Public Companies Accounting Oversight Board (PCAOB) adopted SEC Practice Section membership requirements (d), the first sentence of (f), (l), (m), (n1), and (o).

164 The CPA Profession: Opportunities, Responsibilities, and Services

To date, the PCAOB has promulgated the following standards:

- PCAOB Auditing Standard No. 1, *References in Auditors' Reports to the Standards of the Public Company Accounting Oversight Board*
- PCAOB Auditing Standard No. 2, *An Audit of Internal Control Over Financial Reporting Performed in Conjunction With an Audit of Financial Statements*. This standard provides guidance for implementing the requirements of Section 404 of Sarbanes-Oxley.
- PCAOB Auditing Standard No. 3, *Audit Documentation*
- PCAOB Auditing Standard No. 4, *Reporting on Whether a Previously Reported Material Weakness Continues to Exist*. This standard was approved by the SEC on February 6, 2006, and is effective as of February 6, 2006.

These standards are available on the PCAOB Web site at www.pcaob.org. [It should be noted that the PCAOB's auditing standards apply only to audits of public companies (about 17,000 each year). The auditing standards for private companies (hundreds of thousands each year) are established by the AICPA's Auditing Standards Board.]

With respect to public accounting firms that are registered with the PCAOB to provide public attest services, Section 103 first requires registered public accounting firms to prepare audit work papers and other information related to the audit report to support the conclusions reached in the report. Second, Section 103 requires a second partner review of the work of the primary audit team for each attest engagement. These documents are to be maintained for at least seven years. Third, Section 103 orders the PCAOB to adopt an audit standard for attest firms to conduct a review of the public client's internal control system. The standard will require the auditor to evaluate the internal control structure of the company and provide "reasonable assurance" that (1) the internal procedures produce records that fairly reflect the transactions of the company, (2) the transactions are recorded in a manner that will permit the preparation of financial statements in accordance with generally accepted accounting principles, and (3) any material internal control weaknesses are described. To date, the PCAOB has issued several new auditing standards.

Section 104 orders the PCAOB to conduct inspections of registered public accounting firms. Firms that audit more than 100 public companies are to be reviewed annually. Firms that conduct less than 100 public company audits are to be inspected at least once every three years. The review is to assess the firm's compliance with the requirements of Sarbanes-Oxley, with PCAOB rules, with SEC rules, and with relevant professional standards. To this end, the inspections consist of two types of reviews (1) the firm's policies and procedures and (2) selected engagements.

The review of the firm's policies and procedures seeks to establish how the firm operates. For example, what employee behaviors are rewarded? How are employees trained? How is employee performance monitored? What factors are considered when determining whether a prospective client will be accepted? What factors are considered when determining whether a client will be retained?

In the review of engagements, the inspector is seeking to establish whether the auditors conducted the audit in accordance with generally accepted standards and in accordance with internal firm policies and procedures. Further, the inspector assesses whether the client financial reporting was appropriate. To this end, the PCAOB doesn't re-audit the client, but focuses on the highest risk areas for the selected client. Upon completion of the inspection, the PCAOB issues a report to the registrant firm. The report contains a section that is open to the public and a section that is confidential. The public report contains general information about the inspection and possibly observed departures from GAAP or PCAOB auditing standards (without naming clients). See a recent example of this report (the 2004 report for KPMG) at http://216.6.140.146/PCAOB/documents/PCAOB_2004_KPMG_LLP.pdf. The confidential section contains any criticisms or observed weaknesses in the firm's quality control system. The firm is then given a year to cure the deficiency.[23]

Section 105 orders the PCAOB to establish a fair system for investigating and disciplining registered firms. This section provides the PCAOB authority to require testimony by representatives

---

[23] For additional details, see K. J. Gillan, "Auditing Oversight: Where We've Been and Where We're Going," delivered at the SEC Institute Mid-Year Reporting Forum, San Francisco, June 20, 2005.

of registered firms, to require registered firms to produce documents as requested, and to punish any firm or firm representative that does not cooperate with a PCAOB investigation. Section 105 also sets forth disciplinary sanctions that can be imposed by the PCAOB for violation of the provisions of Sarbanes-Oxley including:[24]

1. Temporary suspension or permanent revocation of registration.
2. Temporary or permanent suspension or bar of a person from further association with any registered public accounting firm.
3. Temporary or permanent limitation on the activities, functions, or operations of such firm or person (other than in connection with required additional professional education or training).
4. A civil money penalty for each violation up to stated maximums.
5. Censure.
6. Required additional professional education or training.
7. Any other appropriate sanction provided for in the rules of the board.

In May 2005, the PCAOB took its first disciplinary actions, revoking the PCAOB registration of the firm Goldstein & Morris CPAs PC, barring the firm's managing partner from practicing, and censuring two other partners.[25] The PCAOB has established a Center for Enforcement Tips, Complaints, and Other Information to encourage a flow of information about potential violations. The Center can be reached on-line at the PCAOB Web site, by e-mail, by letter, or by telephone. See the PCAOB Web site for details.

Section 106 relates to foreign public accounting firms that audit U.S. public companies. The section provides that foreign firms auditing U.S. public companies or foreign subsidiaries of U.S. public companies must register with the PCAOB and are subject to the requirements of Sarbanes-Oxley.

---

[24] Sarbanes-Oxley Act of 2002, Section 105(c)(4).
[25] All disciplinary actions can be viewed on the PCAOB Web site.

Section 107 provides that the SEC will oversee the activities of the PCAOB. This section empowers the SEC to amend PCOAB rules and review sanctions imposed by the PCAOB upon public companies or their auditors.

Section 108 deals with acceptable accounting standards. It amends the 1933 Act by authorizing the SEC to recognize accounting principles as generally accepted that are established by standard-setting organizations that meet certain criteria. Both the FASB and the International Accounting Standards Board (IASB) meet the stated criteria. The SEC has, to date, continued to uphold the FASB standards.

Section 109 details the funding of the PCAOB, which is primarily via fees paid by public companies and public accounting firms. In the first full year of operation, 2003, the PCAOB reported revenues of $54.9 million. About 96 percent of revenues are from issuers and 4 percent from registered accounting firms. In 2004, the PCAOB revenues increased to $101.4 million with 99.7 percent coming from issuers and .3 percent coming from registering accounting firms.

Sarbanes-Oxley Title II: Auditor Independence

Public accounting firms shouldered part of the blame for public company scandals. Sarbanes-Oxley attempts to strengthen auditor performance by providing additional guidance on auditor independence. This guidance is contained in sections 201 through 209.

Section 201 sets forth services that audit firms cannot provide to their attest clients. Among the prohibited services are:[26]

1. Bookkeeping or other serves related to the accounting records or financial statements of the audit client
2. Financial information systems design and implementation
3. Appraisal or valuation services, fairness reports, or contribution-in-kind reports
4. Actuarial services
5. Internal audit outsourcing services
6. Management functions or human resources

---

[26] Sarbanes-Oxley Act of 2002, Section 201 "Services Outside the Scope of Practice of Auditors."

7. Broker or dealer, investment adviser, or investment banking services
8. Legal services and expert services unrelated to the audit
9. Any other services that the PCAOB determines, by regulation, [are] impermissible

It should be noted that the PCAOB has authority to exempt registered firms from these prohibitions. Section 202 authorizes other nonaudit services, such as tax services, provided the services are preapproved by the public company's audit committee and disclosed to investors.

Section 203 mandates that the lead audit partner and the engagement reviewing partner rotate off of the audit every five years. Critics had argued for audit firm rotation rather than audit partner rotation. Many practitioners such as Ernst & Young Vice Chair Beth Brooke called that a "horrible idea" and endorsed the audit partner rotation requirement.[27] Section 204 requires that that auditors report to audit committees all critical accounting policies and practices used, all alternative treatments that are within GAAP and have been discussed with management, and ramifications of the use of the foregone alternative relative to the treatment applied.

Section 206 reduces conflict of interest concerns by providing that the public company's chief executive officer, chief financial officer, controller, chief accounting officer, and other similar officers cannot have been employed by the company's audit firm for the one-year period preceding the audit.

Sarbanes-Oxley Title III: Corporate Responsibility

Company officers are primarily to blame for corporate scandals and frauds. Congress sought to strengthen corporate governance in Title III of Sarbanes-Oxley.

Section 301 seeks to strengthen the oversight of the audit committee of the company's board of directors. First, each member of the audit committee must be an outside member of the board although the SEC can authorize exceptions to this rule. Second, the board's

---
[27] J. Goff, "They Might Be Giants," *CFO* (January 2004): 46.

audit committee is assigned the responsibility to appoint, pay, and oversee the independent auditors. Third, the audit committee is assigned to establish procedures for the receipt, retention, and treatment of complaints received by the Company regarding accounting, internal controls, and auditing. Last, the audit committee is given authority to hire attorneys or other advisers to carry out any of the responsibilities without the consent of management.

Section 302 deals with the company's responsibility for financial reports. It imposes additional accountability on the chief executive officer and chief financial officer by requiring each to certify in writing:

1. They have reviewed the report.
2. They are not aware of any untrue statement of a material fact, any omitted material fact.
3. The financial statements and disclosures "fairly present, in all material respects, the operations and financial condition of the Company."

It should be noted that this certification makes no reference to conformity with generally accepted accounting principles (GAAP). As a result, company officers can no longer use conformity with GAAP as a defense for statements that do not reflect economic reality.

This section also requires the signing officers to certify in writing that:

1. They are responsible for establishing and maintaining a sound internal control system.
2. They have designed the internal control system to ensure that they are aware of relevant material information.
3. They have evaluated the internal controls within 90 days of the financial reports.
4. They have presented in their report their conclusions about the effectiveness of the internal controls. Management must declare any material internal control weaknesses to the audit committee of the company's board of directors as well as the independent auditors.

Section 303 makes it illegal for management to interfere with the conduct of an audit. The exact wording is that it is illegal for management to attempt to "fraudulently influence, coerce, manipulate, or mislead" any auditor to make financial reports misleading. This provision provides the audit firm with a mechanism for stopping clients from "bullying" them.

Section 304 requires the signing officers to repay bonuses, other incentive compensation, and profits from the sale of company stock received in years when the financial statements had to be restated because the company did not comply with relevant financial reporting requirements.

Section 305 makes it easier to prohibit an individual from being an officer or director of a public company by reducing the evidence requirement from "substantial unfitness" to "unfitness" to serve.

Section 306 prohibits directors and officers of the company from selling company shares during any three-day or longer period of time when at least 50 percent of pension plan participants are prevented from trading in the company's shares.

Attorneys have also been intimately involved in fraudulent corporate schemes. Section 307 imposes additional responsibility on attorneys by requiring the SEC to issue guidance for attorneys representing public companies either in an inside or outside counsel role. Unlike auditors who serve an adversarial role, attorneys are advocates for their client. Ultimately, the SEC allowed attorneys great leeway in their advocacy role. Attorneys must report observed violations of state or federal laws, but only have to do so within the client company.

Sarbanes-Oxley Title IV: Enhanced Financial Disclosure

The fourth section of Sarbanes-Oxley is a "catch-all" section designed to further enhance the usefulness of financial disclosures. First, the SEC is called upon to promulgate additional requirements to this end.

One issue at Enron was several million dollars of passed audit adjustments. Sarbanes-Oxley section 401 addresses this problem by requiring that reports reflect "all material correcting adjustments" that have been identified by the auditors. Remember that auditors consider both quantitative as well as qualitative factors when assessing the materiality of an item. Thus, auditors now have legal authority to force the recording of audit adjustments of even small amounts.

Enron also failed to disclose huge amounts of off-balance sheet obligations. Sarbanes-Oxley calls for rules requiring that financial reports disclose all material "off-balance sheet transactions, arrangements, obligations (including contingent obligations), and other relationships of the issuer with unconsolidated entities or other persons" that may have a significant effect on the financial condition or results of operations of the company now or in the future.[28] Section 401 also calls for rules that prohibit companies from issuing untrue, incomplete, or otherwise misleading *pro forma* financial information.

At WorldCom, the board of directors approved loans totaling over $400 million to founder and CEO Bernard Ebbers to help Ebbers pay his broker "margin calls" without selling his shares. Section 402 makes it unlawful for the company to make loans to executives, although some exceptions are provided for.

Section 403 amends the 1934 SEC Act to require that directors, officers, and owners of more than 10 percent of the company's stock report transactions in company shares within two business days. Previously, officers could wait much longer to make these declarations.

Section 404 is the most widely discussed and debated provision of Sarbanes-Oxley. The section is not long, but its ramifications are certainly the most costly and arguably the most significant in the Act. Section 404 requires that management assess the company's system of internal controls and report the following about the control system:

1. An acknowledgment that it is the responsibility of management to establish and maintain adequate internal controls for financial reporting.
2. An assessment of the effectiveness of the internal control system. Auditors must attest to the effectiveness of the internal controls.

This provision has created much work and cost for public companies and has created a great source of revenue for CPA firms.

---

[28] Sarbanes-Oxley Act of 2002, Section 401(j) "Disclosures in Periodic Reports."

Small and mid-sized firms have especially prospered as they are often engaged by companies to help with management's internal control system assessment.

Section 405 exempts investment companies registered under section eight of the Investment Company Act of 1940 from the requirements of sections 401, 402, and 404 of Sarbanes-Oxley.

Section 406 addresses codes of ethics for senior financial officers. Under section 406, the SEC is instructed to issue rules requiring public companies to disclose whether the Company has adopted a code of ethics for senior financial officers and if not, why not. The code is applicable to the principal financial officer, the controller or principle accounting officer, and persons performing similar functions.

Section 407 calls for the SEC to issue rules requiring public companies to disclose whether at least one member of the audit committee is a financial expert. The Act defines what will constitute a financial expert.

Section 408 calls for SEC review of registrants at least once every three years. It holds that the companies with the following characteristics should be considered highest priority for SEC review:[29]

1. Issuers that have issued material restatements of financial results.
2. Issuers that experience significant volatility in their stock price as compared to other issuers.
3. Issuers with the largest market capitalization.
4. Emerging companies with disparities in price to earning ratios.
5. Issuers whose operations significantly affect any material sector of the economy.
6. Any other factors that the SEC may consider relevant.

Section 409 requires companies to disclose information, in plain English and rapidly, on material changes in the financial condition or operations of the company.

---

[29] Sarbanes-Oxley Act of 2002, Section 408(b) "Enhanced Review of Periodic Disclosures by Issuers."

Sarbanes-Oxley Title V: Analyst Conflicts of Interest

Financial analysts are an important source of information about public companies for investors. Several instances of analyst malfeasance in this role were unmasked. The most frequently observed potential conflict of interest involves analysts that work for firms that also seek to provide investment banking services to companies. In these instances, analysts may have been discouraged from issuing negative opinions about the prospects of companies because of the likely loss of investment banking work with that company that would result. In fact, New York Attorney General Eliot Spitzer "launched an all out crusade to eradicate conflicts of interests on Wall Street that he says make analysts biased in favor of potential investment-banking clients at the expense of investors who might act on their recommendations."[30]

Sarbanes-Oxley sought to reduce the likelihood of analyst conflicts by requiring the SEC to issue additional regulation. The SEC responded by adopting Regulation Analyst Certification (Reg AC). This regulation requires that analysts certify that:

1. They believe in the report and the recommendations that they are making.
2. Their compensation is in no way linked to specific recommendations that they make or views that they hold about public companies.

Sarbanes-Oxley Title VI: Commission Resources and Authority

The SEC has oversight authority of public companies on behalf of investors and the public interest. However, the SEC was viewed as understaffed and underfunded, and as a result, may not be able to adequately perform its oversight duties. For example, New York Times reporter Alex Berenson reports that the SEC could only audit about 15 percent of the annual reports that it received and could only investigate a fraction of all allegations of fraud that it received.[31] In

---

[30] Excerpted from R. Sidel, "Sorry Wrong Number: Some Untimely Analyst Advice on WorldCom Raises Eyebrows," *Wall Street Journal* (June 27, 2002): A12.

[31] A. Berenson, "The Number: How the Drive for Quarterly Earnings Corrupted Wall Street and Corporate America," Random House, New York, 2003.

response to this problem, Congress authorized substantial increases in the SEC budget. This section contains provisions that enhance the power of the SEC as well.

Sarbanes-Oxley Title VII: Studies and Reports

In the spirit of continual positive reform, in this section of the Act, Congress calls for several studies by the Government Accountability Office (GAO), the Comptroller General of the United States, and the SEC. Among the mandated studies is a Government Accountability Office (GAO) study of the consolidation in public accounting firms over the past several years and its implications for practice in the public interest. The SEC was ordered to conduct a review and analysis of all of the commission's enforcement actions related to financial statements and reporting requirements. The SEC must also analyze the activities of credit rating agencies and their role in U.S. capital markets. The U.S. Comptroller General must examine whether investment banks assisted public companies in manipulating earnings and obfuscating their true financial condition. The Enron and Global Crossing cases are of particular interest to Congress in this regard. It is expected that other reforms and refinements of Sarbanes-Oxley will be enacted as a result of what is learned from the studies mandated in Title VII of Sarbanes-Oxley.

Sarbanes-Oxley Title VIII: Corporate and Criminal Fraud Accountability

This section of Sarbanes-Oxley is also called the Corporate and Criminal Fraud Accountability Act of 2002. This section creates new securities-related crimes and increases the punishment for violations of existing laws.

Section 802 makes it a felony to knowingly destroy or create documents to impede, obstruct, or influence any existing or contemplated federal investigation. Section 803 provides that fines, judgments, and other debts incurred for violations of securities fraud laws are not dischargeable in bankruptcy. Section 804 extends the statute of limitations for securities fraud. Plaintiffs must sue within two years of the discovery of the fraud and within five years after the fraud violation occurred. Previously, the statute of limitations was one year from the fraud's discovery and three years from the fraud's occurrence. Section 805 calls on the United States Sentencing Commission to review and amend federal sentencing guidelines for obstruction of justice and extensive criminal fraud to ensure that punishments for these offenses are sufficient to deter and appropriately punish these activities. Section 806 allows for civil damage actions to protect corporate whistleblowers in federal securities laws violation cases against retaliation. This section provides additional protection for whistleblowers.[32] Section 807 establishes new crimes for securities fraud and extends existing laws providing for penalties of fines and up to 25 years in prison.

Sarbanes-Oxley Title IX: White-Collar Crime Penalty Enhancements

Title IX of Sarbanes-Oxley is also called the "White-Collar Crime Penalty Enhancement Act of 2002." This Act provides for harsher penalties and more criminal statutes for White-Collar crime as deterrence for future violations. Section 902 holds that people who conspire to commit mail fraud, wire fraud, or securities fraud will be subject to the same punishments as those who commit the offense. Section 903 increases the maximum penalty for mail fraud and wire fraud from five to 20 years. Section 904 increases the maximum prison time for violations of the Employee Retirement Income Security Act of 1974 (ERISA) from one to 10 years, and the maximum fine from $100,000 to $500,000. Section 905 calls on the United States Sentencing Commission to review and amend federal sentencing guidelines for White-Collar offenses to ensure that punishments for these offenses are sufficient to deter and appropriately punish these activities. Section 906 provides the punishments for Chief Executive Officers and Chief Financial Officers that intentionally certify financial reports that do not reflect financial reality. Remember that Section 302 of Sarbanes-Oxley requires these certifications. If the officer is deemed to have "knowingly" certified inaccurate financial reports, the maximum punishment is a fine of up to $1,000,000 and 10 years in prison. If the officer "willfully" certified inaccurate financial reports, the maximum penalty is a fine of up to $5,000,000 and

---

[32] Recall that section 301 requires audit committees to establish procedures to handle whistleblowers' complaints.

20 years in prison. Case law will likely be required to establish the relative meanings of the terms *knowingly* and *willful.*

Sarbanes-Oxley Title X: Corporate Tax Returns

This section simply sets for the Sense of the Senate that the chief executive officer of a corporation should sign the federal income tax return. Thus, this section provides additional evidence of accountability for the CEO should the company file a fraudulent federal tax return.

Sarbanes-Oxley Title XI: Corporate Fraud and Accountability

This section is also called the "Corporate Fraud Accountability Act of 2002." Section 1102 makes it a crime for any person to corruptly alter, destroy, mutilate, or conceal any document with the intent to impair the object's integrity or availability for use in any official proceeding or to otherwise obstruct, influence, or impede any official proceeding. Persons violating this statute may receive a fine and a prison sentence of up to 20 years. Section 1103 authorizes the SEC to temporarily freeze an extraordinary payment to any director, officer, partner, controlling person, agent, or employee of a company during an investigation of possible securities laws violations. Section 1104 once again calls on the United States Sentencing Commission to review and amend federal sentencing guidelines for securities fraud, accounting fraud, and related offenses to ensure that punishments for these offenses are sufficient to deter and appropriately punish these activities. Section 1105 authorizes the SEC to prohibit persons from serving as officers or directors of public companies if the person has committed securities fraud, accounting fraud, or related offenses. A high profile person to be barred under this provision is former ImClone Chairman Sam Waksal. Finally, Section 1107 sets forth criminal penalties for persons that retaliate against whistleblowers. Persons found guilty under this law can be fined an imprisoned up to 10 years.

Impact of Compliance

"One year of implementation has passed. It is no exaggeration to say that every stakeholder hopes the first year will be the hardest."

James Quigley, CEO of Deloitte spoke these words recently, but he wasn't referring to Sarbanes-Oxley. Instead, he was quoting a newspaper article from the 1930s in which an executive was discussing the adjustment to regulation following the stock market crash of 1929.[33]

Needless to say, for every company that is involved in a scandal, tens of thousands are not. However, even these companies felt the effects of the scandals of the 1990s and can reap benefits from compliance with stiffer regulation. For example, Leif Johansson, president of Volvo, pointed out that, "like it or not, all corporations have to reestablish their credibility with investors, other stakeholders, and the broader public." Johansson sees compliance with Sarbanes-Oxley as costly but "worth it." Johansson did echo the complaints of many about the cost of compliance as well as the perception that some of the work is "form over substance." In other words, Johansson and other leaders want to see the reforms accomplish a substantive improvement rather than simply complying with any particular caveat in the law.[34]

Through May 2005, 586 companies had already reported material internal control weaknesses. During all of 2004, only 313 companies reported such weaknesses. Before Sarbanes-Oxley, companies were required to report control weaknesses only if an auditor was terminated. Between January 1, 2004, and May 2, 2005, almost 11 percent of publicly traded companies with market capitalization greater than $75 million reported internal control deficiencies.[35] Hence, the internal control reviews mandated under Sarbanes-Oxley are forcing companies to rigorously review controls and report and correct weaknesses. Also, many companies not subject to Sarbanes-Oxley are voluntarily complying nevertheless. For example, the PriceWaterhouseCoopers survey found that about 30 percent of the nation's fastest growing private companies are adhering to Sarbanes-Oxley. A majority of these companies report improvements related to among several others control documentation and

---

[33] Ellen Heffes, "Audit Firm CEOs speak at FEI Summit," *Financial Executive* (July/August 2005): 14.

[34] Excerpted from the "8th Annual Global CEO Survey" conducted by PriceWaterhouseCoopers.

[35] Results of a Glass, Lewis & Co. shareholder adviser excerpted on CFO.com, "Material Weakness Reports Skyrocket" (July 18, 2005), CFO Publishing.

testing, governance procedures, codes of ethics and conduct. A majority of these companies cited that implementing the best business practice was their primary motivation.[36]

Up-front costs of compliance with the Act are significant. For example, insurance giant AIG reports that it bought over 55,000 hours of accounting services to help with the compliance work.[37] The burden is especially large for small public companies. The problem according to representatives of smaller companies is that the compliance cost has a large fixed component. That is, they believe that the incremental compliance cost for a huge company relative to a mid-cap or small company is not that different.

The regulation has also created some friction between companies and their auditors. A company representative said, "This is probably the largest unintended consequence of Sarbanes-Oxley— companies can no longer consider the Big Four accounting firms their 'trusted business advisers'." Another company representative added that, "public company auditors are now privatized regulators for the Securities and Exchange Commission." Regulation advocates might view this more adversarial relationship a net gain from the additional regulation. The resentment seems to arise primarily from the escalating audit fees caused by additional internal control testing. Surveyors Foley & Lardner found that average audit fees for public companies with less than $1 billion of annual revenues rose by 96 percent while fees for larger companies rose 55 percent.[38] Fortunately, most firms are finding that compliance in subsequent years is less expensive. In interviews with the authors, CFOs of several small, midsize, and large publicly traded companies report that costs of compliance have dropped 20 percent to 40 percent from first-year levels.

Several small public companies have chosen to move from a full reporting public entity to a "pink sheet" public company that doesn't have obligations to file audits or other material information with the SEC (also known as "going dark"). In 2003, about 200 companies

---

[36] PriceWaterhouseCoopers, "30 percent of Fast-Growth Private Companies Applying Sarbanes-Oxley Principles," available at http://www.pwc.com.

[37] *Wall Street Journal* (August 9, 2005): A11. "As Lawyers Invade Accounting, Clarity Flees."

[38] Financial Wire, "SEC Witnesses Worry About Future of Small Public Companies Under Sarbanes-Oxley 404" (June 20, 2005).

"went dark." This was about three times the number that did so in 2002. Michael Scharf, chairman of Niagara Corporation, a company that delisted primarily because of the up-front costs of Sarbanes-Oxley compliance, said, "We have been unable to gain a significant following in the market, yet we have been spending large sums of money for the accounting and legal services needed to maintain our reporting status."[39] Supporters of Sarbanes-Oxley argue that many companies such as Niagara that delist for this reason probably are not ideal public companies anyway. Because of their size, management structure, and relative financial inflexibility, many such companies should rely more on private funding and venture capital rather than being a very small public company. Regardless, the SEC and Congress continue to study the impact of Sarbanes-Oxley and especially smaller companies. It is likely that the law will be tweaked in the near future to decrease its cost burden.

Summary

Investors lost billions of dollars in recent financial scandals. Worse, many investors lost faith in the capital markets. Many were to blame. Certainly greedy, unscrupulous corporate officers and insufficient company internal control systems were most culpable. However, there was plenty of blame to go around. Other parties earning blame include inactive and unqualified corporate boards, less than independent and vigilant auditors, and analysts with conflicting interests. Enron and WorldCom receive the most attention due to the size of the losses related to these scandals.

These and other scandals led Congress to act to shore up investor confidence in the U.S. capital markets. The Sarbanes-Oxley Act of 2002 was the result. This sweeping legislation dealt with many of the issues related to the earlier scandals. Among the ramifications of Sarbanes-Oxley is a reduction in the degree to which the CPA profession is self-regulated. This chapter provides a summary of Sarbanes-Oxley with particular attention to its impact on the CPA profession. While costly, the reforms seemed to be working. Few if any large scandals have surfaced since the Act took effect and investor confidence has rebounded. Certainly, regulators will

---

[39] See footnote 38.

continue to tweak their regulatory measures. However, at the time of this writing the future in the accounting profession looks very bright. Armed with a revised governance structure and a renewed vigilance, CPAs are leading the efforts to restore investor faith in the strongest capital markets in history.

9

A View of the Horizon for the CPA Profession

"Information about money has become as important as money itself."

Walter B. Wriston[1]

Professions must evolve, adapt, and innovate to continue to provide the expert service that is the hallmark of a profession. The accounting profession is no exception. The first years of the 21st century have already produced profound changes for the profession, and the rate of change is not slowing. Some of the larger efforts currently affecting the profession are examined in this chapter, including (1) hiring and employment trends, (2) technological advancements, (3) debate about the optimal philosophical basis for accounting standards, (4) debate about the optimal accounting standards for smaller closely held companies, and (5) convergence of accounting and auditing standards across countries.

---

[1] K. Kelly, "The Don't-Have-to-Work Force," *Wired*, September 1999. Walter B. Wriston (1919–2005) was the Chairman of Citicorp/Citibank (later, Citigroup) at the time of his retirement in 1984.

Hiring and Employment Trends

As discussed in Chapter 3, opportunities for CPAs have rarely or never been more plentiful and this trend shows no signs of slowing. Work related to the Sarbanes-Oxley Act of 2002 added to the already busy audit and attest, tax, and consulting workload and has CPA firms across the country scrambling to add professionals. The Controllers' Leadership Roundtable reports that a CPA looking for a job receives an average of two to four offers, and managers in the Roundtable report that they plan to increase the number of CPAs in their Controllership organization as a percentage of total staff by 34 percent.[2] Reasons cited for the increased CPA hiring include Sarbanes-Oxley related expertise needed; public accounting veterans make excellent candidates for senior management positions; and CFOs need the CPA-specific skill set in their organizations.

In addition, firms have had to rapidly escalate salaries and benefits in the profession to attract talented new CPAs and retain the CPAs that they already have in place. Persons with information technology (IT) auditing expertise are in particularly high demand. For example, according to Robert Half International, new CPAs with IT audit knowledge can expect starting salaries between $67,000 and $94,250, which is an 11 percent increase over the prior year. Other highly desirable skills for the "next generation" accountants are international accounting, internal controls, and anti-fraud knowledge.[3] As always, soft skills such as business professionalism, poise, and written and oral communication will remain critical to a CPAs success.

Accounting programs across the country are providing classes to impart this cutting-edge knowledge to students. The accounting programs at most universities offer majors or courses in accounting information systems (AIS) and have at least one faculty member that conducts AIS related research.[4] Auditing courses have routinely

---

[2] See the Corporate Executive Board's 2005 Controllers' Leadership Roundtable, www.ctlr.executiveboard.com : p. 3.

[3] "Research Identifies Needed Skills for 'Next Generation' Accountants," *SmartPros*, September 7, 2005.

[4] For example, Professor Joseph O'Donnell of Canisius College and Jennifer Moor of Lumsden and McCormick find that 84 percent of large universities offer an AIS course and 79 percent of those schools have at least one full-time faculty member that emphasizes AIS.

focused on internal control concepts. International accounting courses are also offered at many universities and fraud courses are being developed and offered with increasing frequency.

Significant Advances in Technology

The emerging technology that could revolutionize financial reporting and analysis is extensible business reporting language (XBRL). XBRL is a global standard for formatting financial information. It is making reporting and analysis faster, less expensive, and much easier to automate. AICPA President and Chief Executive Officer Barry Melancon said this about XBRL:

> XBRL fundamentally transforms and improves the way companies, investors, lenders, analysts and regulators exchange, aggregate and analyze business information.[5]

A CPA named Charles Hoffman developed XBRL. Hoffman said this about the future with XBRL:

> XBRL will significantly improve the ability of CPA financial managers to distribute information to stakeholders precisely as reported, rather than as condensed or otherwise modified by third-party data aggregators to facilitate distribution. CPAs in public practice will need to know XBRL when working with CEOs and CFOs, who will use it to issue financial reports and to obtain credit from lenders. Members in industry, with corporate management and boards of directors, will use it as a common frame of reference, as will independent auditors working with audit committees. CPA/PFSs will employ XBRL to assess investments for their clients, and accounting educators will prepare students to use XBRL in the marketplace.[6]

The revolution has already begun. For example, beginning in October 2005, financial institutions will be required by the federal banking regulators to file quarterly summaries of their financial condition over the Internet using XBRL format. Also, companies can already file required documents to the SEC online using XBRL.

Currently, users of financial information usually access the information as provided by the company and key it into their models,

---

[5] "XBRL: It's Unstoppable," *Journal of Accountancy*, August, 2005: 32-35.
[6] See footnote 5.

audit applications, and other areas. Hoffman envisions a day when none of these processes are necessary. He foresees users "turning unstructured clusters of text into structured data that computers can process to facilitate their re-use. In such an environment, intelligent software tools driven by XBRL metadata would integrate the various work flow components that contribute to financial reporting, reduce rekeying of data, automate disclosure checklists and automatically validate the complex information contained in financial statements and supporting schedules." Hoffman also foresees that Sarbanes-Oxley compliance work will soon be completed using XBRL. Hoffman's vision extends beyond simple cost savings from reduced analysis time. He sees improvements in analysis resulting from XBRL use as well. Professors Frank Hodge, Jane Kennedy, and Laureen Maines found evidence that this is already occurring. Their research findings suggest that technology helps less sophisticated investors to bring together pieces of related information from various sources. They also find evidence that technology helped investors to use information in the footnotes more often and more effectively.[7]

Principles Versus Rules-Based Guidance

Motivated by recent scandals in which companies seemed to comply with the letter of the rules, but issued statements that did not reflect the economic reality of the company's results of operations and financial position, a debate is ongoing about whether accounting rules should be more principles based or rules based.

Before discussing the current state of the principles versus rules-based debate, it would be appropriate to briefly set forth what is currently the universe of generally accepted accounting principles (GAAP).[8] AU section 411, *The Meaning of* Present Fairly in Conformity With Generally Accepted Accounting Principles, as amended, defines "generally accepted accounting principles" as a

---

[7] F. D. Hodge, J. J. Kennedy, and L. A. Maines, "Does search-facilitating technology improve the transparency of financial reporting?. *The Accounting Review*, 2004, 79(3): 687-703.

[8] For additional detail regarding the generally accepted accounting principles (GAAP) hierarchy see Moehrle et al. (2002) "Is There a Gap in Your Knowledge of GAAP," *Financial Analysts Journal*, 58 (5): 43-47.

"technical accounting term that encompasses the conventions, rules, and procedures necessary to define accepted accounting practice at a particular time." AU section 411 goes on to specify a hierarchy for the various sources of GAAP so that one can determine which principle applies to a particular set of facts. The GAAP hierarchy has five categories. Category A is the highest level of authoritative guidance. It includes Statements of Financial Accounting Standards, Financial Accounting Standards Board Interpretations, Accounting Principle Board Opinions, and Accounting Research Bulletins.

The second highest level of authority in the GAAP hierarchy is called category B. Included in this category are FASB Technical Bulletins, AICPA Industry Audit and Accounting Guides, and AICPA Statements of Position. Category C, the third level in the hierarchy, includes consensus positions of the FASB's Emerging Issues Task Force, and Practice Bulletins issued by the Accounting Standards Executive Committee. The fourth level of accounting authority consists of AICPA accounting Interpretations, FASB Staff Implementation Guides, and "practices that are widely recognized and prevalent either generally or in the industry."[9]

Finally, the lowest level of authoritative GAAP is a catch-all category that includes all other written sources of accounting authority. Examples include FASB Statements of Financial Accounting Concepts, AICPA Issues Papers, International Accounting Standards Committee Statements, Government Accounting Standards Board Statements, Interpretations, and Technical Bulletins, Federal Accounting Standards Advisory Board Statements, Interpretations, and Technical Bulletins, pronouncements of other professional associations or regulatory agencies, AICPA Technical Practice Aids, and accounting textbooks, handbooks, and articles.

Much current authoritative guidance has at least some rules-based characteristics. They are called more rules-based because the rules tend to be written to contain "bright line" specifications of the rules. For example, one more rule-based accounting principle specifies that a lease is a capital lease if the lease term exceeds 75 percent of the economic life of the asset or the present value of the lease payments exceeds 90 percent of the fair value of the asset. A principles-based specification of this determination might prescribe that a lease

---

[9] See footnote 8, 718.

be capitalized if the lease term the whole of the assets useful life or the fair value of the lease payments approximate the amount for which the asset could be purchased outright. In a 2003 white paper on the topic, the Financial Accounting Standards Committee of the American Accounting Association opined that principles-based guidance is conceptually preferable, but will not be easily accomplished.[10] Current FASB Chairman Robert Herz expresses agreement with this position.[11] The firm PriceWaterhouseCoopers also calls for a move toward principles-based system: "Relying on principles will be far more important in the business world that is emerging, in this new era of ideas and imagination where 'tangible' will be far less tangible than it used to be."[12] The high profile nature of the individuals and groups expressing support for principles-based rules suggests that a move in that direction could be possible.

The American Assembly views the debate somewhat differently. They view the international principles as not free from rules and the U.S. principles as replete with principals-based guidance. They view the debate really as the following: "to what degree do we expect the preparers and auditors of financial statements to exercise judgments?"[13] With the question framed in that way, participants at the Assembly favored guidance featuring fewer rules and more preparer/auditor judgment than the current U.S. GAAP.

Private Company Financial Reporting

It was discussed in a previous chapter that the accounting rules for large public companies are also applied to smaller closely held companies. However, in some instances, accounting rules that are optimal for large publicly held companies might not be optimal for privately held companies. Currently a task force from the private firm practice section of the AICPA, chaired by former AICPA Chairman

---

[10] AAA Financial Accounting Standards Committee, "Evaluating Concepts-Based vs. Rules-Based Approaches to Standard Setting," *Accounting Horizons*, 17 (1): 73-89.

[11] R. Herz, "A Year of Challenge and Change for the FASB," *Accounting Horizons*, 2003, 17 (3): 247-255.

[12] See pwc.com/newrealities.

[13] The American Assembly, "The Future of the Accounting Profession", November 13-15, 2003.

James Castellano, is investigating whether certain alternative accounting rules should be developed for privately held companies. Dan Noll, an AICPA staff member that serves on the task force, endorses the concept: "There needs to be a dedicated process to focus on the needs of accounting for private companies." These alternatives are designed to make the financial statements of privately held companies more useful to their owners and stakeholders. Not all see the need for two sets of guidance. For example, Jack Ciesielski, publisher of a popular accounting newsletter, offers this thought: "The financial statements should reflect the worth of the assets and liabilities. If it's a good idea for a public company, it's a good idea for a private company."[14]

The AICPA commissioned a survey of about 1,000 private-company executives, auditors, and financial-statement users to generate information for the task force. While respondents rated GAAP very highly, they indicated some areas where different rules for private companies might be welcomed. Specific accounting topics mentioned include rules for mergers and acquisitions, special purpose entities, lease accounting, goodwill accounting, buy-sell agreements, and rules that call for assets or liabilities to be marked to be revalued to their current market value.[15] Preliminary findings from the Private Company Financial Reporting Task Force should be made public in the near future.

A Global Accounting Community

This book has focused primarily on the organization of the U.S. accounting community. This section describes the organization of the international accounting community and describes efforts afoot to harmonize accounting and auditing standards worldwide.

International Financial Reporting Standards

Like the United States, most countries have accounting and auditing standards for their domestic companies. The accounting standards and resulting accounting reports across countries can vary dramatically. The philosophy of many countries is to produce accounting

---
[14] CFO.com, July 2005.
[15] For additional details see "A GAAP of Their Own," CFO.com, July 2005.

standards that, subject to constraints, attempt to best reflect the economic performance of the entity (for example, United States and United Kingdom). The philosophy of many other countries is to promulgate accounting rules that reflect tax or commercial laws related to the transaction of interest. As a result, the resulting financial reports do not necessarily reflect the economic reality of the entity's performance (for example, Germany and Japan).

These cross-border differences created great challenges for investors as they tried to compare the prospects of companies from various countries and jurisdictions. These challenges are mitigated by the increasing use of International Financial Reporting Standards (IFRS), which are promulgated by the London-based International Accounting Standards Board (IASB). The core objectives of the IASB are the following:

> The Board is committed to developing, in the public interest, a single set of high quality, understandable and enforceable global accounting standards that require transparent and comparable information in general purpose financial statements. In addition, the Board cooperates with national accounting standard setters to achieve convergence in accounting standards around the world.[16]

The 14-member IASB is overseen by the Trustees of the International Accounting Standards Committee. To date, the IASB has issued five International Financial Reporting Standards. In addition, a predecessor organization, the International Accounting Standards Committee (1973-2001) issued 41 International Accounting Standards (IAS). The *Preface to International Financial Reporting Standards* makes it clear that full compliance with IFRSs includes full compliance with all IASs and Interpretations.[17] Reports prepared using IFRSs are designed to, subject to constraints, reflect the economic reality of the entity's operating results and financial position.

International Auditing Standards

International Auditing Standards are promulgated by the International Auditing and Assurance Board (IAASB), which was

---

[16] For additional details, see the International Accounting Standards Board Web site: www.iasb.org.uk.

[17] See the frequently asked questions on the IASB Web site for additional details.

established by the New York-based International Federation of Accountants (IFAC). IFAC is the global organization for the accounting profession. IFAC works with 163 member organizations in 119 countries (including the AICPA) to "protect the public interest by encouraging high quality practices by the world's accountants."[18] IFAC's membership includes approximately 2.5 million accountants employed in public, corporate, and government practice, as well as members from academe.[19]

The mission of the IFAC is the following:

> To serve the public interest, IFAC will continue to strengthen the worldwide accountancy profession and contribute to the development of strong international economies by establishing and promoting adherence to high-quality professional standards, furthering the international convergence of such standards and speaking out on public interest issues where the profession's expertise is most relevant.[20]

IFAC has a Code of Ethics, which encourages accountants worldwide to adhere to the organization's core values: integrity, transparency, and expertise. The IFAC and AICPA Code of Ethics are very similar in spirit as well as substance.

The objective of the IAASB is to "serve the public interest by setting high quality auditing and assurance standards and by facilitating the convergence of international and national standards, thereby enhancing the quality and uniformity of practice throughout the world and strengthening public confidence in the global auditing and assurance profession."[21] The collective IAASB engagement standards come from several sources. International Standards on Auditing (ISAs) are to be applied in the audit of historical financial information. International Standards on Review Engagements (ISREs) are to be applied in the review of historical financial information. International Standards on Assurance Engagements (ISAEs)

---

[18] See the IFAC Web site: www.ifac.org.

[19] It should be noted that a convergence process is currently taking place between ASB and IAASB, to harmonize U.S. auditing standards with international auditing standards. A complete discussion of these talks is beyond the scope of this publication. For additional information, please visit the ASB Web Site at http://www.aicpa.org/members/div/auditstd/index.htm.

[20] See footnote 19.

[21] See the IAASB handbook available at the IFAC Web site: http://www.ifac.org/Members/DownLoads/2005_IAASB_HandBook.pdf

are to be applied in assurance engagements dealing with subject matters other than historical financial information. International Standards on Related Services (ISRSs) are to be applied to compilation engagements, engagements to apply agreed-upon procedures to information and other related service engagements as specified by the IAASB. In addition, the International Standards on Quality Control (ISQCs) are to be applied for all of the above services.[22]

Convergence

Professors Frederick Choi and Gary Meek describe convergence in the accounting context as standards that are "free of logical conflicts, and should improve the comparability of financial information from different countries."[23] In a world of completed convergence, IFRS, U.S. GAAP, U.K. GAAP, and other reporting regimes would apply the same accounting treatment to like transactions. Currently, significant differences remain between IFRS and U.S. GAAP. However, these differences have been reduced over the years and the respective entities each have as a stated objective to continue to work to converge their accounting rules. To this end, the FASB and the IASB recently issued their first joint proposal. The proposal, in exposure draft form at the time of this writing, is designed to improve the accounting and reporting of business combinations. As the issuance of the joint proposal demonstrates, convergence will remain a focus of regulators in upcoming decades.

Summary

Any profession must respond to its changing environment to continue to deliver service worth of the term *professional*. The accounting profession operates in an environment of constant change. As a result, the accounting profession offers continually more opportunities for its members. This chapter summarized four areas to watch over the next several years. The first is technology. Technological advances continue to make the accounting profession more effective and more efficient. Advances that we cannot fathom right now will

---

[22] See footnote 21.
[23] F. D. S. Choi, and G. K. Meek, International Accounting, Fifth Edition, 2005, Prentice-Hall, Upper Saddle River, N.J.

be an integral part of a CPAs toolkit within five years. One such technological advance is XBRL. XBRL has profound potential to change the way companies report to stakeholders and the way CPAs audit the information.

A contemporary debate sets the stage for the second initiative on the horizon for the CPA profession. Currently, much authoritative guidance is written from a rules-based perspective. CPAs across the profession and academe are debating whether a shift to more principles-based guidance is appropriate. Another question being examined is whether small, privately-held companies should use the same accounting rules as large publicly traded companies. A task force of AICPA members chaired by former AICPA Chairman James Castellano is currently investigating this question.

Finally, convergence of accounting and auditing standards across countries is a goal and objective of most accounting regulators. Significant steps toward convergence have occurred in recent years. Current evidence such as the recent joint rule proposal by the FASB and the IASB suggests that convergence will continue and even speed up in future years.

APPENDIX A

AICPA Code of Professional Conduct

AICPA Code of Professional Conduct

Composition, Applicability, and Compliance

The Code of Professional Conduct of the American Institute of Certified Public Accountants consists of two sections—(1) the Principles and (2) the Rules. The Principles provide the framework for the Rules, which govern the performance of professional services by members. The Council of the American Institute of Certified Public Accountants is authorized to designate bodies to promulgate technical standards under the Rules, and the bylaws require adherence to those Rules and standards.

The Code of Professional Conduct was adopted by the membership to provide guidance and rules to all members—those in public practice, in industry, in government, and in education—in the performance of their professional responsibilities.

Compliance with the Code of Professional Conduct, as with all standards in an open society, depends primarily on members' understanding and voluntary actions, secondarily on reinforcement by peers and public opinion, and ultimately on disciplinary proceedings, when necessary, against members who fail to comply with the Rules.

The Code of Conduct includes the following sections

- Introduction
- Section 50—Principles of Professional Conduct
- Section 90—Rules: Applicability and Definitions
- Section 100—Independence, Integrity, and Objectivity
- Section 200—General Standards Accounting Principles
- Section 300—Responsibilities to Clients
- Section 400—Responsibilities to Colleagues
- Section 500—Other Responsibilities and Practices
- ET Appendixes
- ET Topical Index

The complete Code of Conduct, updated for all Official Releases through January 2006, can be accessed on the AICPA's web site at http://www.aicpa.org/about/code/index.htm.

APPENDIX B

CPA Certificate and Permit to Practice Requirements

All CPA candidates must pass the Uniform CPA Examination to quality for the CPA certificate and permit to practice. A majority of states have enacted laws that require CPA candidates to meet the 150-hour education requirement by the year 2000. For information about the requirement in a particular state, please contact the state board of accountancy.

Jurisdiction	Age	Citizen	Required in State: Residency R, Employment E, or Office O
Alabama	19	Yes	Not required
Alaska	19	No	Not required
Arizona	18	No	Not required
Arkansas	N/A	No	R/E/O
California	18 (c)	No	Not required (waiver of exam applicants only)

(continued)

Jurisdiction	Age	Citizen	Required in State: Residency R, Employment E, or Office O
Colorado	N/A	No	Not required
Connecticut	N/A	No	Not required
Delaware	18	No	Not required
Dist. of Columbia	18	No	R/E (6 months)
Florida	N/A	No	Not required
Georgia	18	No	Not required
Guam	N/A	N/A	R (3 mos.)/E/O
Hawaii	18	No	Not required
Idaho	18	No	R (d)
Illinois	18	No	Not required
Indiana	18	No	R (60 days actual or 6 mos. legal residency)
Iowa	N/A	No	R/E/O
Kansas	N/A	No	Not required
Kentucky	18	No	Not required
Louisiana	18	No	R (1 year legal residency)
Maine	18	No	R/E/O
Maryland	18	No	Not required
Massachusetts	18	No	Not required
Michigan	18	No	R/E/O
Minnesota	18	No	R/E/O
Mississippi	N/A	N/A	R
Missouri	21	No	R/E/O
Montana	N/A	No	Not required
Nebraska	N/A	No	R/E/O
Nevada	N/A	No	Not required
New Hampshire	21	No	Not required
New Jersey	18	No	Not required

Appendix B: CPA Certificate and Permit to Practice Requirements

Jurisdiction	Age	Citizen	Required in State: Residency R, Employment E, or Office O
New Mexico	18	No	R/O
New York	21	No	Not required
North Carolina	18	Yes	Not required
North Dakota	N/A	No	R
Ohio	18	No	R/E/O
Oklahoma	N/A	No	R
Oregon	N/A	No	Not required
Pennsylvania	18	No	R/E or O
Puerto Rico	21	Yes	R/E/O
Rhode Island	N/A	No	R/E/O
South Carolina	18	No	Not required
South Dakota	N/A	No	Not required
Tennessee	N/A	No	R/E/O
Texas	N/A	No	Not required
Utah	N/A	No	Not required
Vermont	18	No	E or O
Virginia	N/A	No	Not required
Virgin Islands	21	Yes	R/E or O
Washington	N/A	No	Not required
West Virginia	18	No	R/E or O
Wisconsin	18	No	Not required
Wyoming	19	No	R/E or O

	Education	Experience		Experience That Qualifies	
Jurisdiction	College Education: Years/ Baccalaureate/ Graduate Study	Years	License/ Permit to Certificate	Public Accounting Experience Required to Practice	Acceptable Nonpublic Accounting Experience as Deemed Acceptable by the Board
Alabama	Baccalaureate 150-hours graduate	0	2	2	5
Alaska	Baccalaureate	2-3	2-3 (a)	2-3	4-6 (b)
Arizona	Baccalaureate	2	2 (a)	2	2
Arkansas	Baccalaureate	0	2	2	2
	Graduate	0	1	1	1
California	2	2-4	2-4	2-4	2-4
	Baccalaureate	2-3	2-3 (a)	2	2-4
Colorado	Baccalaureate	1	1 (a)	1	1
	Graduate	0	0 (a)	0	0
Connecticut	Baccalaureate	2-3	2-3	3	3
Delaware	2	0	2-4	4	4
	Baccalaureate	0	2	2	4
	Graduate	0	1	1	2
Dist. of Columbia	Baccalaureate	0	2	2	2
Florida	Baccalaureate	0	0 (a)	0	Not acceptable
	Graduate	0	0 (a)	0	0

Appendix B: CPA Certificate and Permit to Practice Requirements 199

Education

Jurisdiction	College Education: Years/ Baccalaureate/ Graduate Study
Georgia	Baccalaureate
Guam	Baccalaureate
	Graduate
Hawaii	Baccalaureate
	Graduate
Idaho	Baccalaureate
Illinois	Baccalaureate
Indiana	Baccalaureate
	Graduate
Iowa	Baccalaureate
Kansas	Baccalaureate
Kentucky	Baccalaureate
Louisiana	Baccalaureate
	Graduate

Experience

Years	License/Permit to Certificate
0	2
0	2
0	1
4.5	4.5 (a)
2	2 (a)
1	1 (a)
0	1
3	3 (a)
2	1
0	2
0	1-2 (l)
1-2	2 (a)
0	2
0	1

Experience That Qualifies

Public Accounting Experience Required to Practice	Acceptable Nonpublic Accounting Experience as Deemed Acceptable by the Board
2	5
2	2
1	1
4.5	Not acceptable
2	Not acceptable
2	2 (e)
1	1
3	3-6
3	3-6
2	Not acceptable
1-2 (l)	
(m)	2 (m)
2	Allowed (h)
1	Allowed (h)

(continued)

200 The CPA Profession: Opportunities, Responsibilities, and Services

	Education	Experience			
				Experience That Qualifies	
Jurisdiction	College Education: Years/ Baccalaureate/ Graduate Study	Years	License/ Permit to Certificate	Public Accounting Experience Required to Practice	Acceptable Nonpublic Accounting Experience as Deemed Acceptable by the Board
Maine	Baccalaureate	2	2	2	Allowed
	Graduate	1	1 (a)	1	Allowed
Maryland	Baccalaureate	0	0	0	0
Massachusetts	Baccalaureate	3	3 (a)	3	6-9
	Graduate	2	2 (a)	2	4-6
Michigan	Baccalaureate	2	2 (a)	2	2
		1	1 (a)		
Minnesota	0	5	1	6	Not acceptable
	2	3	2	5	Not acceptable
Mississippi	Baccalaureate + 150-hour rule	0	1	1	1
Missouri	Baccalaureate	0	2-4	2	2-4
Montana	Baccalaureate	0	1-2	1	2
Nebraska	Baccalaureate	0	2	2	3-3.5
Nevada	Baccalaureate	2	2 (a)	2	Allowed

Appendix B: CPA Certificate and Permit to Practice Requirements

Jurisdiction	Education: College Education: Years/ Baccalaureate/ Graduate Study	Experience Years	Experience License/ Permit to Certificate	Public Accounting Experience Required to Practice	Acceptable Nonpublic Accounting Experience as Deemed Acceptable by the Board
New Hampshire	Baccalaureate	0	2 (i)	2	2 (j)
	Graduate	0	1	1	11
New Jersey	Baccalaureate	1	1	2	2-4
New Mexico	Baccalaureate	1	1	1	3
New York	0	15	15(a)	15	Not acceptable
	Baccalaureate	2	2 (a)	2	2
	Graduate	1	1 (a)	1	1
North Carolina	2	4	4 (a)	4	Not acceptable
	Baccalaureate	2	2 (a)	2	5
	Graduate	1	1 (a)	1	4
North Dakota	0	4	4	4	4 (k)
	Baccalaureate	0	0	0	0
Ohio	Baccalaureate	2	2	2	6
	Graduate	1	1	1	4
Oklahoma	Baccalaureate	0	0	0	0
Oregon	Baccalaureate	2	2	1	1
	Graduate	1	1	1	1

(continued)

Jurisdiction	Education: College Education: Years/ Baccalaureate/ Graduate Study	Experience Years	Experience License/ Permit to Certificate	Experience That Qualifies Public Accounting Experience Required to Practice	Experience That Qualifies Acceptable Nonpublic Accounting Experience as Deemed Acceptable by the Board
Pennsylvania	Baccalaureate	2	2 (a)	2	2
	Graduate	1	1 (a)	1	1
Puerto Rico	Non-Accounting Baccalaureate	8	8 (a)	8	16
	Baccalaureate	0	0 (a)	0	0
Rhode Island	Baccalaureate	2	2 (a)	2	Not acceptable
	Graduate	1	1 (a)	1	Not acceptable
South Carolina	Baccalaureate	2	2 (a)	2	2
South Dakota	Associate	0	2	2	Not acceptable
	Baccalaureate	0	1	1	Not acceptable
Tennessee	Baccalaureate	0	1	1	Not acceptable
	150 hours	2	2 (a)	2	2-3
	Graduate	1	1 (a)	1	2
Texas	Baccalaureate	2	2 (a)	2	2
	150 hours	1	1 (a)	1	1
	Graduate	1	1 (a)	1	1
Utah	Baccalaureate	1	1	1	3
Vermont	60 semester hours	2	2	2	Acceptable

Appendix B: CPA Certificate and Permit to Practice Requirements

Education / Experience / Experience That Qualifies

Jurisdiction	College Education: Years/Baccalaureate/Graduate Study	Years	License/Permit to Certificate	Public Accounting Experience Required to Practice	Acceptable Nonpublic Accounting Experience as Deemed Acceptable by the Board
Virginia	Baccalaureate	1	1	1	3
Virgin Islands	0	6	6	6	Not acceptable
Washington	Baccalaureate	3	3	3	3
	Graduate	2	2	2	2
Washington	Baccalaureate	0	1	1	1
West Virginia	Baccalaureate	0	2	2	2
Wisconsin	Baccalaureate	3	3 (a)	3	3
Wyoming	Baccalaureate	0	2	2	Not acceptable

(a) There is no distinction between a license and a certificate.
(b) Based on the point system in which different kinds of experience carry with them different point values, one must accumulate 4 to 8 experience points according to the level of education attained.
(c) There is no minimum age to sit for the Uniform CPA Examination. However, one must be over 18 to be issued a certificate.
(d) Residency is required for examination applicants only.
(e) Equivalent experience may be longer than 2 calendar years.
(f) Person must have 6 months' auditing experience.

(continued)

(g) Only in certain agencies of state government, or 4 years experience and successful completion of the IRS examination.
(h) Acceptable equivalent experience may be 4 calendar years.
(i) In New Hampshire the license is referred to as a certificate.
(j) Governmental only qualifies.
(k) Governmental accounting or auditing can qualify.
(l) One year accounting experience under direct supervision of licensed CPA for permit to do tax and compilation work. Two years' accounting experience; one year with CPA firm, full-time, including 1,000 hours auditing, all under direct supervision of licensed CPA for permit to do all accounting, including audits and reviews.
(m) Candidates must be supervised by a CPA with an active permit to practice.

Source: Digest of State Accountancy Laws and State Board Regulations, American Institute of CPAs and National Association of State Boards of Accountancy, 1996, pp. 119-121. Reprinted with permission.

APPENDIX C

State Boards of Accountancy

Alabama State Board of Accountancy
RSA Plaza
770 Washington Avenue
Montgomery, AL 36130
Att: Boyd E. Nicholson, Jr., CPA
　Executive Director
Telephone: (334) 242-5700
Fax: (334) 242-2711

Alaska State Board of Public Accountancy
Department of Commerce and
　Economic Development
Division of Occupational Licensing
P.O. Box 110806
Juneau, AK 99811-0806
Att: Steven B. Snyde
　Licensing Examiner
Telephone: (907) 465-2580
Fax: (907) 465-2974
Web Site: http://www.state.ak.us/
　local/adpages/commerce/occ/
　ic.htm

Arizona State Board of Accountancy
3110 N. Nineteenth Avenue
Suite 140
Phoenix, AZ 85015-6038
Att: Ruth R. Lee
　Executive Director
Telephone: (602) 255-3648
Fax: (602) 255-1283

Arkansas State Board of Accountancy
101 East Capitol, Suite 430
Little Rock, AR 72201
Att: Rollie L. Friess, CPA
　Executive Director
Telephone: (501) 682-1520
Fax: (501) 682-5538

California State Board of Accountancy
2000 Evergreen Street, Suite 250
Sacramento, CA 95815-3832
Att: Carol B. Sigmann
 Executive Director
Telephone: (916) 263-3680
Fax: (916) 263-3674
E-mail: casboa@casboa.ca.gov

Colorado State Board of Accountancy
1560 Broadway, Suite 1370
Denver, CO 80202
Att: Mary Lou Burgess
 Administrator
Telephone: (303) 894-7800
Fax: (303) 894-7790
Web site: http://www.state.co.us

Connecticut State Board of Accountancy
Secretary of the State
30 Trinity Street, P.O. Box 150470
Hartford, CT 06115-0470
Att: David L. Guay
 Executive Director
Telephone: (860) 566-7835
Fax: (860) 566-5757

Delaware State Board of Accountancy
Cannon Building, Suite 203
P.O. Box 1401
Dover, DE 19903
Att: Sheila H. Wolfe
 Administrative Assistant
Telephone: (302) 739-4522
Fax: (302) 739-2711
E-mail: @board@prof#reg

District of Columbia Board of Accountancy
Department of Consumer and
 Regulatory Affairs
614 H Street, N.W., Room 923
c/o P.O. Box 37200
Washington, D.C. 20013-7200
Att: Harriette E. Andrews
 Administrator
Telephone: (202) 727-7468
Fax: (202) 727-8030

Florida Board of Accountancy
2610 N.W. 43rd Street
Suite 1A
Gainesville, FL 32606-4599
Att: Martha P. Willis
 Division Director
Telephone: (352) 955-2165
Fax: (352) 955-2164

Georgia State Board of Accountancy
166 Pryor Street, S.W.
Atlanta, GA 30303
Att: Barbara W. Kitchens
 Executive Director
Telephone: (404) 656-2281
Fax: (404) 651-9532

Guam Territorial Board of Public Accountancy
P.O. Box 5753
Agana, GU 96910
Att: Todd S. Smith, CPA
 Chairman
Telephone: (671) 646-3884
Fax: (671) 649-4932

Hawaii Board of Public Accountancy
Department of Commerce and
  Consumer Affairs
P.O. Box 3469
Honolulu, HI 96801-3469
Att: Verna Oda
  Executive Officer
Telephone: (808) 586-2694
Fax: (808) 586-2689

Idaho State Board of Accountancy
P.O. Box 83720
Boise, ID 83720-0002
Att: Patricia L. Johnson
  Executive Director
Telephone: (208) 334-2490
Fax: (208) 334-2615

Illinois Board of Examiners
10 Henry Administration Building
506 S. Wright Street
Urbana, IL 61801-3260
Att: Joanne Vician
  Executive Director
Telephone: (217) 333-4213
Fax: (217) 333-3126

Illinois Department of Professional Regulation
Public Accountancy Section
320 West Washington Street,
  3rd Floor
Springfield, IL 62786-0001
Att: Judy Vargas
  Manager
Telephone: (217) 785-0800
Fax: (217) 782-7645

Indiana Board of Accountancy
Indiana Professional Licensing
  Agency
Indiana Government Center South
302 West Washington Street,
  Room E034
Indianapolis, IN 46204-2246
Att: Nancy Smith
  Exam Coordinator
Telephone: (317) 232-5987
Fax: (317) 232-2312

Iowa Accountancy Examining Board
1918 S.E. Hulsizer Avenue
Ankeny, IA 50021-3941
Att: William M. Schroeder
  Executive Secretary
Telephone: (515) 281-4126
Fax: (515) 281-741 1
E-mail: bschroe@max.state.ia.us
Web site: http://www/state.ia.us/
  governmentacct/com/prof/
  acct.htm

Kansas Board of Accountancy
Landon State Office Building
900 S.W. Jackson, Suite 556
Topeka, KS 66612-1239
Att: Glenda S. Moore
  Executive Director
Telephone: (913) 296-2162

Kentucky State Board of Accountancy
332 West Broadway, Suite 310
Louisville, KY 40202-2115
Att: Susan G. Stopher
  Executive Director
Telephone: (502) 595-3037
Fax: (502) 595-4281

State Board of CPAs of Louisiana
1515 World Trade Center
2 Canal Street
New Orleans, LA 70130
Att: Mildred M. McGaha, CPA
 Executive Director
Telephone: (504) 566-1244
Fax: (504) 566-1252

Maine Board of Accountancy
Dept. of Professional & Financial
 Regulation
State House Station 35
Augusta, ME 04333
Att: Sandra Leach
 Board Clerk
Telephone: (207) 624-8603
Fax: (207) 624-8637

Maryland State Board of Public Accountancy
501 St. Paul Place, 9th Floor
Baltimore, MD 21202-2272
Att: Sue Mays
 Executive Director
Telephone: (410) 333-6322
Fax: (410) 333-6314
Web site: http://www.dllr.state.md.us/dllr

Massachusetts Board of Public Accountancy
Saltonstall Building, Government
 Center
100 Cambridge Street, Room 1315
Boston, MA 02202
Att: Leo H. Bonarrigo, CPA
 Executive Secretary
Telephone: (617) 727-1806
Fax: (617) 727-0139

Michigan Board of Accountancy
Department Of Commerce-BOPR
P.O. Box 30018
Lansing, MI 48909-7518
Att: Suzanne U. Jolicoeur
 Licensing Administrator
Telephone: (517) 373-0682
Fax: (517) 373-2795

Minnesota State Board of Accountancy
85 East 7th Place, Suite 125
St. Paul, MN 55101
Att: Dennis J. Poppenhagen
 Executive Director
Telephone: (612) 296-7937
Fax: (612) 282-2644

Mississippi State Board of Public Accountancy
653 North State Street
Jackson, MS 39202
Att: Susan M. Harris, CPA
 Executive Director
Telephone: (601) 354-7320
Fax: (601) 354-7290

Missouri State Board of Accountancy
P.O. Box 613
Jefferson City, MO 65102-0613
Att: William E. Boston III
 Executive Director
Telephone: (573) 751-0012
Fax: (573) 751-0890
E-mail: bboston@mail.state.mo.us

Montana State Board of Public Accountants
Arcade Building, Lower Level
111 North Jackson
P.O. Box 200513
Helena, MT 59620-0513
Att: Susanne M. Criswell
  Administrator
Telephone: (406) 444-3739
Fax: (406) 444-1667

Nebraska State Board of Public Accountancy
P.O. Box 94725
Lincoln, NE 68509-4725
Att: Annette L. Harmon
  Executive Director
Telephone: (402) 471-3595
Fax: (402) 471-4484

Nevada State Board of Accountancy
200 S. Virginia Street, Suite 670
Reno, NV 89501-2408
Att: N. Johanna Brand
  Executive Director
Telephone: (702) 786-0231
Fax: (702) 786-0234

New Hampshire Board of Accountancy
57 Regional Drive
Concord, NH 03301
Att: Louise O. MacMillan
  Executive Assistant to the Board
Telephone: (603) 271-3286
Fax: (603) 271-2856

New Jersey State Board of Accountancy
P.O. Box 45000
Newark, NJ 07101
Att: Jay J. Church
  Executive Director
Telephone: (201) 504-6380
Fax: (201) 648-3355

New Mexico State Board of Public Accountancy
1650 University N.E., Suite 400-A
Albuquerque, NM 87102
Att: Trudy Beverley
  Executive Director
Telephone: (505) 841-9108
Fax: (505) 841-9113

New York State Board for Public Accountancy
State Education Department
Cultural Education Center,
  Room 3013
Albany, NY 12230
Att: C. Daniel Stubbs, Jr., CPA
  Executive Secretary
Telephone: (518) 474-3836
Fax: (518) 473-6995

North Carolina State Board of CPA Examiners
1101 Oberlin Road, Suite 104
P.O. Box 12827
Raleigh, NC 27605-2827
Att: Robert N. Brooks
  Executive Director
Telephone: (919) 733-4222
Toll Free: (800) 211-7930
  Licensing & Exam Applications
  Only
Fax: (919) 733-4209
E-mail: 75361.3404@compuserve.com

North Dakota State Board of Accountancy
2701 South Columbia Road
Grand Forks, ND 58201
Att: Jim Abbott
  Executive Director
Telephone: (701) 775-7100
Fax: (701) 775-7430
E-mail: 103132.2525@compuserve.com

Accountancy Board of Ohio
77 South High Street, 18th Floor
Columbus, OH 43266-0301
Att: Timothy D. Haas
  Executive Director
Telephone: (614) 466-4135
Fax: (614) 466-2628

Oklahoma Accountancy Board
4545 Lincoln Boulevard, Suite 165
Oklahoma City, OK 73105-3413
Att: Diana Collinsworth
  Executive Director
Telephone: (405) 521-2397
Fax: (405) 521-3118

Oregon Board of Accountancy
3218 Pringle Road SE, Suite 110
Salem, OR 97302-6307
Att: Karen DeLorenzo
  Administrator
Telephone: (503) 378-4181
Fax: (503) 378-3575
E-mail: www.boa@teleport.com

Pennsylvania State Board of Accountancy
613 Transportation & Safety
  Building
P.O. Box 2649
Harrisburg, PA 17105-2649
Att: Dorna J. Thorpe
  Board Administrator
Telephone: (717) 783-1404
Fax: (717) 787-7769

Puerto Rico Board of Accountancy
Box 3271, Old San Juan Station
San Juan, PR 00902-3271
Att: Antonio Cruz Murphy
  Director
Telephone: (787) 722-2122
Fax: (787) 721-8399

Rhode Island Board of Accountancy
Department of Business
  Regulation
233 Richmond Street, Suite 236
Providence, RI 02903-4236
Att: Norma A. MacLeod
  Executive Secretary
Telephone: (401) 277-3185
Fax: (401) 277-6654

South Carolina Board of Accountancy
Board of Accountancy
Suite 101
P.O. Box 11329
Columbia, SC 29211-1329
Att: Robert W. Wilkes, Jr.. CPA
  Administrator
Telephone: (803) 734-4228
Fax: (803) 734-9571

South Dakota Board of Accountancy
301 East 14th Street, Suite 200
Sioux Falls, SD 57104
Att: Lynn J. Bethke
  Executive Director
Telephone: (605) 367-5770
Fax: (605) 367-5773

Tennessee State Board of Accountancy
500 James Robertson Parkway,
  2nd Floor
Nashville, TN 37243-1141
Att: Darrel Tongate, CPA
  Executive Director
  Don Hummel
  Director of Administration
Telephone: (615) 741-2550
Fax: (615) 532-8800

Texas State Board of Public Accountancy
333 Guadalupe Tower III, Suite 900
Austin, TX 78701-3900
Att: William Treacy
  Executive Director
Telephone: (512) 505-5500
Fax: (512) 505-5575

Utah Board of Accountancy
160 East 300 South
P.O. Box 45805
Salt Lake City, UT 84145
Att: Dan S. Jones, Esq.
  Administrator
Telephone: (801) 530-6720
Fax: (801) 530-6511

Vermont Board of Public Accountancy
Pavilion Office Building
Montpelier, VT 05609-1106
Att: Loris Rollins
  Staff Assistant
Telephone: (802) 828-2837
Fax: (802) 828-2496

Virginia Board for Accountancy
3600 West Broad Street
Richmond, VA 23230-4917
Att: Nancy T. Feldman
  Assistant Director
Telephone: (804) 367-8590
Fax: (804) 367-2474

Virgin Islands Board of Public Accountancy
P.O. Box 3016, No 1 A Gallows Bay
  Mkt, Plaza Christiansted
St. Croix, VI 00822
Att: Pablo O'Neil, CPA
Telephone: (809) 773-4305
Fax: (809) 773-9850

Washington State Board of Accountancy
P.O. Box 9131
210 East Union, Suite A
Olympia, WA 98507
Att: Carey L. Rader, CPA
  Executive Director
Telephone: (360) 753-2585
Fax: (360) 664-9190
E-mail: 103124.2013@compuserve.com

West Virginia Board of Accountancy
200 L&S Building
812 Quarrier Street
Charleston, WV 25301-2695
Att: JoAnn Walker
  Executive Director
Telephone: (304) 558-3557
Fax: (304) 558-1325

Wisconsin Accounting Examining Board
1400 East Washington Avenue
P.O. Box 8935
Madison, WI 53708-8935
Att: Patricia H. Reuter
  Bureau Director
Telephone: (608) 266-1397
Fax: (608) 267-0644

Wyoming Board of Certified Public Accountants
First Bank Building
2020 Carey, Suite 100
Cheyenne, WY 82002
Att: Peggy Morgando
  Executive Director
Telephone: (307) 777-7551
Fax: (307) 777-3796
E-mail: pmorga@missc.state.wy.us

Source: Digest of State Accountancy Laws and State Board Regulations, American Institute of CPAs and National Association of State Boards of Accountancy, 1996, pp. 159-162. Reprinted with permission. Updated by the authors for this volume, 2006.

APPENDIX D

State/Jurisdiction CPA Societies

Alabama Society of CPAs
1103 South Perry Street
Montgomery, AL 36103
Phone: (334) 834-7650
E-mail: webmaster@ascpa.org
http://www.ascpa.org

Alaska Society of CPAs
341 West Tudor, Suite 105
Anchorage, AK 99503
Phone: (907) 562-4334
　　　　(800) 292-1754
Fax: 　 (907) 562-4025
E-mail: akcpa@alaska.net
http://www.accountingnet.com/
　society/ak/

Arizona Society of CPAs
432 N. 44th Street, Suite 300
Phoenix, AZ 85008-7602
Phone: (602) 273-0100
　　　　(888) 237-0700
　　　　In State Only
Fax: 　 (602) 275-2752
http://www.ascpa.com

Arkansas Society of CPAs
415 North McKinley, Suite 970
Little Rock, AR 72205-3022
Phone: (501) 664-8739
　　　　(800) 482-8739
　　　　In State Only
Fax: 　 (501) 664-8320
E-mail: ascpa@arcpa.org
http://www.arcpa.org

California Society of CPAs
E-mail: wiremail@calcpa.org
http://www.calcpa.org
Main Office
275 Shoreline Drive
Redwood City, CA 94065-1412
Phone: (415) 802-2600
Fax: (415) 802-2225
Glendale Office
330 North Brand Boulevard,
  Suite 710
Glendale, CA 91203-2308
Phone: (818) 246-6000
Fax: (818) 246-4017
Sacramento Office
1201 K Street, Suite 1000
Sacramento, CA 95814-3922
Phone: (916) 441-5351
Fax: (916) 441-5354

Colorado Society of CPAs
7979 East Tufts Avenue, Suite 500
Denver, CO 80237-2843
Phone: (303) 773-2877
  (800) 523-9082
Fax: (303) 773-6344
E-mail: cpa-staff@cscpa.denver.
  co.us
http://www.cocpa.org

Connecticut Society of CPAs
179 Allyn Street, Suite 201
Hartford, CT 06103
Phone: (860) 525-1153
  (800) 232-2232
  In State Only
Fax: (860) 549-3596
E-mail: cscpa@cs-cpa.org
http://www.cs-cpa.org

Delaware Society of CPAs
28 The Commons
3520 Silverside Road
Wilmington, DE 19810
Phone: (302) 478-7442
Fax: (302) 478-7412
http://www.accountingnet.com/
  society/de

Florida Institute of CPAs
325 West College Avenue
Tallahassee, FL 32301
Phone: (904) 224-2727
Fax: (904) 222-8190
E-mail: webmaster@ficpa.org
http://www.ficpa.org

Georgia Society of CPAs
3340 Peachtree Road NE,
  Suite 2700
Atlanta, GA 30326-1026
Phone: (404) 231-8676
  (800) 330-8889
  In State Only
Fax: (404) 237-1291
E-mail: gscpaweb@gscpa.org
http://www.gscpa.org

Greater Washington Society of CPAs
1023 15th Street N.W. 8th Floor
Washington, D.C. 20005-2602
Phone: (202) 789-1844
Fax: (202) 789-1847
E-mail: info@gwscpa.org
http://www.gwscpa.org

Guam Society of CPAs
361 South Marine Drive
Tamuning, GU 96911
Phone: (671) 646-3884
Fax: (671) 649-4265

Appendix D: State/Jurisdiction CPA Societies

Hawaii Society of CPAs
P.O. Box 1754
Honolulu, HI 96806
Phone: (808) 537-9475
Fax: (808) 537-3520
http://www.accountingnet.com/society/hi

Idaho Society of CPAs, Inc.
250 Bobwhite Court, Suite 240
Boise, ID 83706
Phone: (208) 344-6261
Fax: (208) 344-8984
http://www.idcpa.org

Illinois CPA Society
http://www.icpas.org
Chicago Office
222 S. Riverside Plaza, 16th Floor
Chicago, IL 60606
Phone: (312) 993-0393
        (800) 993-0393
        In State Only
Fax: (312) 993-9432
Springfield Office
511 W. Capitol, Suite 101
Springfield, IL 62704
Phone: (217) 789-7914
        (800) 572-9870
        In State Only
Fax: (217) 789-7924

Indiana CPA Society
8250 Woodfield Crossing Blvd., No. 305
Indianapolis, IN 46240-2054
Phone: (317) 726-5000
Fax: (317) 726-5005
E-mail: info@incpas.org
http://www.incpas.org

Iowa Society of CPAs
950 Office Park Road, Suite 300
West Des Moines, IA 50265-2548
Phone: (515) 223-8161
Fax: (515) 223-7347

Kansas Society of CPAs
400 Croix P.O. Box 5654
Topeka, KS 66605-0654
Phone: (913) 267-6460
Fax: (913) 267-9278
http://www.copilot.greensoft.com/kscpa

Kentucky Society of CPAs
1735 Alliant Avenue
Lousville, KY 40299-6326
Phone: (502) 266-5272
        (800) 292-1754
        In State Only
Fax: (502) 261-9512
E-mail: kycpa@kycpa.org
http://www.kycpa.org

Society of Louisiana CPAs
2400 Veterans Blvd., Suite 500
Kenner, LA 70062
Phone: (504) 464-1040
Fax: (504) 469-7930

Maine Society of CPAs
153 US Rt. 1, Suite 8
Scarborough, ME 04074-9053
Phone: (207) 883-6090
        (800) 660-2721
        In State Only
Fax: (207) 883-6211
http://www.mecpa.org

Maryland Association of CPAs
1300 York Road, Building C
P.O. Box 4417
Lutherville, MD 21094
Phone: (410) 296-6250
Fax: (410) 296-8713
E-mail: Info@macpa.org
http://www.macpa.org

Massachusetts Society of CPAs, Inc.
105 Chauncy St.
Boston, MA 02111
Phone: (617) 556-4000
Fax: (617) 556-4126
E-mail: mscpa@mscpaonline@org
http://www.mscpaonline.org

Michigan Association of CPAs
28116 Orchard Lake Road
Farmington Hills, MI 48333-9054
Phone: (248) 855-2288
Fax: (248) 855-9122
E-mail: macpa@michcpa.org
http://www.michcpa.org

Minnesota Society of CPAs
7900 Xerxes Ave. So. STE 1230
Bloomington, MN 55431
Phone: (612) 831-2707
(800) 331-4288
In State Only
Fax: (612) 831-7875
http://www.accountingnet.com/society/mn

Mississippi Society of CPAs
Highland Village, Suite 246
Jackson, MS 39236
Phone: (601) 366-3473
(800) 772-1099
In State Only
Fax: (601) 981-6079
E-mail: mscpa@compuserve.com
http://www.accountingnet.com/society/ms

Missouri Society of CPAs
275 N. Lindbergh Blvd., Suite 10
P.O. Box 419042
St. Louis, MO 63141-9042
Phone: (314) 997-7966
(800) 264-7966
http://www.accountingnet.com/society/mo

Montana Society of CPAs
P.O. Box 138
Helena, MT 59624-0138
Diamond Block, 3rd Floor, 44 West 6th Ave.
Helena, MT 59601
Phone: (406) 442-7301
Fax: (406) 443-7278
http://www.accountingnet.com/society/mt

Nebraska Society of CPAs
635 South 14th Street, Suite 330
Lincoln, NE 68508
Phone: (402) 476-8482
Fax: (402) 476-8731

Nevada Society of CPAs
5250 Neil Road, Suite 205
Reno, NV 89502
Phone: (702) 478-7442
(800) 554-8254
Fax: (702) 826-7942
http://www.accountingnet.com/society/nv

New Hampshire Society of CPAs
Three Executive Park Drive
Bedford, NH 03110
Phone: (603) 622-1999
Fax: (603) 626-0204
E-mail: info@nhscpa.org
http://www.nhscpa.org

New Jersey Society of CPAs
425 Eagle Rock Avenue
Roseland, NJ 07068
Phone: (201) 226-4494
Fax: (201) 226-7425

New Mexico Society of CPAs
1650 University NE, Suite 450
Albuquerque, NM 87102-1733
Phone: (505) 246-1699
(800) 926-2522
In State Only
Fax: (505) 246-1686
E-mail: nmcpa@nmcpa.org
http://www.nmcpa.org

New York State Society of CPAs
530 Fifth Avenue, Fifth Floor
New York, NY 10036-5101
Phone: (212) 719-8300
Fax: (212) 719-3364
http://www.nysscpa.org

North Carolina Society of CPAs
P.O. Box 80188
Raleigh, NC 27623
3100 Gateway Center Blvd.
Morrisville, NC 27560
Phone: (919) 469-1040
Fax: (919) 469-3959
E-mail: ncacpa@interpath.com
http://www.ncacpa.org

North Dakota Society of CPAs
2701 South Columbia Road
Grand Forks, ND 58201
Phone: (701) 775-7100
Fax: (701) 775-7430
http://www.ndscpa.org

Ohio Society of CPAs
535 Metro Place South
P.O. Box 1810
Dublin, OH 43017-7810
Phone: (614) 764-2727
(800) 686-2727
Fax: (614) 764-5880
E-mail: oscpa@ohio-cpa.com
http://www.ohioscpa.com

Oklahoma Society of CPAs
1900 NW Expressway St., Suite 910
Oklahoma City, OK 73118-1804
Phone: (405) 841-3800
(800) 522-8261
In State Only
Fax: (405) 841-3801
http://www.oscpa.com

Oregon Society of CPAs
P.O. Box 4555
Beaverton, OR 97076-4555
10206 SW Laurel Street
Beaverton, OR 97005-3209
Phone: (503) 641-7200
(800) 255-1470
In State Only
Fax: (503) 626-2942
E-mail: oscpa@orcpa.org
http://www.orcpa.org

Pennsylvania Institute of CPAs
1608 Walnut Street, 3rd Floor
Philadelphia, PA 19103-5457
Phone: (215) 735-2635
(888) 272-2001
In State Only
Fax: (215) 735-3694
http://www.picpa.com

Colegio de Contadores Publicos Autorizados de Puerto Rico
Call Box 71352
San Juan, PR 00936-1352
Edif. Capital Center Ave.
Arterial Hostos No. 3
Buzon 1401
Hato Rey, PR 00918
Phone: (809) 754-1950
Fax: (809) 753-0212
http://www.prccpa.org

Rhode Island Society of CPAs
One Franklin Square
Providence, RI 02903
Phone: (401) 331-5720
Fax: (401) 454-5780
http://www.accountingnet.com/
    society/ri

South Carolina Association of CPAs
570 Chris Drive
West Columbia, SC 29169
Phone: (803) 791-4181
Fax: (803) 791-4196
E-mail: info@scacpa.org
http://www.scacpa.org

South Dakota CPA Society
P.O. Box 1798
Sioux Falls, SD 57101-1798
1000 West Ave. North No. 1000
Sioux Falls, SD 57104
Phone: (605) 334-3848
Fax: (605) 334-8595

Tennessee Society of CPAs
201 Powell Place
P.O. Box 187
Brentwood, TN 37024-0187
Phone: (615) 377-3825
(800) 762-0272
In State Only
Fax: (615) 377-3904
E-mail: tncpa@tncpa.org
http://www.tncpa.org

Texas Society of CPAs
14860 Montfort, Suite 150
Dallas, TX 75240
Phone: (972) 687-8500
(800) 428-0272
Fax: (972) 687-8646
http://www.tscpa.org

Utah Association of CPAs
455 East 400 South, Suite 202
Salt Lake City, UT 84111-3011
Phone: (801) 359-3533
(800) 676-2776
Fax: (801) 359-3534
http://www.uacpa.org

Vermont Society of CPAs
100 State Street
Montpelier, VT 05602
Phone: (802) 229-4939
Fax: (802) 223-0360
E-mail: vscpa@sover.net
http://www.accountingnet.com/society/vt

Virginia Society of CPAs
P.O. Box 4620
Glen Allen, VA 23058-4620
4309 Cox Road
Glen Allen, VA 23060
Phone: (804) 270-5344
Fax: (804) 273-1741
http://www.vscpa.com

Virgin Islands Society of CPAs
P.O. Box 1734
Kings Hill
St. Croix, VI 00851
Phone: (809) 776-1852
Fax: (809) 776-1845

Washington Society of CPAs
902 140th Avenue NE
Bellevue, WA 98005-3480
Phone: (425) 644-4800
Fax: (425) 562-8853
E-mail: memberservices@wscpa.org
http://www.wscpa.org

West Virgiana Society of CPAs
P.O. Box 1142
Charleston, WV 25324
Phone: (304) 342-5461
               (800) 352-3855
Fax: (304) 344-4636
http://www.wvscpa.org

Wisconsin Society of CPAs
P.O. Box 1010
Brookfield, WI 53008-1010
235 N. Executive Drive, No. 200
Brookfield, WI 53005
Phone: (414) 785-0445
Fax: (414) 785-0838

Wyoming Society of CPAs
1721 Warren Avenue
Cheyenne, WY 82001
Phone: (307) 634-7039
Fax: (307) 634-5110

Source: Compiled by Gokhan Alanya, Graduate Assistant, University of Miami, 1997. Updated by the authors for this volume, 2006.

APPENDIX E

A Historical Perspective

> *Throughout the last hundred years, the profession has made a significant contribution not only to the operations of the capital markets but also to society as a whole. The certified public accountant has long held a position of great responsibility and trust, serving the public by assuring that the highest standards are maintained in the preparation of financial statements.*
>
> William S. Kanaga, J. Michael Cook, and Philip B. Chenok, 1987[1]

Introduction

This appendix gives a perspective on the origin, development, and ethical concepts of the CPA profession. This background should help you to understand the profession's current structure. The personal responsibility of today's CPAs to their peers, clients, and the public are part of a system of oversight by governmental and self-regulatory institutions that have developed over the past century. Writing in 1904, Arthur Lowes Dickinson, one of the profession's early leaders noted:

---

[1] William S. Kanaga, J. Michael Cook, and Philip B. Chenok, "Letter to the Membership," *Journal of Accountancy*, (May 1987): 9.

The Profession of Public Accountant, in the modern sense of the term, is a product of the Nineteenth Century, and owes its existence and progress to the great expansion of industry and commerce for which that period is remarkable, and in particular to the rapid growth of . . . the joint stock company or industrial corporation.[2]

Similarly, the services offered by CPAs today are a product of the development of the industrial enterprise and the capital markets in the United States.

Where and When Did the Profession Begin?

The roots of the CPA profession lie in the United Kingdom. Individuals holding themselves out as public accountants were noted to exist in the early 1700s in both the United States and United Kingdom. However, the organization of individuals into professional groups began at a later date.[3] Scholars trace the organized profession to a U.S. visit in 1886 by Edwin Guthrie, a U.K. chartered accountant.[4] In the United Kingdom, several societies of chartered accountants were in place by 1880. Formed under royal grants or "charters" that constituted public recognition of their professional status, these societies operated privately, without formal legislative licensure.

Societies developed the chartered accountant (CA). The societies assumed responsibility for evaluating and regulating entry-level competence for professionals. They were also responsible for the ongoing regulation of the United Kingdom accountancy professional in these early times and continue to maintain the emphasis on professional self-regulation today. The British government has never attempted to regulate conditions for entry to the accountancy profession. These conditions have remained under the control of the

---

[2] Arthur L. Dickinson, *The Duties and Responsibilities of the Public Accountant* (Price Waterhouse & Co., 1904).

[3] Gary J. Previts and Barbara D. Merino, *A History of Accounting in America* (John Wiley & Sons, Inc., 1979): 9.

[4] James D. Edwards and Paul J. Miranti, Jr., "The AICPA: A Professional Institution in a Dynamic Society," *Journal of Accountancy*, (May 1987): 22.

accountancy bodies.[5] The role of legislation in the United Kingdom, however, did assist the profession's development, since legislative initiatives created the market for the CA's services by mandating, in 1948, that audits of public companies be conducted by chartered, incorporated, or certified accountants.[6]

In the United States, private-sector activity during the post-Civil War period included groups such as the Institute of Accounts (New York). The Institute was originally formed as the Institute of Accountants and Bookkeepers in 1882 to provide accounting education and literature, and it remained in operation until 1908.[7] Private-sector activity in the organized public accountancy profession continued with the formation in 1887 of the American Association of Public Accountants (AAPA).

Rivalry existed between these two organizations. The Institute of Accounts promoted a CPA law in New York which required, among other things, that a CPA be a U.S. citizen. This was disadvantageous to the many British members of the AAPA. Ultimately, the two groups reached a compromise and the final legislation required that New York CPAs either be U.S. citizens or have duly declared to become a citizen. Unlike in the United Kingdom, the U.S. CPA designation was a result of legislative authority, rather than professional associations.

How Did the Certification Requirements Evolve?

Initially, the Institute of Accounts and American Association of Public Accountants provided certificates of proficiency to their members based on examination or experience.[8] Possession of such a certificate might indicate proficiency in the subject. However, it did not qualify the certificate holder to perform any duties beyond those of "noncertified" accountants.

---

[5] R. H. Parker, "The Development of the Accountancy Profession in Britain to the Early Twentieth Century Monograph Five" (The Academy of Accounting Historians, 1986, School of Accountancy James Madison University): 46.

[6] See footnote 5, p. 39.

[7] Previts and Merino, *A History of Accounting in America*: 93.

[8] Dale L. Flesher, Paul J. Miranti, and Gary J. Previts, "The First Century of the CPA," *Journal of Accountancy* (October 1996): 51.

The first state law establishing the CPA was approved in New York on April 17, 1896. Legislation provided that individuals practicing public accounting since January 1, 1890, could waive the CPA examination. In 1896 and 1897, 108 individuals obtained the certificate under this provision. Another four individuals received certificates upon completing the first CPA examination, offered in December 1896.[9] After passage of the New York legislation, the other states passed similar provisions. By 1967, with passage in Guam, 54 states and jurisdictions (for example, Puerto Rico, Virgin Islands) had CPA legislation.[10]

Siegel and Rigsby studied the development of education and experience requirements for CPAs from 1915 through 1985. In 1915, 26 out of 38 states required at least a high school education for the CPA certificate. At that time, college was not required. By 1985, 47 out of 54 states and jurisdictions required some college education, while the remaining seven required a high school education. Experience requirements also existed during this period. Seigel and Rigsby report that, on average, 1.79 years of experience were required for the CPA in 1915. This number has varied over time and in 1985 was 2.39 years on average. Before 1969 continuing education was not required. By 1985, 45 out of 54 states or jurisdictions had legislated continuing education requirements.[11]

The passage of legislation restricted the use of the CPA designation to those who met the regulations of the state or jurisdiction. Additionally, it restricted certain activities like attest services to CPAs. Legislation, therefore, provided the CPA with a "franchise" to perform services. These services could only be performed by CPAs.

The formation of state CPA societies followed CPA legislation. The New York State Society of Certified Public Accountants (NYSSCPA) was formed in 1897 by five individuals, four of whom were members of the Institute of Accounts.[12] One of the principal functions of the NYSSCPA was to promote the CPA designation as the

---

[9] Previts and Merino, *A History of Accounting in America*: 98.

[10] Philip H. Seigel and John R. Rigsby, "An Analysis of the Development of Education and Experience Requirements for CPAs," *Research in Accounting Regulation* (Volume 3, 1989): 45-68.

[11] See footnote 10.

[12] Larissa S. Kyj and George C. Romeo, "Paving the Way for the NYSSCPA: The Institute of Accounts," *The CPA Journal* (June 1997): 11.

"sole badge of professional competence."[13] Similar societies appeared in other states as CPA legislation was adopted throughout the country. Over time, these societies have promoted the CPA and provided a source of support and education for practicing CPAs. For example, today state societies provide extensive continuing education courses to update the accounting, audit, tax, and consulting skills of CPAs.

How Did Professional Services Evolve in the Early Years of the Profession?

Professional accountants were providing a wide variety of services before receipt of the legislative franchise discussed above. As early as 1718, individual accountants advertised their services in such activities as keeping merchant and shopkeeper books.[14] In the early 1800s, other professional services included serving as a trustee for estates, creditors, bankruptcies, and partnership dissolutions. The conclusion of the Civil War in 1865 led to an increase in the scope of CPA services, as noted by Mednick and Previts:

> The industrialization following the Civil War set the stage for expanded accounting services in an economy that had previously been characterized substantially by trading and agricultural activities. As railroads, steel mills and fabricating and manufacturing companies emerged, complex cost and other calculations became necessary. At the same time, providers of business capital, including the banking community and investors, began to concern themselves with measuring the results of operations of major corporate enterprises in which large debt and equity positions were held. The need for consistent, impartial and accurate financial reports, which could be used to evaluate these investments, created steady demand for the services of public accountants who were both competent and free of undue influence—having no axe to grind.[15]

---

[13] Paul J. Miranti, *Accountancy Comes of Age: The Development of an American Profession, 1886-1940* (The University of North Carolina Press, 1990): 58.

[14] Previts and Merino, *A History of Accounting in America*: 9.

[15] Mednick, Robert and Gary J. Previts, "The Scope of CPA Services: A View of the Future From the Perspective of a Century of Progress," *Journal of Accountancy* (May 1987): 222.

An analysis of services provided in 1880 by a large U.K. accounting firm shows that 72 percent of fees resulted from insolvency work, while 10 percent came from auditing services.[16] Over the next 25 years the proportion of auditing work grew substantially to about 58 percent of services. An advertisement by Selden R. Hopkins in 1880 reflects the type of services provided at that time by a sole practitioner:

> Will render assistance to lawyers in the examination of accounts in litigation; aid agents and administrators of estates in adjusting accounts. Will give counsel upon improved methods of keeping the accounts of corporated companies. Assists book-keepers and business men in straightening out intricate and improperly kept books. Adjusts complicated partnership accounts. Examines books for stockholders and creditors.[17]

The appearance and growth of audit services in this period was independent of any legal requirements for an audit. The need for audit service increased with the passage of the Securities Acts of 1933 and 1934. The Securities Acts followed the 1929 stock market crash and the failure of a pyramid scheme created by Ivan Kreuger using stock in a publicly traded company.

The Securities Acts required that financial statements of public companies be certified by independent public or certified public accountants. The passage of these acts gave public accountants an expanded franchise and emphasized the importance of the concept of independence. The formation of the Securities and Exchange Commission (SEC) to oversee these acts provided additional regulatory structure and responsibilities to the profession. CPAs are subject to the authority of the SEC as it relates to the SEC's oversight of capital markets. Additionally, while the SEC has the legal authority to establish accounting principles for publicly traded entities, the SEC has largely delegated that responsibility to the accounting profession.

Other legislation enacted throughout the years created new opportunities for CPAs to use their skills in providing additional services to clients. The passage of tax legislation is one of the main

---

[16] See footnote 15.

[17] Advertisement by Selden R. Hopkins in *The Book-keeper*, November 23, 1880, as cited in Mednick and Previts, "The Scope of CPA Services," (May 1987): 222.

sources of opportunity. Beginning in 1861 a variety of tax acts was passed. Initially taxes were of a temporary nature or applied only to businesses. With the passage of the Sixteenth Amendment to the Constitution, taxation of individuals became common. The importance of taxes to both individuals and corporations has grown over time:

> In 1939 fewer than 6% of all individuals in the United States were legally required to pay any federal income tax. By the end of World War II, over 74% of a larger population had to pay it. During these six years, the top marginal rate on taxable corporate income doubled, from 19% to 38%, while the top marginal rate on individual incomes increased from 79% to 94%. This rapid expansion in the taxpaying population, along with the exceedingly high marginal rates for individuals, soon made the federal income tax dominate the U.S. tax system....
>
> The rapidly increasing complexity of the income tax rules between 1945 and 1986 therefore made the services of the CPA and other tax practitioners indispensable for many taxpayers. Sophisticated investors as well as general business managers soon discovered that it is unwise to engage in even routine business or personal transactions without first consulting tax advisers to determine the most advantageous ways of arranging them.[18]

Through the years, CPAs have offered a variety of services other than audit and tax. Today these services are generally classified in the broad category term, *consulting*. While, for a time, audit and tax services dominated CPA services, consulting began to play a major role during the 1950s and 1960s.[19] This growth caused concern since a CPA often provided attest (audit) and consulting services to the same client, which created the appearance of a potential conflict. On the other hand, the provision of such services improved the CPA's ability to understand the client's business and, therefore, provide a more effective audit. The Independence Standards Board operates in the AICPA and under the oversight of the SEC to deal with these types of issues. The issue of independence came to the forefront in recent years as consulting revenues began to exceed audit revenues in many cases. As a result, most large accounting firms have spun off

---

[18] Ray M. Sommerfeld and John E. Easton, "The CPA's Tax Practice Today—and How It Got That Way," *Journal of Accountancy* (May 1987): 166.

[19] Robert Mednick and Gary J. Previts, "The Scope of CPA Services," (May 1987): 226-7.

their consulting businesses into separate and autonomous companies. This development is examined throughout this publication.

The types of services within each area (attest, tax, and consulting) have evolved and continue to evolve. While the focus of an audit was initially on financial statements, complex business transactions and the need by capital markets for information (other than items such as profit and loss or total assets) have led to greater disclosures of both financial and nonfinancial information.

Increased disclosure has provided additional responsibilities as well as opportunities for CPAs. Recent professional committees, such as the AICPA Special Committee on Financial Reporting and the AICPA Special Committee on Assurance Services, are evidence of the further expansion of CPA services. The Special Committee on Financial Reporting (also known as the Jenkins Committee) demonstrated a need to move from financial reporting to business reporting, incorporating the need for more nonfinancial types of information. The Special Committee on Assurance Services (also known as the Elliott Committee) proposed broadening the scope of attest services to areas outside the traditional financial statement audit.

How Did CPA Ideals Evolve?

Ethical rules are a way to explicitly state a CPA's duties and responsibilities to others. The codification of ethical rules for CPAs happened well after the first CPA examination was administered in December, 1896. Nevertheless, first question in the auditing section of the first CPA examination was: "Give a brief outline of the duties of an auditor and his responsibilities." The recommended answer provided what we might call the traditional altruistic view:

> In the absence of any legal or specific definement, the duties as well as the responsibilities of an auditor must be regarded from purely ideal and moral stand points. . . .[20]

The emphasis on personal responsibility based on ideal and moral standpoints is key. It represents a belief in the role of the individual and the values that educated professionals were expected to

---

[20] F. Broaker and R. Chapman, *The American Accountants Manual*, Vol. 1. (New York: 1897): 45.

uphold. These values were similar to those which were the basis of audit practice in the more established British profession.

The accountancy profession in Britain, formed in the Victorian era, demonstrated an orientation to the reputed high virtue of that period. Professor Dicksee was a British author of a series of texts on auditing which were also widely read in the United States. He listed the desirable qualities of an auditor as follows: "Tact, caution, firmness, fairness, good temper, courage, integrity, discretion, industry, judgment, patience, clear-headedness and reliability." And, he said, ". . . in accountancy . . . it is only he who aims at absolute perfection who can expect to attain even to a decent mediocrity."[21]

Considering the times, this form of rhetoric was not uncommon, and reflected the serious commitment made by early practitioners and professors to the ideals of client and public service in the practice of auditing that comprised the principal economic and statutory activity of CPAs.

Robert Montgomery edited Dicksee's American version through a collaboration arranged by Arthur Lowes Dickinson. Montgomery, a native-born American, and Dickinson, an Englishman, worked together in early professional organizations which later established ethics committees and self-regulatory processes.

Early Professional Control

Lowe, writing in 1987 about the first CPA ethics committee, observed the following:

> In 1906 the AAPA established a formal committee on ethics to develop standards to which members should adhere. It wasn't until 10 years later, though, that this committee was officially empowered to consider and evaluate a member's conduct in terms of compliance with those standards.[22]

The yearbook for the 1907 AAPA meeting contains a substantial section dealing with professional ethics. The major paper was presented by Joseph E. Sterrett, who relied heavily on the experiences of what he termed "older professions" and gave examples from ethical

---

[21] Lawrence R. Dicksee, *Auditing: A Practical Manual for Auditors*, ed. R. H. Montgomery, Authorized American Edition (New York, 1905): 260.
[22] H. J. Lowe, "Ethics in Our 100-Year History," *Journal of Accountancy* (May, 1987).

canons, codes and drafts of bar associations, medical associations and the Institute of Electrical Engineers. He further developed his commentary into three categories of conduct:

1. Duties and Responsibilities of a Public Accountant in Relation to His Clients
2. The Accountant's Relation to the Public
3. The Accountant's Relation to His Professional Brethren

The five rules of professional ethics adopted by the AAPA in 1907 were prohibitions, each beginning "No member shall. . . ." The rules prohibited:

1. AAPA identity from being used by anyone but members
2. Sharing professional fees with the laity
3. Incompatible occupations
4. Certifying of accountancy work without proper involvement or supervision of an AAPA member
5. Members from using CPA or similar (CA) designations in business advertisements or recognizing any organization using same unless said designation is authorized by law in the state[23]

The fact that the recently established CPA profession emphasized prohibitory, self-regulatory rules to control use of the CPA identity (while pioneering its own code of ethics) is understandable given that, as of 1912, Montgomery noted:

American courts have never laid down specific rules regulating the duties or obligations of public accountants. . . .[24]

Montgomery argued that it was desirable to weed out poor work because "a few irresponsible men can offset the good work of ten

---

[23] Joyce Lambert and S. J. Lambert, "The Evolution of Ethical Codes in Accounting," Working Paper 23, (The Academy of Accounting Historians Working Paper Series, vol. 2, 1979, School of Accounting, James Madison University).

[24] R. H. Montgomery, *Auditing Theory and Practice* (New York: Ronald Press, 1912), 571 ff.

times their number."[25] The logic is that self-regulation is proper given the CPAs duty to others, and it also helps the profession as business persons to weed out incompetence, and as professionals to do more for clients than the law requires.

Early Cooperation Between National and State Societies

At the 1908 AAPA annual meeting, a report from the ethics committee noted that state societies had been requested to provide their views on issues to be addressed, including "whether or not it is desirable that recognized bodies of accountants throughout the United States should adopt a code of ethical rules suitable to the profession of public accounting."[26]

Responding to the request, the Illinois Society indicated its support for a code, and also noted concerns about the use of the corporate form by audit firms. In the Illinois Society's view, this was particularly important when the corporate form included a board of directors that was used to solicit business.

Such early efforts at coordination between the national and state professional groups in matters of ethics established the pattern for the present system of joint enforcement.

By 1916, when the American Institute of Accountants (AIA) had succeeded the AAPA, the ethics committee was officially empowered to consider and evaluate a member's conduct, and the AIA governing council served as a trial board to provide a panel of peers in the event of a hearing.[27]

The Profession Develops

As the number of individuals in the CPA profession grew from a few hundred to thousands, the courts, Congress, and state and federal governmental agencies became more involved in specifying the role of CPAs. This was first done for the attest functions, and eventually for tax and consulting. During both World War I and World War II, war-related government work by CPAs increased the professional exposure of CPAs to oversight of technical standards and rules of conduct.

---

[25] See footnote 24.

[26] Report of the Committee on Ethical Rules, *Twenty-First Anniversary Year Book*, (The American Association of Public Accountants, 1908), 98-100.

[27] See footnote 22.

The public's image of the duties of a CPA during this growth period remained simple. A CPA was often viewed as a well-paid person who performed accounting or tax work, and perhaps also as one who was dedicated and trustworthy, but not necessarily a broad-thinking or creative individual. This stereotype limited the ability of the CPA profession to impress upon the public its true value and ability (because of the perception of the limitations on creativity). This is a problem that lingers somewhat even today. Yet, there is another side to the coin. The public already had developed an expectation of trustworthiness of CPAs—high praise and a valuable label indeed.[28]

CPA—Protecting and Developing the Name Through Ethics

During the period 1930 through 1952, the CPA profession grew at increasing annual rates from thousands to tens of thousands. This rapid growth was accompanied by an expanded scope of services and a need to specify practitioner standards. The *CPA Handbook*, issued in 1952, addressed the subject. By 1960, several important publications on accounting ethics had been printed.[29]

The first known work written in this country and dedicated solely to CPA Ethics was written in 1931 by A. P. Richardson, an Englishman who served as the Institute's first permanent secretary or principal staff person. Entitled *The Ethics of a Profession* and published by the Institute, it contained 159 pages on topics including solicitation, advertising, fees, contingent fees, secrecy, and bidding. In the Foreword, Richardson observes:

> In accountancy, which is the newest of the professions, it has been rather easier to adopt high ethical standards than in any other profession, but that does not imply that those standards have been invariably observed. There are men and women calling themselves accountants

---

[28] Report from Louis Harris and Associates, American Institute of Certified Public Accountants, Council, Minutes of Meeting (October 18, 1986): 6-8.

[29] *The Ethical Problems of Modern Accountancy* (Lectures delivered in 1932), (New York: Ronald Press, 1933) (Reprint 1980 New York: Arno Press Co.), Carey, J. L., *Professional Ethics of Public Accounting* (New York: American Institute of [Certified Public] Accountants, 1946), Carey, J. L., *Professional Ethics of Certified Public Accountants*, (New York: American Institute of Certified Public Accountants, 1956).

who deride the argument that accountancy is a profession at all. They say, with a fair amount of apparent justification, that the accountant is merely engaged in a business service very much like that of an appraisal company or a statistical venture; that be should perform his work honestly, of course, and to the best of his ability, but that to consider himself on a plane with the lawyer, the physician or surgeon is preposterous. The greater number of accountants, however, are firmly convinced that the practice of accountancy is professional purely, and they are supported by statute and judgement.[30]

By 1946, when John L. Carey, one of the architects of CPA ethics, wrote his first work on ethics, the post-war expansion of the profession's members and activities had begun. During this era, the foundation of professional ethics was the personal commitment and character of the individual practitioner. The existing code of ethics consisted of enforceable rules and focused on ethical concerns in the fashion devised by Sterret, that is, (1) those related to the public, (2) those related to the client, and (3) those related to peers.

A cornerstone ethical concept of the post-war period was *independence*, which evidenced the view of the public that auditing is the franchise of public practice.[31] Many individuals have wrestled with the issues surrounding independence and the concept has a literature of its own. It is safe to argue that historical evidence suggests that the meaning of independence has evolved over time and continues to evolve even today.

Carey, who served many years as the AICPA's chief staff officer, wrote the following about the meaning of *independence*:

> Independence is an abstract concept, and it is difficult to define either generally or in its peculiar application to the certified public accountant. Essentially it is a state of mind. It is partly synonymous with honesty, integrity, courage, character. It means in simplest terms, that the certified public accountant will tell the truth as he sees it. And will permit no influence, financial or sentimental, to turn him from that course.[32]

---

[30] A.P. Richardson, *The Ethics of a Profession* (New York: The Century Co., 1931).

[31] Bruce Edward Committee, "Independence of Accountants and Legislative Intent," *Administrative Law Review* (Winter 1989): 33-57.

[32] John L. Carey, *Professional Ethics of Public Accounting*, (New York: American Institute of Accountants 1946): 7.

Writing nearly a generation later (in 1985) on the subject of independence Carey observed:

> This is a word with at least 15 different meanings. The word independent was first used in conjunction with "accountant" (i.e. independent accountant) in the same sense as in the phrase independent contractor—as the dictionary says, "not subject to another's authority." But the noun form, "independence" also denotes the admirable quality of being "not influenced or controlled by others in matters of opinion or conduct." It was not difficult, by subtle thought transmission, for independent accountants, perhaps with some self-satisfaction, to invest themselves with the admirable quality of independence.

Carey continues:

> However, in the absolute and literal sense, it is obviously impossible for any human being except a hermit to avoid being influenced by others to some extent—not necessarily for evil.
>
> .... In the *Tentative Statement of Auditing Standards*, issued in 1947, independence was equated with complete intellectual honesty, honest disinterestedness, unbiased judgment, objective consideration of facts, judicial impartiality.
>
> .... We can say with confidence that audit independence means integrity and objectivity.
>
> .... But alas, the discussion cannot end here.[33]

Nor should it be expected to—for to seek a *solution* to an individual case is one matter, but to expect a *conclusion* to the cornerstone issue of the CPA profession would suggest stagnation of practice and of the profession. The definition of independence may be expected to acquire added meanings as the relationships of practitioners encounter new circumstances.[34]

---

[33] John L. Carey, "The Independence Concept Revisited," *The Ohio CPA Journal* (Spring, 1985): 5-8.

[34] Bruce E. Committee,, "Independence of Accountants and Legislative Intent," *Administrative Law Review* (Winter, 1989): 33-59. Writing in 1944, Maurice Peloubet, a practitioner, commented as follows: It is not really independence, which some glib and uninformed writers discuss so freely, it is rather integrity, which is so necessary to the practice of the profession. "Independence—A Blessed Word," *The Journal of Accountancy* (January, 1944): 69.

Carey further notes that the federal Securities Acts' administrative regulations introduced the distinction between independence in fact (a state of mind) and the *appearance of independence*. In these 1985 writings, he warned of the ethical, legal, and semantic morass that results from this distinction between reality and perception.

Early court cases decided during the period, along with statutory requirements, expanded the responsibility of the CPA as auditor. As a result, the CPA-auditor became more exposed to lawsuits from a broader element within the investment community. While the Securities Acts increased the demand for audit services, a corresponding increase occurred in expectations for, and oversight of, the professional conduct and competence of CPAs providing professional services to public companies. Carey depicted the ethical view of the post World War II era as follows:

> A professional attitude must be learned. It is not a natural gift. It is natural to be selfish and greedy—to place personal gain ahead of service.... The rules of ethics are guides to right action that will develop the professional attitude, and thus win public confidence.[35]

In the 1970s, the base of Institute ethical rules which members were required to observe was expanded so that violations of generally accepted accounting principles and auditing standards by members were considered a breach of ethics.

Beginning with a salvo of accusations in a congressional staff study entitled *The Accounting Establishment*, issued in October, 1976, and continuing through the 1980s, which included a study by the Treadway Commission, a private sector group, the activities of CPAs in public accounting and corporate practice were subjected to extensive review in hearings and studies. The aftermath of these reviews resulted in a series of unprecedented self-regulatory initiatives by professional organizations, principally the AICPA and state societies. These initiatives included the establishment of a Division for Firms within the AICPA. This division enrolled practice units as members based upon the client base, that is, a Private Companies Practice Section and an SEC Practice Section.

---

[35] J. L. Carey, "Practical Applications of Professional Ethics," Chapter 5, *CPA Handbook*, (American Institute of [Certified Public] Accountants, 1952): 2.

Public practice specialization reflecting the changing scope of services also led the Institute to formally establish practice divisions for taxation, advisory services, and financial planning.

In October, 1983, the AICPA established a Special Committee on Standards of Professional Conduct for CPAs, chaired by former AICPA chairman George Anderson, to evaluate the need for a major revision of the code of ethics because of the changing scope of public practice and the increasing number of CPAs in corporate practice. Membership data indicated that, as the profession entered the 1980s, the AICPA was identified with careers not only in public practice, but also in corporate practice as financial managers, corporate reporting executives and chief financial officers.

In late 1987 and early 1988, the AICPA membership overwhelmingly approved six changes to the code of ethics and membership requirements, based upon recommendations by the Anderson Committee. The recommendations:

1. Updated the rules of conduct and emphasized positive goal oriented statements including integrity, objectivity, and competence as the basis for all CPA services.
2. Established a practice monitoring program for members in public practice.
3. Restructured the joint Trial Board and reduced duplication of enforcement procedures.
4. Established minimum continuing professional education (CPE) requirements for members in public practice.
5. Established minimum CPE requirements for members not in public practice.
6. Adopted a membership admission requirement that, after the year 2000, applicants must have at least 150 collegiate-level semester hours, including a bachelor's degree or its equivalent.

A large number of state CPA societies subsequently voted to conform their state society requirements to those adopted by the AICPA membership referendum.

A seventh Anderson recommendation, that a member practicing with a firm with one or more SEC clients may retain that membership only if the firm is a member of the SEC Practice Section, was approved as part of a separate ballot in late 1989. The Anderson initiatives focused on the need for recognition of several fundamental ideals such as integrity, objectivity, and competence as a basis for professional qualification and proper conduct.[36] Bringing these ideals into the professional culture was necessary for CPAs just as it was for physicians (for example, patient well-being above self-interest of the doctor) and lawyers (for example, advocacy at law above self-interest of the lawyer). There can be no capital market activity on a large scale if the information profession is not functioning with integrity and objectivity.

The Treadway Commissioners released their final report in October, 1987. Their recommendations for improvements in the financial reporting system and to reduce fraudulent financial reports encompassed four areas: (1) the public company itself, (2) independent public accountants, (3) the SEC and others involved in establishing the regulatory environment, and (4) the education community.[37]

The CPA profession is currently emerging from recent challenges to the CPA name. For a broader discussion of this issue, see Chapter 8, *Developments in the Profession: Enron, WorldCom, Arthur Andersen, and Sarbanes-Oxley*.

Summary

Past events in the development of the CPA profession remain an important part of the prologue to the contemporary practice environment and serve to explain how things came to be as they are. These past events in the financial and investment community reinforce the need for the positive influence of the CPA professional and the need for the integrity and objectivity set forth in the code of conduct.

---

[36] "Restructuring Professional Standards to Achieve Professional Excellence in a Changing Environment," Report of the Special Committee on Standards of Professional Conduct for Certified Public Accountants, AICPA, New York, 1986. See also the *CPA Letter* of the AICPA dated May 29, 1987, for detailed results of the balloting.

[37] Report of the National Commission on Fraudulent Financial Reporting, October 1987, National Commission on Fraudulent Financial Reporting, 1701 Pennsylvania Avenue N. W., Washington D.C. 20006.

The current code of ethics is being reexamined in light of recent high-profile accounting scandals. The tradition of our profession does provide a strong basis from which to meet these difficult challenges. Despite recent problems, CPA counsel and attestation continues to be highly valued by the public. All in the profession must act with honesty and integrity to ensure that accountants regain their undisputed perch at the top of the list of honest professionals.

APPENDIX F

World Wide Web Sites

This is a sampling of World Wide Web Internet sites containing information relevant for current and prospective CPAs. Many of the sites, particularly those under General Accounting Sites, have extensive links to other accounting sites such as CPA firms, corporate employers and universities. Internet sites for state boards of accountancy and state CPA societies are provided in Appendixes C and D, when available.

CPA Examination Sites

CPA Examination
   http://www.cpa-exam.org

Professional Accounting Associations and Related Sites

AICPA
   http://www.aicpa.org

American Institute of Certified Public Accountants Career Initiatives
   http://www.aicpa.org/members/div/career/index.htm

American Institute of Certified Public Accountants State and Jurisdiction Specific Information
   http://aicpa.org/states/stmap.htm

British Accounting Association
  http://www.bham.ac.uk/BAA

Certified General Accountants Association of Canada
  http://www.cga-canada.org

Canadian Institute of Chartered Accountants
  http://www.cica.ca/new/index.htm

European Accounting Association
  http://www.bham.ac.uk/EAA/homepage.htm

The Institute of Chartered Accountants in Ireland
  http://www.icai.ie

National Association of State Boards of Accountancy
  http://www.nasba.org

The Academy of Accounting Historians
  http://weatherhead.cwru.edu/Accounting

International Federation of Accountants
  http://www.ifac.org

Standard Setting Groups

Public Company Accounting Oversight Board
  http://www.pcaob.org

Financial Accounting Standards Board
  http://www.fasb.org

Governmental Accounting Standards Board
  http://www.financenet.gov/gasb.htm

International Accounting Standards Committee
  http://www.iasc.org

International Accounting Standards Board
  http://www.iasb.org

Governmental Agencies

Securities and Exchange Commission
  http://www.sec.gov

Internal Revenue Service
  http://www.irs.ustreas.gov

General Accounting Sites Including Employment Information

Rutgers Accounting Web
   http://www.rutgers.edu/Accounting

Accountingnet
   http://accountingnet.com

Tax and Accounting Sites Directory
   http://www.uni.edu/schmidt/sites.html

ANET
   http://anet.scu.edu.au/anet

Robert Half International and Accountemps
   http://www.rhii.com
   http://www.accountemps.com

Academic-Related Sites

Beta Alpha Psi
   http://www.bap.org

American Accounting Association
   http://www.rutgers.edu/Accounting/raw/aaa

Journals

Accounting Today/Faulkner and Gray
   http://www.electronicaccountant.com

Journal of Accountancy
   http://www.aicpa.org/pubs/jofa/joahome.htm

The *CPA Letter*
   http://www.aicpa.org/pubs/cpaltr/index.htm

The *Practicing CPA*
   http://www.aicpa.org/pubs/tpcpa/index.htm

Research in Accounting Regulation
   http://weatherhead.cwru.edu/dept/rar

Related Professional Associations and Designations

Association for Investment Management and Research (CFA)
   http://www.aimr.org

CFP Board
   http://www.cfp-board.org
Association of Certified Fraud Examiners
   http://www.acfe.org
The Institute of Internal Auditors
   http://www.theiia.org
Institute of Management Accountants (CMA)
   http://www.rutgers.edu/Accounting/raw/ima

APPENDIX G

Chapter Discussion Questions

The following discussion questions can be used for classroom instruction, testing, or in-firm training purposes. The question modules are arranged by chapter for ease of reference.

Chapter 1: Introduction to the CPA Profession

1. Define a profession and indicate in what respects accountancy may or may not fit that definition.
2. What constitutes a professional? Do you feel that CPAs are professionals or simply employees of organizations? Why?
3. Explain what is meant by the "information right" of individuals.
4. Why is it important for CPAs to have a commitment to serve?
5. Describe the three "Es" necessary to attain professional competency as a CPA.
6. What is the difference between integrity and objectivity?
7. What is the principal objective and concern of the CPA in today's society?
8. List and describe the principal personal attributes necessary to the practitioner in fulfilling the principal objective and concern of the CPA in today's society.

9. Why is a written code of ethics a necessary part of the culture of a profession? Are there any disadvantages related with providing a written set of ethical rules?
10. What is the AICPA? What is its mission? How does the AICPA achieve its mission?
11. List and describe the six key principals for CPAs set forth in the Code of Professional Conduct.
12. Find an example of a CPA's ethical/unethical behavior taken from a recent news report. Who was most affected by the CPA's behavior.

Internship-Related Discussion Questions

1. Does your firm have a stated code of conduct or commitment statement? If so, what does it say and how does it impact your practice on a daily basis?
2. How does your firm develop professional competence at the early stages of your career?

Chapter 2: Qualities of a CPA: Commitment to Serve, Competence, Integrity, and Objectivity

1. List and describe the key qualities of a CPA.
2. Describe the CPA's commitment to serve.
3. List the "3 Es" that refer to the processes in place to help the aspirant to develop competency to practice accountancy.
4. List and describe the four parts of the Uniform CPA Examination.
5. What are the education requirements in the state where you intend to practice for receiving a CPA license or permit to practice?
6. What is the experience requirement in the state where you intend to practice for receiving a CPA license or permit to practice? Must the experience be in public accounting?
7. What is the continuing education requirement in the state where you intend to practice for maintaining a CPA license or permit to practice.
8. Distinguish between independence in fact and independence in appearance.

9. Discuss the relevance of independence in a CPA's integrity and objectivity.
10. Describe a paradigm for making difficult decisions on behalf of clients when substantial uncertainty exists.
11. In each of the following independent cases, opine whether the CPA firm's independence is impaired. You are encouraged to consult the details of revised Rule 101, "Independence" in the AICPA Professional Standards to obtain the definition or additional details regarding any rule specified in this text. (AICPA Adapted[1]):
   a. A bank retains a CPA firm to perform an audit. During the period of the professional engagement, a manager in the CPA firm obtains a mortgage from the bank. He works in the same office as the lead partner on the audit but does not provide any services to the bank. Is the firm's independence impaired?
   b. A CPA firm performs an audit of a large manufacturing company. One of the firm's managers, who plans to provide a significant amount of tax services to the company, has a spouse who inherited a small amount of stock in it. The manager does not work in the same office as the lead audit partner. Is the firm's independence impaired?
   c. A CPA firm is considering hiring the controller of one of its audit clients as a part-time independent contractor during tax season. She would help prepare tax returns for other clients of the CPA firm, all of which are nonattest clients. The firm has two offices and she would be working out of the one that does not provide any services to her primary employer. If she is hired, would the CPA firm's independence be impaired with respect to that client?
   d. A small manufacturing company has asked a CPA firm to perform an audit. The company's controller is the engagement partner's mother-in-law. Would the firm be considered independent for purposes of accepting the audit engagement?
   e. A partner in a multioffice CPA firm owns 2% of a potential audit client. The audit would be conducted by an office with

---

[1] Adapted from Goria, J. *Journal of Accountancy*, October 2002, 104(4): 110-111.

which he is not associated. The partner would not provide any services to the client nor be in a position to influence the engagement team. Is the firm independent?
f. A manager in a multioffice CPA firm serves on the board of directors of a potential review client. The manager would not be assigned to provide services to the client nor located in the office that would perform the engagement. Is the firm independent to perform the review?
g. A partner's dependent son works as an inventory clerk during the summer months for an audit client of the firm. The partner is located in the office in which the lead audit engagement partner practices. Is the firm independent?

Internship-Related Discussion Questions

1. Describe your view of the professional culture as it relates to the CPA profession.
2. Describe your view of the personal culture at your firm.
3. At what level is the person at your firm that has been most instrumental in introducing you to the culture of the firm as it relates to the CPA profession and service in the public interest.
4. Describe an important learning experience in which you learned something from a supervisor. What was the nature of the lesson and was the lesson delivered in a constructive or negative way?

Chapter 3: CPA Careers

1. What is meant by a CPA being in "public practice"?
2. What is meant by a CPA being in "private or corporate practice"?
3. What are the names of the four largest CPA firms?
4. What is the largest firm (in terms of revenues and professionals) in your city that is not one of the four largest CPA firms?
5. What are the traditional departments within CPA firms?
6. What are the three traditional services offered through a CPA firm's Accounting and Auditing department?
7. What specialty designations are currently accredited by the AICPA?
8. What are the traditional levels in CPA firms?
9. How many years does it traditional take to reach the partnership level in CPA firms?

10. What are the traditional levels/position titles for CPAs in corporate practice?
11. How does the Center for Excellence in Financial Management support CPAs in corporate practice?
12. What other professional organizations serve and support the needs of CPAs in corporate practice?
13. What positions do CPAs hold in government practice?

Internship-Related Discussion Questions

1. What are the names of the positional levels at your firm?
2. How many partners does your office have? In what area do these partners specialize?
3. What is the average number of years required to reach partner level at your firm?
4. If your internship is with a Corporation, describe the career path to the Vice-President level in your operating unit.

Chapter 4: The Scope of CPA Services

1. Distinguish between audit, attest, and assurance.
2. What are the two primary components of tax practice and who do CPAs compete with in servicing the needs of the public?
3. Describe the rise of the "consulting" practice within CPA firms. How did the events surrounding Sarbanes-Oxley impact these practices?
4. What services to attest clients are specifically prohibited by Sarbanes-Oxley?
5. Describe the role of Certified Financial Planners.
6. What is the role of those who hold the Accreditation in Business Valuation credential?
7. Describe the specialized expertise held by CPAs that are also Certified Information Technology Professionals.
8. What are the requirements for CPAs to obtain the CFP, ABV, or CITP credential.
9. What is forensic accounting and fraud examination?
10. How might a Certified Fraud Examiner be valuable to an organization that has not been the victim of a fraud?
11. How does being a CPA add value to the role of the CFO? Do you think the capital markets care whether the CFO is a CPA?

12. What issues are raised about CPA auditor independence when the auditor provides NAS services to an audit client?

Internship-Related Discussion Questions
1. Describe your ideal career path at your current firm or company.
2. What services does your firm offer?
3. Is your firm a PCAOB registered firm? If so, how often does the firm undergo PCAOB inspection and when is the next inspection expected?
4. What area(s) of expertise (or industry of expertise) does your firm feature?

Chapter 5: Accountability: Personal Oversight

1. What are the principal forces directing the behavior of all professionals—CPAs included?
2. What do we mean by "personal integrity"?
3. How does the relationship between a professional and a client differ from the relationship between a salesperson and a customer? In what ways may the two be the same?
4. Who is to judge whether a professional is able to perform the services that he or she holds out to the public as being able to perform?
5. Would CPAs and their clients be better served if the profession had no articulated rules of conduct? Why or why not?
6. Why has the AICPA Code of Professional Conduct been extended explicitly to cover CPAs not in public practice?
7. To what extent is it necessary or desirable that a candidate obtain "experience" under the direction of a CPA before being granted a license? If so, should that experience be in a particular area of expertise, such as performance of the attest function, for all candidates?
8. Discuss the three areas of responsibility falling to a supervisor in guiding the experience of a CPA candidate.
9. Describe from your own experience a situation involving ethical choices, and consider how that situation might have been resolved using the approach described in the text. Would you have reached the same or a different answer?

10. Develop your own definition of professional "failure." How would you surface and deal with it in the best interests of the public served by the CPA?
11. Why does the AICPA Code of Professional Conduct contain both "principles" and "rules"?
12. Select one of the Code's "rules" and trace the changes in that rule over time, as influenced by professional and legal developments affecting CPAs.
13. Several of the rules (e.g., Rule 101, Independence) refer to compliance with ". . . standards promulgated by bodies designated by Council." What is the significance of this reference? What are "bodies designated by Council"?
14. How do you think standards and rules regarding independence should be formulated and enforced?
15. What are the public policy aspects of the ethical rules regarding confidentiality for a CPA in public practice? For those CPAs in other circumstances?
16. Is it ever acceptable to break the confidentiality barrier when dealing with a client? When working in an employee status for an employer? In the case of a former employer? Be specific.
17. Should communications between CPAs and their clients have the same protected ("privileged") status as those between a doctor and patient or a lawyer and client? Why or why not?

Internship-Related Discussion Questions

1. Does your firm have a written Code of Conduct or Ethics? If so, what does it say?
2. Was your training from your firm in professional responsibilities and ethics formal or informal? Explain.
3. Identify a person that you view as the model of ethics. How does this person manifest his/her high standards in their day-to-day activities?
4. Describe strategies for dealing with an ethical dilemma that you would face at your firm?

Chapter 6: Accountability: Professional (Peer) Oversight

1. What do we mean when we talk about "regulation?"
2. List the key activities involved in self-regulation of the accounting profession by members of the accounting profession.

3. Has the accounting profession been forced into changing its behavior by outside forces (reactive) rather than taking the initiative in doing so (proactive)? Is this a good or a bad thing?
4. What is the relationship between the accounting profession and the SEC?
5. Why has the SEC been so interested in the structure and operation of the CPCAF of the AICPA, and particularly in the peer review process?
6. List and discuss the key technical activities carried out the AICPA.
7. Which body currently sets the generally accepted auditing standards? Is this a private sector or public sector body?
8. Which body currently sets the generally accepted financial accounting principles? Is this a private sector or public sector body?
9. Why should private companies, not registered with the SEC, be concerned with the activities of the SEC in accounting and auditing matters?
10. How does the SEC's authority in the development of accounting principles differ from its authority in the development of auditing practices?
11. Is there a difference between regulation of the technical aspects of a profession and its commercial aspects? Should there be? What effect has the consent agreement between the AICPA and the FTC had on the practice of public accountancy?
12. Describe the organizational structure of the AICPA and the place of the peer reviews in the self-regulatory process.
13. What are the two peer review processes available to CPA firms and how do they differ?
14. Why were the AICPA's Committee on Accounting Procedures and its successor, the Accounting Principles Board, ultimately replaced by the Financial Accounting Standards Board?
15. Outline the principal arguments for and against setting accounting and auditing standards in the private sector. What changes, if any, would you make to this process as it now exists?
16. Which organization establishes the auditing standards for public companies? Which organization establishes the auditing standards for nonpublic organizations?

Internship-Related Discussion Questions

1. Is your firm peer reviewed by the CPCAF PRP or the AICPA PRP or neither?
2. What year did your firm last undergo a peer review? Did the report identify any operating weaknesses? If so, what changes did the firm make in their operating policies and procedures?

Chapter 7: Accountability: Public Oversight

1. What are some of the social and economic factors that have led to an expansion of the CPA's legal responsibilities and liabilities?
2. Why do even members of otherwise autonomous occupations often actively seek governmental intervention in their activities?
3. Does a business failure indicate an audit failure? Could an audit failure lead to a business failure?
4. Discuss an auditor's responsibility to detect fraud, and ability to do so.
5. What are the implications to the practice of public accountancy of increasing legal exposure and high damage awards? Direct consequences? Indirect consequences?
6. What is "due care," and what legal implications arise from the failure of the CPA to exercise it in providing professional services?
7. Differentiate a CPA's liability under common law to clients and to third parties not in privity. How has this evolved over time?
8. State in your own words the present status of the common law liability of CPAs.
9. Differentiate the liability of CPAs under the Securities Act of 1933 and the Securities Exchange Act of 1934. What are the standards of proof required of plaintiffs and the standards of defense required of defendants under the respective acts?
10. Why is the case of *United States v. Arthur Young & Co.*, simply a case limited to the access to audit working papers granted the IRS, so important in defining the function and responsibilities of CPAs?
11. List five significant developments from Sarbanes/Oxley that directly impact CPAs.
12. Would you make any changes to the legal responsibilities and duties of the CPA as they presently are understood? If so why and in what respect?

13. How and in what respect should CPAs in industry, government and academe be concerned with the legal responsibilities and potential liabilities of CPAs in public practice?
14. Discuss some of the reasons for the apparent increase over time in cases against CPAs in public practice. Is this a good or bad thing for the profession? For society at large?
15. What important changes were made in the application of the federal securities acts by the *Private Securities Litigation Reform Act of 1995*?
16. What are LLPs? What is the significance of this new form of organization for CPAs?
17. What are LLCs? What is the significance of this new form of organization for CPAs?
18. Discuss the dilemma that a CPA might face when deciding whether to provide attest services to a potential client.
19. Review the accountancy act and the rules of the board of accountancy in your state.
20. Identify the names of the members of the State Board of Accountancy in your state.
21. Report on a meeting of the State Board of Accountancy or its disciplinary committee.

Internship-Related Discussion Questions

1. How is your firm organized (e.g., corporation, partnership, LLP, LLC, other)? In what year was this formal organization completed?
2. Is your firm a defendant in legal proceedings? If so, is it a civil or criminal case?
3. How has the passage of Sarbanes-Oxley impacted the work load in your firm?

Chapter 8: Developments in the Profession: Enron, WorldCom, Arthur Andersen, and Sarbanes-Oxley

1. Describe aspects of the business environment that contributed to the high profile scandals of the 1990s.
2. Define earnings management and describe how it contributed to the dramatic stock price increases in the 1990s.

3. Discuss how reduced investor faith in the capital markets increases the cost of funds for companies.
4. Describe how successful accounting and financial regulation and internal controls can save companies money via reduced cost of funds.
5. Describe the relation between non-audit related CPA services and reduced audit quality that is alleged to exist before recent professional reforms.
6. Describe the role and charge of the PCAOB.
7. What CPA firms are reviewed and evaluated by the PCAOB? How often are CPA firms inspected by the PCAOB?
8. Describe the relationship between the PCAOB and self-regulating units of the accounting profession—the FASB and the AICPA.
9. Section 201 of Sarbanes-Oxley sets forth services that audit firms cannot provide to attest clients. List these services and explain how each can impair independence to provide audit and attest services.
10. Section 404 is the most widely discussed provision in Sarbanes-Oxley. Discuss what section 404 requires. Do you think that the benefits of the work required by section 404 justify the cost compliance?

Internship-Related Discussion Questions

1. If you work for a CPA firm, does your firm provide Sarbanes-Oxley related services? If so, which services are provided? Describe any experiences that you have providing such services.
2. If you work for a corporation, is your company required to comply with Sarbanes-Oxley? If so, what is the estimated cost of compliance?
3. If you work for a corporation that is not required to comply with Sarbanes-Oxley, does it voluntarily comply with some or all of the Act's provisions? If so, which provisions and what is the cost of compliance? Are company officers satisfied with the changes brought about by compliance?
4. What internal operating policies and procedures have changed in response to recent accounting scandals.
5. If you work for a CPA firm, has your firm dropped any clients because of the risk posed by providing their audit?

Chapter 9: A View of the Horizon for the CPA Profession

1. What is XBRL?
2. Describe your vision of feasible developments in financial reporting using the XBRL technology.
3. What constitutes the universe of U.S. generally accepted accounting principles?
4. Describe the principles-based versus rules-based accounting guidance and indicate which position you support.
5. Describe what is meant by the "Big GAAP / Little GAAP" debate.
6. Describe the structure of the international accounting community.
7. In the accounting context, what is meant by the term convergence? Describe efforts underway to achieve convergence.

Internship-Related Discussion Questions

1. Do you see growth, steady state, or contraction in the size of your firm or department?
2. What opportunities might the proliferation of XBRL bring for your firm and for you?
3. Does your firm more often employ "Big GAAP" or "Little GAAP"? Explain.